Behind the Intifada

———————————

PRINCETON STUDIES ON THE NEAR EAST

Behind the Intifada

LABOR AND WOMEN'S MOVEMENTS
IN THE OCCUPIED TERRITORIES

Joost R. Hiltermann

PRINCETON UNIVERSITY PRESS
PRINCETON, NEW JERSEY

Library of Congress Cataloging-in-Publication Data

Hiltermann, Joost R.
Behind the Intifada : labor and women's movements in the occupied
territories / Joost R. Hiltermann.
p.   cm.
Includes bibliographical references and index.
1. West Bank—Politics and government.   2. Labor movement—
Political aspects—West Bank.   3. Women, Palestinian Arab—West
Bank—Political activity.   4. Gaza Strip—Politics and government.
5. Labor movement—Political aspects—Gaza Strip.   6. Women.
Palestinian Arab—Gaza Strip—Political activity.   7. Intifada, 1987–
I. Title.
DS110.W47H55   1991   322.4'4'095694—dc20   91-14181

ISBN 0-691-07869-6 (alk. paper)

*This book is respectfully dedicated
to the memory of*

*Tamam Miz'el Ghanam al-Furoukh
(Um Jamal)
(Sa'ir, 1944–Ramallah, 1986)*

_____

CONTENTS

PREFACE

FEW ARE THE RESEARCHERS who find themselves graced with a subject population that, on completion of the research project, rises in unison and validates the study's main findings. I am one of those who have been so fortunate, although I must confess at the outset that my subjects' behavior had less to do with their feelings about my research (of which the great majority were blissfully unaware) than with the concrete conditions they had been forced to endure in their everyday lives for decades. No sooner had I completed a study of mass mobilization in the West Bank and Gaza Strip than the Palestinian population rose in mass protest to reject and undo the structure of Israel's military occupation, coordinating its collective effort through the very infrastructure of popular organizations that, I had concluded in my study, had come to constitute the backbone of Palestinians' resistance to Israel's occupation in the 1980s.

I had arrived in the West Bank in the autumn of 1984 with the firm plan of spending no more than a year conducting field research for a doctoral dissertation in sociology on the blocked proletarianization of the Palestinian peasantry. Lacking friends and an institutional affiliation in my new abode, I was fortunate to make the acquaintance of activists in a local human-rights organization called Law in the Service of Man during the first month of my stay. Soon they asked me to contribute to a research project in which a colleague of theirs was involved. In the following months, a strong bond was forged between this organization (later to be renamed Al-Haq) and me, a bond that continues to this day.

Through my association with and work for Al-Haq my academic research became suffused with a new concern, not merely for socioeconomic processes or the historic injustice inflicted on the Palestinians, but more important, for Palestinians' efforts to assert and actualize their right to change adverse conditions and resist unjust rule. Thus my focus shifted from analyzing the political obstacles that have blocked the process of proletarianization under occupation to studying the mechanisms used by Palestinian activists to mobilize the masses in an attempt collectively to resist an oppression whose outstanding feature is a peculiar combination of colonial exploitation and military rule.

This has not been an easy study to undertake. Aside from the language barrier (which did not begin to crumble until I had completed the bulk of my fieldwork), I found in my path two hurdles: people's initial uneasiness concerning the foreigner's "true intentions," and factional infighting that renders all information one collects automatically suspect. The first hurdle I cleared—to the extent one can—once I had succeeded in establishing myself in the local community, and had made friends. But I stumbled badly on the second.

In the early stages of my research I was drawn like a magnet to those who were most eager to provide me with the type of data I was seeking. One particular group of activists was more open and willing to be interviewed than others. My mistake was to believe that these were the only data that mattered, and that the picture I had pieced together at that point was complete. The result was that in an article published in *MERIP Reports* in the autumn of 1985 I leaned heavily toward an interpretation of political mobilization in the West Bank that appeared favorable to one particular faction of the Palestinian national movement. At least I was accused of having done so by one of the aggrieved factions. That it had not been my intention to play partisan politics mattered little. In an area that has become so profoundly politicized and emotionally charged as the West Bank and Gaza, to allot a fair amount of space to discussing one side at the expense of another is tantamount to taking sides. It is also, I must add, a reflection of poor scholarship and poor judgment.

I believe I have rectified my initial erring in the course of later research and writing, although I now fear that by favoring no one I may incur the wrath of all. That, however, is one of the hazards of academic research.

This is perhaps the place to clarify my role in the Palestinian community, which has played host to me so generously for more than five years. I am not an active participant in the Palestinian struggle for national liberation, however sympathetic I may be to that unfortunately elusive goal. My only task has been to contribute in a minor way to the writing of a collective historical document about the Palestinians' struggle to throw off the yoke of foreign occupation. I have done so in my research by recording a particular aspect of this struggle, the mobilization of workers and women in trade unions and women's committees.

Such documentation is long overdue. The field of Middle Eastern studies has been cluttered with discussions about the parameters of the Palestinian-Israeli conflict rather than clarified by in-depth field studies. It has also been dominated by writers whose prejudice against Arabs has colored their findings. Because these writers generally receive an uncritical reception in the West, they have helped shape the negative perceptions that prevail in the United States and Western Europe of Palestinians and their struggle. One of the early and significant victories, therefore, of the Palestinian uprising that began in December 1987 was that Palestinians for the first time succeeded in convincing the West that there was more than just one side to the issue. By compelling journalists and others to cover the uprising, they set in motion the process of decolonizing their own history. Palestinians no longer have to waste their energy arguing that they have a case and that they deserve to be heard. They are now being heard and can argue their case.

This, I believe, is a momentous change that will shape discourse on the issue in the years to come. I am happy to have been a witness to this metamorphosis, which was long overdue but sudden all the same, and I will be satisfied if the present study contributes to a better understanding in the West of how Palestinians went about taking their fate into their own hands.

Research for this book was made possible by grants from the International Organisation for the Elimination of All Forms of Racial Discrimination (EAFORD) in London and the Transnational Institute in Amsterdam.

A number of people in the West Bank provided invaluable help collecting and processing data: Khaled 'Omar and his friend 'Issa from Jalazon refugee camp, Yusef Nimr from Kharbata, and 'Adnan Isma'il from Sa'ir. Others helped me with the translation of interviews and articles: Serin Heleileh, Muhammad Mas'ad, Wadah 'Abd-al-Salam, Musaddaq al-Masri, Hisham De'is, Akram Safadi, and Khaled Hassan. I want to thank them for their crucial assistance during my fieldwork.

I could not have written this book if my "employers" at Al-Haq in Ramallah had not given me their personal support and allowed me to use office time and resources, even during the early months of the intifada when there were pressing demands on our time and resources. I want to thank especially Raja Shehadeh, Emma Playfair, and Mona Rishmawi. I also wish to thank Suheil Jaber, whose house in Ramallah was partially demolished by the Israeli army in June 1987, for letting me use one of his computers for half a year out of pure generosity, despite all his problems.

I am very grateful to those who reviewed the various drafts of what was first a Ph.D. thesis and then a book. I thank especially Salim Tamari, who teaches sociology at Bir Zeit University. He first got me excited about the subject and provided support along the way, if not always by reading drafts, then at least by telling good jokes. I owe him a good deal more than the few cigars I bring him from Schiphol Airport each time I travel. I also wish to thank Walter Goldfrank, who guided me through my graduate career at the University of California, Santa Cruz; Lisa Taraki at Bir Zeit University; Barbara Harlow at the University of Texas, Austin; Zachary Lockman at Harvard University; Susan Rockwell in Ramallah; and my editors, Jane Lincoln Taylor and Margaret Case at Princeton University Press. They are in no way responsible for any errors.

I also want to give a special word of thanks to three Palestinians for the assistance they gave me in my research. One is 'Ali Abu-Hilal, the head of the Workers' Unity Bloc in 1985, who was always ready to talk to me and help me. He was issued a deportation order by the Israeli military authorities at the end of October 1985—coincidentally, a few hours after I had left his house in al-Bireh, where we had chatted about developments in the labor movement under the "Iron Fist." The Iron Fist came knocking that night; he was deported to Jordan in January 1986.

The second person is 'Adnan Dagher of the Construction Workers' Union in Ramallah, who supplied me with a wealth of information about the labor movement, and who ran one of the most active unions in the West Bank. 'Adnan was deported to Lebanon in 1988 for alleged membership in the Unified National Leadership of the Uprising. I was both pleased and sad to see him again, in Moscow in September 1990, where he is now working as a journalist, unable to return home.

The third person is Sami Kilani, a poet from the village of Ya'bad, who teaches at Al-Najah University in Nablus when it is open. Sami has been a friend since I met him in 1985. He helped me in setting up my research when I arrived; he arranged interviews; and he distributed my questionnaires in Ya'bad, producing some of the richest material of all my research in the West Bank. Sami has had regular run-ins with the military authorities. He was under town arrest in Ya'bad for three and a half years, and was then placed in administrative detention, without charges or trial, on several occasions. I owe him and his wonderful family in Ya'bad special thanks for their friendship and encouragement.

Finally, my most heartfelt thanks go to my friends who put up with me on a daily basis, in the West Bank and in Washington, D.C. They know who they are, but I would like to single out Susan Rockwell, Joe Stork, and Priscilla Norris for their extraordinary forbearance in the face of my usual antics.

This book is respectfully dedicated to the memory of Tamam Miz'el Ghanam al-Furoukh, or Um Jamal, into whose house I once dashed, rather irresponsibly, as I was being pursued by soldiers during a curfew in Ramallah in April 1985. From that moment she considered me part of the family and treated me like a son, while her own sons intermittently disappeared behind bars. She died too young, too soon. I shall not forget her.

INDEX OF ORGANIZATIONS

POLITICAL ORGANIZATIONS

ANM: Arab Nationalist Movement, an organization espousing Arab nationalism in the 1950s and 1960s. Precursor of the PFLP faction of the PLO.

Ba'ath: Political movement in Syria and Iraq. The Syrian version was a precursor of the Saiqa faction of the PLO.

DFLP: Democratic Front for the Liberation of Palestine, a left-wing faction of the PLO. Was first to propose the "national authority"/two-state solution in the early 1970s. Supports armed struggle. Marxist-Leninist in ideology. Has traditionally backed Soviet policy in the Middle East. Leader: Nayef Hawatmeh. Illegal in the Occupied Territories; underground.

Fatah: Largest PLO faction, founded in 1965. Has controlled the PLO since 1969. Mainstream movement, comprising groups from across the ideological spectrum, from Marxists to Islamic fundamentalists. Has supported the two-state solution since the mid-1970s, and has advocated a combination of political and armed struggle to attain national liberation. Leader: Yasser Arafat. Illegal in the Occupied Territories; underground.

GUPW: General Union of Palestinian Women, the women's organization of the PLO. Also: the General Union of Palestinian Workers, the trade-union arm of the PLO, later renamed the PTUF.

HAMAS: Arabic acronym for the Islamic Resistance Movement (Haraket al-Muqawwamet al-Islamiyya). Founded in early 1988, it is the political organ of the Muslim Brotherhood. Supports armed struggle in pursuit of the liberation of all of Palestine, and the establishment of an Islamic state.

Islamic Jihad: A small but very militant Islamic fundamentalist organization that supports the establishment of an Islamic state in all of Palestine. Banned by the military authorities in 1990.

JCP: Jordanian Communist Party, the continuation of the PCP in Jordan (including the West Bank) after 1948. The West Bank and East Bank parts of the JCP were separated by the 1967 war. The West Bank JCP was eventually renamed the PCP.

NGC: National Guidance Committee, a pro-PLO leadership committee founded in the West Bank and Gaza in 1978. Operated openly until outlawed by the military authorities; disappeared in the early 1980s.

NLL: National Liberation League, an offshoot of the PCP formed in 1944.

PCP: Palestine Communist Party. Founded during the British Mandate, it merged with the JCP in the West Bank after 1948. It continued to be referred to as the JCP during the first decade of Israeli occupation, but then reverted to its original name. A member of the PLO since the eighteenth PNC meeting in Algiers in April 1987, it has been active primarily inside the Occupied Territories, unlike the other PLO factions. Marxist-Leninist in ideology, at least until 1990 when changes in Eastern Europe forced a reevaluation of the party's constitution and program. Has opposed armed struggle and supported the two-state solution. Leader: Suleiman al-Najjab. Illegal in the Occupied Territories; underground.

PDFLP: Popular Democratic Front for the Liberation of Palestine, the precursor of the DFLP.

PFLP: Popular Front for the Liberation of Palestine, a left-wing faction of the PLO. Longtime advocate of a secular national state in all of Palestine, but threw its support behind the two-state solution at the nineteenth PNC meeting in Algiers in November 1988. Calls for armed struggle. Marxist-Leninist in ideology. Has traditionally backed Soviet policy in the Middle East. Leader: George Habash. Illegal in the Occupied Territories; underground.

PLO: Palestine Liberation Organization, the executive organ of the Palestine national movement. Founded in 1964. Chairperson: Yasser Arafat. Illegal in the Occupied Territories; underground.

PNC: Palestine National Council, effectively the Palestinian parliament-in-exile.

PNF: Palestine National Front, a pro-PLO leadership committee founded in the West Bank in 1973. Semiclandestine until its demise in the late 1970s.

PTUF: Palestine Trade Union Federation, the trade-union arm of the PLO.

PWA: Palestine Women's Association, a women's organization established in the West Bank in 1964. Banned by the Jordanian authorities in 1966. Ideological precursor of the modern women's movement in the Occupied Territories.

UNLU: Unified National Leadership of the Uprising, a pro-PLO leadership committee founded in the West Bank and Gaza during the uprising in 1988. Illegal in the Occupied Territories; underground.

POPULAR ORGANIZATIONS

Action Front: Popular movement supportive of the PFLP.

AWC: Arab Workers' Congress, a Palestinian trade-union movement after 1945, replacing the FATULS.

FATULS: Federation of Arab Trade Unions and Labor Societies, a Palestinian trade-union movement in the Mandate period that was founded, in 1942, as a rival to the PAWS. It continued as the AWC after 1945.

FPWAC: Federation of Palestinian Women's Action Committees, the women's organization of the Unity Bloc. First such organization to be founded in the Occupied Territories, in 1978. Focuses on organizing housewives in addition to working women.

GFTU: General Federation of Trade Unions, a formal trade-union structure that incorporates West Bank trade unions. Established according to the Jordanian labor law. Headquartered in Nablus.

GFTU-Ghanem: Separate GFTU comprising the PWB, the WUB, the PUAF, and the WVB under Secretary-General 'Adel Ghanem from August 1981 to September 1985. Headquartered in Nablus.

GFTU-PWB: Separate GFTU controlled exclusively by the PWB from September 1985 to March 1990. Headquartered in Nablus.

GFTU-WUB: Separate GFTU controlled exclusively by the WUB since January 1986. Headquartered in Ramallah.

GFTU-WYM: Separate GFTU controlled exclusively by the WYM from August 1981 to March 1990. Headquartered in Nablus.

HWC: Higher Women's Council, a coordinating committee incorporating the four strands of the women's movement in the Occupied Territories. Established in December 1988, at the height of the intifada.

PAWS: Palestinian Arab Workers' Society, the first Arab trade union in Palestine, established in Haifa in 1925.

Progressive Bloc: Popular movement supportive of the PCP.

PUAF: Progressive Unionist Action Front, the unionist arm of the Action Front.

PWB: Progressive Workers' Bloc, the unionist arm of the Progressive Bloc. Oldest of the union movements in the Occupied Territories.

"Reunified" GFTU: Separate GFTU comprising all main trade-union blocs except the WUB, as well as some smaller groups whose unionist character remains unclear. Established on 1 March 1990.

Unity Bloc: Popular movement supportive of the DFLP.

UPMRC: Union of Palestinian Medical Relief Committees, a grass-roots organization of health professionals in the Occupied Territories, established in 1981.

UPWC: Union of Palestinian Women's Committees, the women's organization of the Action Front.

UPWWC: Union of Palestinian Working Women's Committees, the women's organization of the Progressive Bloc. It has focused on organizing working women.

Vanguard Bloc: Popular movement borrowing its ideology from the ANM of the 1950s and 1960s. Historically close to the Syrian Ba'ath, it currently has few active supporters in the Occupied Territories.

WCSW: Union of Women's Committees for Social Work, the women's organization of the Youth Movement.

WUB: Workers' Unity Bloc, the unionist arm of the Unity Bloc. Founded in 1978, it has focused on organizing Palestinian migrant workers employed in Israel.

WVB: Workers' Vanguard Bloc, the unionist arm of the Vanguard Bloc.

WWC: Women's Work Committee, a women's organization set up in 1978, later renamed the FPWAC.

WYM: Workers' Youth Movement, the unionist arm of the Youth Movement.

Youth Movement: Popular movement supportive of Fatah.

Foreign and International Organizations

FNV: Federatie Nederlandse Vakverenigingen, a Dutch trade-union federation.

Histadrut, the largest Israeli trade-union federation, an affiliate of the ICFTU in Brussels.

ICFTU: International Confederation of Free Trade Unions, an international trade-union federation based in Brussels.

ICRC: International Committee of the Red Cross, a Swiss relief organization with a mission in Israel and the Occupied Territories.

ILO: International Labor Organization, a United Nations organization headquartered in Geneva. It sends an annual fact-finding mission to Israel and the Occupied Territories.

UNRWA: United Nations Relief and Works Agency for Palestinian Refugees, headquartered in Vienna, with operations in several Arab countries and the Occupied Territories.

WCL: World Confederation of Labor, an international trade-union federation based in Prague. The PTUF is one of its affiliates.

Behind the Intifada

———————————

Chapter One

MASS MOBILIZATION UNDER OCCUPATION

THE START of the Palestinian uprising in December 1987 sent persons both inside and outside the Israeli-occupied territories scrambling for explanations as to why the uprising occurred when it did and, to a lesser extent, how it occurred at all. Explanations focused on possible influences, like the successful hang glider penetration of Israel's northern border in November 1987, which punctured the myth of Israeli invincibility, and catalysts, like the incident in the Gaza Strip when an Israeli truck driver allegedly swung his vehicle directly into the path of a vanload of Palestinian laborers returning from work in Israel, killing four. The incident sparked demonstrations in Jabalya refugee camp on 9 December, which spread to other areas of the Gaza Strip, and soon thereafter to the West Bank as well.[1]

Many Western observers have also pointed to the "Extraordinary Arab Summit" in Jordan earlier that fall as another spark that helped ignite the uprising. Palestinians, they said, finally saw, through the lack of attention paid to the question of Palestine and King Hussein's snub of PLO leader Yasser Arafat, that they could not rely on the Arab states to help them in their struggle for national liberation. The summit reinforced Palestinians' disillusionment with the Arab regimes and, it was said, Palestinians realized that they had to take their struggle completely into their own hands.[2]

For many Palestinians in the Occupied Territories, however, the greatest surprise, with hindsight, was that the uprising had not occurred before December 1987. Smaller uprisings, usually lasting not more than one or two months, had repeatedly broken out in the preceding decade, led by political organizers linked to the Palestine Liberation Organization (PLO). From late 1986 on, there was definitely "something in the air," with continual demonstrations in various locations in the Occupied Territories fueled by ever-harsher Israeli military reprisals and encouraged by the crucial reconciliation of PLO factions at the eighteenth meeting of the Palestine National Council (PNC) in Algiers in April 1987.

Only a decade earlier, however, the assessment was that no collective action against the occupation could occur. In 1981, Palestinian sociologist Salim Tamari remarked in reference to social changes in the Occupied Territories that a number of analysts had concluded "that there is wide-scale differentiation leading to proletarianization, that this proletarianization automatically gives rise to a new class consciousness, and that this, in turn, translates into resistance against occupation." Tamari claimed to the contrary that this "is not borne out by analysis of political events. The main source of resistance has been the towns, and not the country-side. . . . Indeed, shopkeepers have played a major role in shaping and leading urban strikes, whereas peasant workers and migrant workers to Israel have, in general, been rather quiet in these movements." One of the reasons for this, according to Tamari, was that the number of union-ized workers remained very small, and urban-based unions were unable to recruit effectively in the villages. "Thus, peasant consciousness remains the main force among Palestinians employed in Israel."[3]

The question then arises of what took place within Palestinian society during that brief ten-year period that allowed the uprising to occur, given that mass mobilization is a complex phenomenon requiring that numerous stages of recruitment, organization, and perceptions of common interest reach levels sufficient to ignite and sustain a national movement. Why the uprising started when it did becomes secondary to the question of how the elements necessary to enable it to take place at all emerged within the specific socioeconomic formation of the West Bank and Gaza Strip.

The Palestinian struggle for national liberation is articulated by a na-tional movement that falls squarely in the classic twentieth-century tra-dition of national movements arising in colonial settings, but it has fea-tures that differ significantly from those of other movements of national liberation because of its unusual inside and outside wings, and the partic-ular conditions created by a prolonged military occupation. In order to analyze the Palestinian national movement in the context of other such movements, it is necessary to mention briefly a number of crises in Pal-estinian history that caused the development of the Palestinian movement to differ from other movements that may exhibit a more "regular" pattern of development. These crises, stemming both from wars and from an ac-tive policy of the occupier further to dispossess the Palestinian popula-tion, resulted in large parts of Palestinian territory being alienated from Palestinian control, and in the expulsion and dispersal of thousands of Palestinians.

The first such crisis, the war and subsequent establishment of the state of Israel in 1947–48, an event referred to by Palestinians as the Disaster (al-Nakba), not only dealt a severe setback to the national movement that had emerged from the wreckage of the Ottoman Empire; it altered the terms of the conflict in the area.[4] While first a native population had found itself pitted against white settlers protected by a European power, it was now dispersed and placed under the rule of various Arab governments while the settlers ensconced themselves in their own state. The colonizers and the colonized, except for the small and powerless Palestinian minority in Israel, were no longer interspersed. As a result, resistance to colonialism took the form not of guerrilla warfare leading to mass insurrection and revolution in a nationalist context, but—to the extent possible, given Palestinians' dependence on the Arab governments that hosted them—of commando attacks across national boundaries.

The particular character of Israeli colonialism, and the destruction and exile of Palestinian society, gave rise to an idiosyncratic Palestinian nationalist movement, first embodied by Fatah, the organization established by Yasser Arafat in 1965. It was a movement that opposed imperialism, and in particular Israel as imperialism's beachhead, but it was faced with an enemy that was organized in a coherent, relatively homogeneous society enjoying overwhelming support from the world community, the Soviet Union not excluded. This, in other words, was not a colonialist regime desperately clinging to its remaining, and weakening, ties with the metropolis, as had become the pattern in most of Africa and Asia in the 1960s. This was not simply an outgrowth but truly an organ of the West, implanted in foreign soil. Fatah, on the other hand, which in the late 1960s took control of the PLO, lacked the coherent societal base that other movements of national liberation found in their home societies, and it was forced to use the entire Arab world, in all its diversity and contradictions, as a base for its operations, recruiting supporters from among the Palestinian masses in refugee camps in Lebanon, Syria, and Jordan.[5]

The second crisis, the June War of 1967, both worsened the Palestinian predicament—through more dispossession, expulsion, and dispersal—and for the first time made it possible to opppose the colonial enemy from within, as the two populations, Israeli and Palestinian, became progressively interspersed during the next two decades of Israeli military occupation of the West Bank and Gaza Strip. Only in the 1970s, after more than five decades of Palestinian nationalism, did a nationalist movement of classic design begin to emerge in what remained of Palestine. This movement, however, had to exist in the shadow of the preexisting, overarching Palestinian movement led by the PLO that matured in the diaspora and whose program and ideology reflected that of the diaspora. The local movement consisted of two branches: the underground military-political branch, whose members adhere directly to one of the factions of the PLO and carry out resistance operations on the orders of their commanders, who are usually outside the area; and the semilegal social-political branch, consisting of institutions and popular organizations set up by local activists who have attempted to mobilize the Palestinian masses by offering them services that were otherwise not available, while articulating nationalist concerns and aspirations as part of their day-to-day work. It is especially the second branch, the popular movement in the Occupied Territories,

that provided the local institutional infrastructure as well as the leadership
for the uprising that began in December 1987.

How was this movement born? What has its trajectory been? Its character? And how is it linked to the Palestinian national movement? To answer these questions, it may be helpful to look at some comparative cases,
using a model developed by Jeffery Paige in his seminal study, *Agrarian
Revolution*.[6] Paige studied particular forms of agricultural organization
and rural class conflict in the Third World, drawing correlations between
"different forms of political action and different configurations of interests," and then predicting actions from interests.[7] We will look only at
those economic systems dominated by landed estates employing a migratory wage-labor force, because these, despite considerable differences,
come closest to the Palestinian situation.

Although in the Palestinian case there are no landed estates in the Occupied Territories like the grape estates of colonial Algeria or the coffee
estates of colonial Kenya, a parallel structure of a Palestinian migratory
wage-labor force employed in Israeli enterprises prevails. Most Palestinians employed in Israel work on agricultural estates like the kibbutzim and
moshavim, on construction sites, in industrial enterprises like textile companies, and in hotels and restaurants. What these workplaces have in common is that they, like the colonial landed-estate system, are economically
weak and cannot survive without a cheap, disenfranchised labor force.
While Israeli employers may not have had to use legal or extralegal force
to secure a ready supply of labor as in the colonial tradition,[8] the Israeli
state has instituted mechanisms of labor control to ensure a constant flow
of cheap and unorganized labor from the Occupied Territories to Israel. It
should be remembered that the availability of Palestinian labor results in
large part from continued expropriation of Palestinian lands, with Israel
currently in control of over 50 percent of West Bank lands.

In explaining the occurrence of revolts in societies where migrant labor
predominates, Paige notes that since the work force must return to sub-
sistence agriculture during the landed estate's off-season, workers remain
dependent on the villages from which they hail. According to Paige, when

> revolutionary movements do form in such systems, they are therefore likely
> to combine both wage laborers and traditional communal organizations. The
> ideology uniting these disparate elements cannot be based on class but can be
> based on national or racial hatred of a settler class. Settler-owned estates
> affect not only the wage laborers but the traditional subsistence cultivators
> they frequently displace. Thus revolutionary movements in migratory wage
> labor estate systems are likely to involve coalitions based on communal ties.[9]

In the Palestinian case, workers' ties with their communities are reinforced, not by the off-season in Israeli agriculture, but by the irregularity

of work in Israeli construction and agriculture, the high turnover of workers due to their uncertain legal status as "frontier workers," and the seasonal need for Palestinians to be employed temporarily in agriculture in the Occupied Territories themselves, especially in the crucial olive harvest every two years. In addition, the experience of work in Israel (higher wages, a different worldview) is radically altering the structure of leadership in the villages as the power of the landed elites is being eroded by the new class of migrant workers.

Itinerant day labor in Israel has constituted the backbone of the Palestinian economy for the past two decades. As such, it became the source of the fundamental developments that made collective action possible. From the migratory wage-labor force stemmed the Palestinian labor unions, which arose, in part, from the failure of organized labor in Israel to protect the rights of Palestinian workers. These unions have proven particularly adroit in linking the workers' daily experience to the military occupation, thereby placing their programs within the overall nationalist framework. Through alliances with other sectors of the population (organized in service-oriented popular committees, such as women's committees and medical relief committees), they became a mainstay of the national movement in the Occupied Territories.

However, as Paige has argued, given the disparate nature of the migrant-labor community, which militates against the effective mobilization of its members, political organization must be introduced from outside the workers' community. In his analysis this role is played by the traditional agrarian elite.[10] In the Palestinian case, however, there is hardly an agrarian elite left that is strong enough, compared with other social sectors in Palestinian society, to serve as a powerful partner in a coalition with the migrant-labor force. In its place, however, a petite bourgeoisie of traders, merchants, labor contractors, and professionals, which in other social formations might be relegated to a secondary position behind the main social classes, in the West Bank and Gaza Strip constitutes the main pillar of the Palestinian national movement next to the "working class" of itinerant and locally employed workers. In the Occupied Territories, as in Angola and elsewhere, a dynamic coalition emerged that was based not on class but on a shared perception of a common enemy, and a commonality of interest in fighting that enemy.

Paige's model posits other prerequisites for successful mobilization and collective action. One is the presence of political structures that can provide the organizational and ideological framework for the popular movement.[11] In the Palestinian case, this framework exists in the form of the PLO and its institutions, which have formulated strategy and tactics for Palestinians both in the Occupied Territories and in the diaspora. In the West Bank and Gaza Strip, some local political structures already existed from the pre-1967 period; these were mobilized for the national cause, while activists who identified with the PLO began organizing the masses in new structures in the mid-1970s.

Lack of local economic development is another structural precondition. This tends to lessen class differences in colonial situations, and may give rise to a national alliance of classes opposed to the colonial power.[12] In the Palestinian case, the Israeli authorities have laid obstacles in the path of economic development in the Occupied Territories, especially in commodities that compete with Israeli production, and have generally made acquisition of permits conditional on "good behavior" and payment of taxes (during the intifada). This has brought collective hardship to the Palestinian community, and has thereby reinforced alliances across class lines, enabling collective action against the occupation. For example, the trade unions in the West Bank decided in the early 1970s to "freeze the class struggle" and to engage in a "national alliance of classes" with the Palestinian managerial sector, creating social peace as the requisite environment for collective struggle against the common enemy.

The crucial point in Paige's analysis is the blurring of class lines in the face of wholesale dispossession and exploitation, and the emergence of class coalitions opposed to the settler society. The struggle of the Palestinians against the occupier does not arise directly out of the relations of production. In the words of Roger Simon, who analyzes Antonio Gramsci's theory of hegemony and the "war of position,"

> hegemony has a national-popular dimension as well as a class dimension. It requires the unification of a variety of different social forces into a broad democratic alliance expressing a national-popular collective will, such that each of these forces preserves its own autonomy and makes its own contribution in the advance towards socialism. It is this strategy of building up a broad bloc of varied social forces, unified by a common conception of the world, that Gramsci called a war of position.[13]

It may not be socialism that Palestinians (or at least followers of the dominant trend in the Palestinian movement) are after, but the basic features of a movement that entrenches itself to undermine the prevailing relations of power appear to be present in the Palestinian case. Again, it is the idea of "freezing the class struggle" that is significant here.

Who are the main actors in this nationalist coalition? Historical examples support the Palestinian case. In colonial Africa, according to Immanuel Wallerstein, social and economic changes brought about by colonial rule led to the growth of a new elite that began to challenge both traditional sources of authority and the colonial power itself.[14] In the case of the West Bank, labor migration in the 1950s and 1960s further undermined the power of the landed elite, which was already weakened by land fragmentation and a discriminatory Jordanian policy against the West Bank economy. Some urbanization took place (though probably not to the extent witnessed in African countries), and growing numbers of Palestinians sought a formal education. At the time Israel occupied the West Bank in 1967, it found two elites vying for power: the traditional landed families and a new group of urban traders. The military authorities banked on the former for support (through patronage, and by offering them leadership in indirect-rule schemes), which helped push the new elite into the nationalist camp; this accounts for the strong showing of this pro-PLO elite in the municipal elections of 1976.

The changes described by Wallerstein not only led, in the case of the West Bank and Gaza, to the emergence of new leaders in the Palestinian community; it also gave rise to a generation of grass-roots organizations that provided those services to the population that were not provided by the occupying power. This too has clear parallels with the African case.[15] In the West Bank, social changes in the countryside gave rise to a host of new organizations, the majority of which were based in the urban centers, but which were increasingly extended into the rural areas in the late 1970s and 1980s. The trade unions were the most obvious example, providing health insurance and other basic services to their members. But as in Africa, it was the educated elite that took the lead in establishing organizations other than trade unions. Some of the first grass-roots organizations in the West Bank, for example, were voluntary work committees that sprang from the Community Work Program sponsored by the first Palestinian institute of higher learning in the Occupied Territories, Bir Zeit University. Professional associations preceded mass organizations like the women's committees and, in the late 1970s, the revitalized trade unions. In fact, such organizations initially provided the national leadership in the Occupied Territories, as in the municipal elections, while the organizations that mobilized the masses (including in the villages and refugee camps) did not start producing a national leadership until the mid-1980s.

We have, in short, in the specific socioeconomic formation of the Occupied Territories in the 1970s and 1980s an insurgent nationalist movement based on an alliance of workers (both migrant and nonmigrant) and a new petite bourgeoisie consisting of merchants, traders, educators, and other professionals, much as in African countries. In this arrangement, the petite bourgeoisie provided the leadership, while the workers helped cement the mass base of the movement through their own organizations. The question remains how—by what mechanisms—this coalition was able to translate mass mobilization into collective action, as witnessed in the popular uprising that began in 1987.

The most basic of all ingredients for collective action is a population (a group, class, or society) that has acquired a shared perception of its situation, and is prepared to let itself be organized for the attainment of a common goal to transcend the situation it finds intolerable. This "human base" alone (without people to organize it) is not enough, just as revolutionaries operating in a social vacuum have little chance of realizing their goals. In the words of William Friedland, "while social groups are capable of providing the human base for a revolutionary transformation . . . and models for organizing conscious revolutionaries . . ., revolutionaries must face the problem of developing revolutionary consciousness and action in the people while translating action into strategies to effect the transformation of state power."[16]

In the first instance what counts is how individuals can overcome their dependence on others, because this will shape their sense of what is possible. In the Palestinian case, the migration of men for purposes of finding work pulled women out of their homes and pushed them into the labor market, often over the objections of male family or community members, as new economic imperatives started to shatter established customs. This physical step produced a transformation of women's understanding of their role in Palestinian society. It is exactly these women who began to be recruited by the women's committees in the late 1970s. On the societal level, the absence of basic services gave rise, rather spontaneously, to voluntary work groups in the early 1970s, which then mushroomed as more and more people realized that the only way to have existing conditions improved was to improve them themselves.

The organizers of such groups were Palestinians who in one way or another had attained a consciousness of their situation and who were willing to make the necessary sacrifices to foment change. Often they were educators or those in the process of being educated—high-school and college students. Some of the voluntary work effort, as stated before, grew out of community programs developed as part of the formal Bir Zeit University curriculum. These programs combined teachers and students in an effort to resolve concrete problems, first on a limited level (problems students themselves faced), and then on a wider scale (problems in the community at large). The founders of the first network of women's groups, the Women's Work Committee (WWC), were graduates of Bir Zeit University and other professional women, some of them educators, in the Ramallah area, but the movement soon included working women, from the services sector down to the shop floor.

From the individual experience, the process goes up one step to the group experience. For Gramsci, the crucial link between the individual and the group is the transformation of what he calls "common sense," defined by Roger Simon as "the uncritical and largely unconscious way in which a person perceives the world, often confused and contradictory, and compounded of folklore, myths and popular experience." This "common sense" has to be turned into a coherent ideology.[17] Workers consti-tute one obvious group. In the absence of a proletariat in the Western sense, workers, according to John Iliffe, will create their own organization and group consciousness of their interests, "and organise to advance these interests . . . in response to their common status."[18] In the Palestinian case, the Israeli occupation stimulated the rise of migrant labor. Since these workers could not be reached by organizers in their places of work, unionists in the late 1970s began to organize them in their villages, offer-ing some of those benefits the workers were unable to obtain from their employers or the Israeli state. Unions developed programs directed to-ward the specific needs of these workers, thus reinforcing their identity as migrant laborers, while raising their consciousness about their rights and how to realize them. In the process, the definition of a union was ex-panded, as happened, for example, as well in South Africa where "black worker interests extend beyond the factory . . . to the ghetto where black workers stay together in hotels under squalid conditions."[19]

Other groups in Palestinian society shared identities and structures, and they were among the first to be mobilized: professionals (doctors, lawyers, engineers), students, women workers, merchants, artists, and writers, even—to an extent—housewives. In all cases organizers at-tempted to make a link between people's daily experiences and the mili-tary occupation, and while offering concrete services to their members, they firmly placed their organizations' programs within the overall na-tionalist framework.

On the next level up, the societal level, the various groups have to be held together. Nationalism can be the necessary glue. How does nation-alism come about? According to Friedland, "the social practices of colo-nialism inflict on the indigenous people a host of daily indignities. Even where there is no sense of nationhood before the establishment of the colony, colonialism creates it. It accomplishes this by treating all indige-nous residents with equal contempt."[20] This by itself may not be enough. In the words of Barrington Moore, Jr.:

> Once a critical mass of potentially discontented people has come into exis-tence through the working out of large-scale institutional forces the stage is set for the appearance of "outside agitators." . . . Their task is to find and articulate latent grievances, to challenge the dominant mythology, to organ-ize for a contest with the dominant forces around them. The outside agitators do the hard work of undermining the old sense of inevitability. They are also the traveling salesmen for the new inevitability.[21]

In Palestinian society, nationalism grew out of the systematic repres-sion exercised by the Israeli military occupation. The successes of outside organizers, primarily the PLO under Arafat, in the international arena in the early 1970s enhanced nationalism's appeal in the local population, and the PLO's decision in 1974 to redirect its energies and resources to the Occupied Territories and the subsequent adoption by mass organizers of nationalist symbols and programs helped unify the ranks behind the PLO's banner.

For Charles Tilly, mobilization denotes the extent to which a population succeeds in gaining collective control over resources, which include such factors of production as land, labor, and capital. The effectiveness of mobilization can be measured by determining the sum of the market value of these factors of production that are in the collective control of the population and the population's ability to make these resources available for use when needed.[22] A more general definition of resources would include the number of organizations, the size of their membership, the degree of their membership's commitment, and the amount, scale, and quality of their activities.

In the Palestinian case, a conscious decision was made by the PLO in 1974 to begin mobilizing the masses in the Occupied Territories in popular organizations. The PLO sought to set up new organizations and, more importantly, to infuse the existing ones with a new ideology—to transform them in the service of nationalism. During the following years, an intensive recruitment drive took place among students, workers, professionals, and others around issues of common concern. Organizations proliferated, not only in the urban centers but in the rural areas as well. Their membership increased dramatically, and their activities expanded. By the mid-1980s one can speak of the existence of a network or infrastructure of organizations that had a popular base and were able to provide the basic services lacking in the community, and also to lead the masses in times of direct confrontation with the occupier.

An important aspect of mobilization is the coherence of the participants. As stated before, a nationalist movement rests on an alliance of classes that, because of shared oppression, have momentarily set aside their differences—that have chosen, in the words of Palestinian unionists, to "freeze the class struggle." Once an alliance has been established, a common strategy must be developed with clear goals and means of realizing them. In a nationalist movement, the strategy has three interrelated, and indeed overlapping, elements: assailing the hegemony exercised by the state (or occupying power) and its institutions, outadministering the enemy by setting up "parallel hierarchies," and creating a new hegemony of the nationalist movement. It is crucial to undermine the hegemony of the state because the movement's ultimate goal, seizure of state power, is often too far removed, or even elusive, to ensure the full commitment at all times of a movement's membership. In addition, state power tends to be diffuse, spread through a number of institutions, and its control over the population is exercised not only physically, through institutions and coercive measures, but, more importantly, by ideological means, which are not readily recognized for what they are. According to Friedland, "seizing the state is not a simple physical activity; post offices, radio stations, governmental buildings, work places and corporate offices may be occupied, but the ideological assumptions and habitual behavior that underlie the manner in which these institutions operate are more difficult to uproot."[23]

A strategy aimed, ultimately, at seizing state power must therefore rely on intermediate steps. The power of the state, which is diffuse and sometimes hidden, must, according to Friedland, "be challenged wherever it is exercised and whenever feasible."[24] It is necessary, in Moore's words, to take concrete measures and effect concrete changes that, by their example, will help people "overcome the illusion that the present state of affairs is just, permanent, and inevitable."[25] This process is referred to by Eqbal Ahmad as "outadministering" the enemy. According to Ahmad, a revolutionary guerrilla movement "concentrates on outadministering, not on outfighting the enemy."[26] The aim, says Ahmad, is not "simply to inflict military losses on the enemy," which is usually "vastly superior" in military terms, but "to destroy the legitimacy of its government and to establish a rival regime through the creation of 'parallel hierarchies.'"[27]

Concretely, what is needed are organizations that at once provide essential services and, through the provision of these services, undermine the legitimacy of the adversary. Most important, these organizations must be able to operate openly in order to be effective. They must therefore work within the existing legal framework. In the Palestinian case, the continued absence of an independent national authority that could regulate society has meant that basic services not provided by the foreign ruler had to be furnished by Palestinians themselves, in informal ways. Consequently, Palestinians began setting up organizations like trade unions. In Western democratic countries these play a role complementary to that filled by the state and constitute a counterweight to the state's transgressions. In the Palestinian case they have played a substitute role under military occupation, filling the gaps created by the occupier. Organizations like trade unions have fought for basic rights, including health insurance, workers' compensation, and the right to organize.

For all intents and purposes, these organizations have also gone further: they have provided the economic, social, and political infrastructure of Palestinian society. They have outadministered the Israeli occupation by reaching those areas of daily life the occupier could not reach, and by mobilizing people whose loyalty the occupier could never gain. As such, these organizations, which in the 1980s included trade unions, voluntary work committees, women's committees, and medical relief committees, became an institutional infrastructure of resistance to the Israeli military occupation. At the same time, these organizations groomed a new leadership, one that gradually wrested the initiative in the Palestinian national movement from the outside leadership in the 1980s, as demonstrated by the organization of the popular uprising that began in December 1987. The ramifications of this in the Palestinian movement are yet unclear, but the emergence of this leadership structure, this "parallel hierarchy" that has come about democratically through periodic elections in the unions and committees, poses a serious, long-term challenge to Israeli power in the West Bank and Gaza; it is raising the cost of occupation and thus, eventually, may bring an end to it.

Finally, the effectiveness of a revolutionary or nationalist movement is contingent on the clarity of its vision or ideology as expressed through its leadership, and on the democratic process of its institutions. In the words of Eqbal Ahmad, "only a relationship of mutuality, identification and coperformance between leaders and masses can release the creative energies necessary for the constant improvisations and the steady flow of new leaders (their attrition rate being very high) so crucial in revolutionary warfare."[28] In addition, "the most successful guerrilla movements . . . evince deep respect for local autonomy, self-management, rapid social mobility, egalitarianism, and accountability of leaders and cadres to the populace."[29]

In the Palestinian case, no popular organizations of any size and influence existed until the late 1970s. In the organizations that did exist, leadership came about nominally through elections, but in effect by prior arrangement between the various factions. In the 1980s the new organizations were characterized by a higher degree of democratic process. Power was decentralized, and the rotation of leaders, in part due to the repressive practices of the occupying regime, was accelerated. Although the leaders inside the Occupied Territories firmly pledge their allegiance to the PLO, a division of labor has developed whereby the inside leadership directs the masses on a day-to-day basis, while the PLO leadership outside provides the strategic framework for the movement and presents itself as the official Palestinian side in peace negotiations.

The questions that remain are why, in the Palestinian case, there has been as much mobilization as there has been, and at the same time, why there has not been more. In other words, one must determine the parameters of mass mobilization. In the West Bank and Gaza, it is easy to see why people would want to organize against the occupation. But this in itself does not explain the level of organization. As has been argued, however, the right conjunction of forces occurred in the Occupied Territories for an organized mass movement to arise: there was a discontented human base that, through the shared oppression it suffered, could be organized collectively when outside leaders gave the green light and provided the minimally necessary resources to inside activists in the mid-1970s. The size of the movement, and the democratic process that characterizes it, as well as the (essentially legal) nature of its activities, have made it difficult for the military authorities to suppress it, although they have never ceased to try to do so.

It is, in fact, surprising that there has not been more mobilization, or, to state it more precisely, why the movement has been so singularly incapable of getting significantly closer to its stated goal of establishing an independent Palestinian state. Part of the reason lies in the situational field of opportunity (in the Tillyan sense) in which the movement has found itself. Although the military authorities have been unable to suppress the movement, they have at the same time managed to keep it off balance by decapitating the leadership as soon as it emerges, ipso facto forcing others to maintain a low profile, which reduces their effectiveness. More important, the dichotomy between inside and outside leadership, dictated by the geographic realities of the conflict, has not helped the movement's effectiveness, which is hindered by problems in communication and the provision of resources, and the variance of conditions in which the dispersed Palestinian communities have found themselves.

The nationalist movement in the Occupied Territories is a relatively minor actor in the larger scheme of things, where the PLO is subjected to the whim of the Arab governments that host it, while the Israeli state has received the unwavering support (economic, military, institutional, ideological) of the United States. The Palestinian movement may raise the cost of military occupation and thus force the occupying power to change its policies, or perhaps even to withdraw behind the pre-1967 border, but it cannot alter the overall balance of forces, and it can therefore not bring about the ultimate goal of Palestinian nationalism: a Palestinian state in all of Palestine.

At the same time, it would be a mistake to ignore concrete obstacles to the mobilization of the Palestinian masses generated in the Occupied Territories themselves. Some of the organizations in the vanguard of the national movement in the West Bank and Gaza are dominated by Palestinians who consider themselves Marxist-Leninists and, just as important, are seen to be so by a population that harbors suspicions of any foreign ideology, especially an atheistic one. Unionization itself is a foreign idea in a rural society, and although the situation is changing, many workers still prefer to fall back on their familial and village networks rather than on unions for support. Strikes are not the customary method of seeking redress; one operates through established channels, calling on trusted mediators to reconcile between the two sides in a conflict. Unionization is a rare phenomenon in most of the Middle East, and indeed it could be argued that the presence of a nationalist struggle in the Occupied Territo-

ries has enhanced recruitment in trade unions where otherwise little unionization would have taken place.

There are also other factors: the geographic spread of the work force,
the methods of recruiting workers, the relationship between employers
and employees, the isolation of housewives in the villages, the stigma
attached to women's participation in public activities. Some of these will
be discussed at greater length in the chapters that follow. The main point
is that despite these obstacles, a mass-based movement emerged in the
West Bank and Gaza in the 1970s and 1980s that—though unable to ac-
complish its ultimate goal, the establishment of a Palestinian state, because of the presence of a military occupation—succeeded in reaching
such levels of cohesiveness and organization that it could lead the popular
uprising that started in 1987.

Chapter Two

THE STRUCTURAL CONTEXT

As WE HAVE SEEN, successful organization and mobilization that will lead to collective action can occur only if certain conditions obtain. Most important among these is a human base dissatisfied with its own condition. In the West Bank and Gaza Strip, the Palestinian population has not only lived under harsh military occupation; it has also suffered economic exploitation, blocked development, and discrimination in services.

THE ECONOMICS OF MILITARY OCCUPATION
AND THE LABOR FORCE

In the June War of 1967, Israel occupied, among other territories, the remaining parts of Palestine not yet under its control, the West Bank and Gaza Strip. During the following years, the military occupation permitted the Israeli authorities to carry out a wide-ranging scheme of colonization under the guise of law.[1] With the progressive Israeli takeover of Palestinian resources in the Occupied Territories, the social, political, and economic infrastructure of the Occupied Territories underwent a dramatic transformation. Of particular importance are the socioeconomic developments of the post-1967 period in the West Bank and Gaza Strip, as well as the major demographic trends, in particular with relation to the labor force, stemming from these developments.

Israeli Economic Policy and Labor

The 1967 war and its aftermath gave new impetus to the Israeli economy, which had suffered two years of deep depression, including mass layoffs of workers. With the influx of international capital in the aftermath of the war (especially United States economic and military aid, which increased dramatically),[2] investments were redirected toward services and industry, revitalizing these sectors, especially the armaments industry. These changes were accompanied by a continuing drop in Jewish participation in the wage-labor force, by a low rate of Jewish immigration to Israel, and by a strong pull for Jewish labor emanating from those industries either designated as strategic (thus excluding non-Jews) or requiring a high level of technical competence. At the same time, other high-growth sectors such as food processing, textiles, tourism, and—most important—construction were faced with an increasing shortage of unskilled labor. A major result, therefore, of the post-1967 boom was the new and high demand for a cheap, mobile, unskilled, and unorganized labor force. This Israel found in the population of the newly occupied West Bank and Gaza Strip.

The economic situation in the Occupied Territories differed sharply from that in Israel in June 1967. Under Jordan, the West Bank had been an economic backwater, playing the role of "supplier of agricultural produce to the East Bank, where some industrialization occurred."[3] Consequently, the period 1948–67 was one of high unemployment in the West Bank; many Palestinians left the area in search of jobs elsewhere, mostly in the East Bank and in the Persian Gulf states.[4]

The economic situation in the Gaza Strip was worse. Whereas the West Bank experienced at least a degree of industrialization, concentrated in small workshops, in Gaza "there was no industrial sector at all." The main economic sectors were agriculture (mostly citrus growing) and trade.[5] Unemployment was high, with those who worked employed in commerce, a few small workshops, the citrus harvest, and the Egyptian army.

Given economic conditions in the West Bank and Gaza on the one hand and in Israel on the other, and given the differential impact of the 1967 war on the economies of the two areas, Israel was able to take the upper hand in the economic future of the Occupied Territories. In the words of Ibrahim Dakkak, the "superiority of the Israeli system over the Palestinian system and the emergence of a sophisticated industrial, agricultural, and military complex in the former, facilitated Israeli dominance over the West Bank and the integration of its economy into the Israeli framework."[6]

Although the integration was an economic (and administrative) process, the policies that made it possible were based on solid political considerations. The main Israeli policy that set the tone for the first two decades of occupation crystallized within a year after the war. Its architect was the minister of defense, Moshe Dayan. The latter's view was, according to Elie Rekhess, that "the division between the Israeli economy and that of the areas [sic] should be functional, not territorial; capital and labour should move freely, regardless of political geography."[7] An important security consideration underlay this reasoning: "It was believed that the improvement of economic and social conditions . . . would be a means to minimize grievances and to blanket resentments. It would, therefore, become difficult for the fida'iyyun [resistance fighters] to find sympathizers among the inhabitants."[8]

Other motives doubtless played a role, including the Israelis' long-term desire to integrate their economy with that of the Arab world, and to impose an Israeli peace on the area. In the Occupied Territories the erasure of economic barriers would lead to a subsequent erasure of the geographic borders (the 1949 Armistice—or "Green"—Line). According to a study by the RAND Corporation, "Moshe Dayan seems to be aiming at an arrangement in which the issue of territorial sovereignty will be submerged in the welter of economic and personal ties that will have been created in the area. . . . In this fluid creation, in the process of integration, or what the ECONOMIST has called 'osmosis,' particular boundaries will assume secondary significance."[9]

Dayan's policy was based, according to Rekhess, on three principles: "*non-presence* (minimizing visible signs of the Israeli authorities to lessen friction and conflict with the population); *non-interference* (placing responsibility for economic and administrative activities in Arab hands); and *open bridges* (renewing personal and economic contacts between the population and the Arab world)."[10] In 1980, the Israeli ministry of defense went so far as to suggest that as a result of the policy of "minimal interference" in the lives of Palestinians, "the 'green line' actually disappeared, 'de facto' if not 'de jure,'" during the first decade of military occupation.[11]

By 1977, with the ascendancy of the right-wing and ultranationalist Likud, Israeli designs for the Occupied Territories changed, with the government pursuing an official policy of settling "Greater Israel." Using elaborate military legislation enabling the appropriation of land,[12] the limiting of Palestinian agriculture and industry,[13] the imposition of new taxes,[14] and the withholding of basic social services,[15] Israel rendered the economy of the Occupied Territories subservient to its own in an artificial "common market" arrangement. In addition, land alienation (amounting to over 52 percent of West Bank land in 1985)[16] and restrictions on agriculture led to the decline of the agricultural sector, forcing the agrarian population to look for alternative sources of income. In 1970, according to official Israeli statistics, 38.7 percent of Palestinians employed in the Occupied Territories were employed in agriculture. In 1986, their numbers had declined to only 25 percent.[17]

The Occupied Territories' industrial sector was unable to absorb this new pool of labor. The contribution of industry to the West Bank's gross domestic product was less than 7 percent in 1985.[18] In 1986 only sixty-four establishments in the West Bank and eighteen establishments in Gaza employed twenty or more workers; this involved mostly garment factories producing clothes for the local market, as well as for the Israeli and foreign markets through subcontracts with Israeli firms.[19] Investments in industry have been few, due to the unstable political climate and the difficulty in obtaining permits for productive projects from the military authorities. Minister of Defense Yitzhak Rabin declared unequivocally in February 1985 that "there will be no development in the Occupied Territories initiated by the Israeli government, and no permits given for expanding agri-

culture or industry, which may compete with the State of Israel."[20] Under
such conditions the Palestinian industrial sector, according to Meron Benvenisti, has been "unable to withstand Israeli competition. Moreover, the
industry has lately had to compete with Israeli enterprise located in the
settlements enjoying far-reaching incentives and subsidies."[21] The overall
result has been, in the words of Hillel Frisch, that "contrary to accepted
norms of growth, the rapid rise in income per capita in the West Bank was
not accompanied by comparable growth in its industrial sector, but rather
[by] that sector's relative decline."[22] In 1986, only 16.3 percent of the total
West Bank work force was employed in industry; the corresponding figure
for Gaza was 17.6 percent.[23]

Unable to find work in the undeveloped industrial sector, many Palestinians joined the ranks of those who, since 1968, have made a daily journey across the Green Line in search of jobs in Israel.

Work across the Green Line

Following the 1967 war, the Israeli economy generated a demand for
manual, mostly unskilled labor. To satisfy this new demand, legislation
was introduced in 1968 to enable Palestinians from the West Bank and
Gaza to work in Israel, in accordance with Moshe Dayan's overall policy
in the Occupied Territories. However, the inflow of Palestinian labor was
restricted by a quota requirement[24] (replaced after a few years by the requirement to hire Israelis before Palestinians), and the need to obtain a
work permit specifying the employer.[25] To control the flow of workers, the
government set up labor exchanges. By 1975, there were twenty-four
such exchanges in the West Bank and twelve in Gaza.[26] By 1988, there was
a total of thirty-nine exchanges.[27]

There has never been a shortage of Palestinians from the Occupied Territories willing to work in Israel. According to official Israeli statistics, in
1968, 5,000 Palestinians from the Occupied Territories were employed in
Israel. By 1974 this figure had risen to 69,000; by 1986, 94,700 Palestinians were working across the Green Line. In 1970, they made up 12
percent of the total labor force in the West Bank and Gaza. In 1974, it was
32 percent; in 1986, it was 36.3 percent.[28] These figures constitute an
underestimate, however.[29] Palestinian estimates, including estimates
made by trade unionists, indicate that an annual average of 120,000 workers from the Occupied Territories are employed in Israel; this number
fluctuates seasonally, reaching possible peaks of 150,000 during the summer and fall harvests when children temporarily join the work force. In
1989, at the height of the uprising, the Israeli government conceded that
as many as 116,000 Palestinians were regularly employed in Israel, only
45,000 of whom had registered with the labor exchanges.[30]

Israel's specific need for manual, mostly unskilled, labor has led to a concentration of Palestinians in the labor-intensive sectors of the Israeli economy, invariably in subordinate, nonmanagerial occupations. Most Palestinians are employed in construction (48 percent). The remainder are evenly divided among industry (17.4 percent), agriculture (15.8 percent), and other branches (18.8 percent), which include services and jobs in hotels and restaurants.[31] Construction is preferred because of the high demand in this sector; because few skills are needed; and because these jobs, which are temporary, allow part-time farmers to return to their agricultural activities during the harvest season.

A number of mechanisms of control were introduced by the authorities to ensure that only a particular type of worker would enter the job market, and only enough to satisfy labor demand. One of the most common criteria for hiring employees is the requirement that the job applicant present evidence of Israel Defense Forces (IDF) service along with a security clearance. A security clearance is rarely issued to Palestinians, especially not to Palestinians from the Occupied Territories, and Palestinians cannot serve in the Israeli military. The IDF service criterion applies to all industries and services labeled "strategic," and it is up to the Israeli state to decide which industries are "strategic" and which are not.[32] As a result, according to Moshe Semyonov and Noah Lewin-Epstein, in 1982 Palestinians from the Occupied Territories "were still unable to penetrate nineteen occupational categories out of the eighty-three that were defined."[33] A more subtle exclusionary technique is the employers' oft-expressed preference for "local workers." Since most industries are located in urban areas predominantly populated by Jews, Palestinians can effectively be kept out of almost any job when demand for labor is low and Jewish workers must be shielded from unemployment. This criterion has been codified in the Employment Service Law, which applies to all Palestinians who are registered with the official labor exchanges.[34]

One of the main functions of the labor exchanges is to screen workers. Their role has not been to find work for Palestinian job-seekers, but rather to register those workers who have already found work with Israeli employers on their own, and to find additional workers for Israeli employers whenever the need arises. After a worker's security record has been checked, the worker is issued a work permit,[35] which must be renewed periodically contingent on the employer's approval.[36]

Palestinian workers, like all residents of the Occupied Territories, are not allowed to stay overnight in Israel (between one and five o'clock in the morning) unless they have obtained an additional permit from the labor office in the town where they work following approval by the police and a factory inspector. Many workers, especially from Gaza, have been compelled to stay overnight in Israel without a permit, often with the connivance of their employers, because of the long commute and, since the up-rising, because of strikes and army curfews in the Occupied Territories.[37]

The Israeli government has had a strong interest in channeling workers from the Occupied Territories through the exchanges. The government has thus controlled wage rates and wage payments, effectively preventing Palestinian workers from undercutting Jewish labor, while deducting sums for social security and insurance purposes from the workers' wages; these sums, for the most part, are not returned to them in any form. Nom-inally, Palestinian workers from the Occupied Territories receive the same wages as do Israeli workers in order to protect the latter's economic position, by decree of the Economic Affairs Committee of the Israeli Knesset in 1968.[38] Palestinians' net wages are much lower than those earned by their Israeli colleagues in the same jobs, however, because of the deductions.

Official deductions consist of three parts: income taxes, national insur-ance fees, and pension contributions. Income tax deductions are the same for Israelis and Palestinians; it is in the area of national insurance that the two population groups are treated differently. National insurance fees for Palestinian workers have been grouped under the name "Deduction Fund," which has been defined as "the sum equivalent to that intended to cover the insurances of the National Insurance Institute for the Israeli workers."[39] It amounts to about 20 percent of the worker's gross wage. The difference is that Palestinians are eligible for only two percent of this in-surance, while Israelis are eligible for the full 20 percent. Official Israeli documents state that the remaining 18 percent is used to promote invest-ment and development in the Occupied Territories. For this reason, the money is transferred from the Employment Service, not to the National Insurance Institute, but to the Israeli Treasury. It has been calculated, however, that as much as 80 percent of this money is not transferred from the Treasury to the Israeli Civil Administration in the West Bank and Gaza, as it is supposed to be, but is kept in the Treasury for use in Israel itself.[40] In addition, Palestinian workers from the Occupied Territories are not eligible for the benefits received by Israeli workers: old-age allow-ances, allowances for surviving relatives, general disability benefits, un-employment benefits, and wage compensation.[41]

The second area of wage deductions in which Palestinians face discrim-ination is that of social security contributions. Totaling about 32 percent of the Palestinian workers' gross wages (before taxes), these contributions are collected, not to provide the worker with a pension on retirement, but to "create equality between the cost of an Israeli worker and a worker from the Occupied Territories, so as not to give the latter an advantage."[42] The ultimate destination of these contributions remains shrouded in mystery. They are reportedly deposited in workers' funds controlled by the Employment Service rather than by the Histadrut (the largest Israeli trade-union federation), and the individual Palestinian worker has no access to them, pending—or so the Israeli authorities claim—a final settlement of the Palestinian-Israeli conflict.[43]

In short, the stated Israeli aim to equalize nominal wages of Israelis and Palestinians from the Occupied Territories is offset by a number of factors that militate against equalization of take-home wages and benefits. There is therefore a large wage differential between Israeli and Palestinian workers. According to Emanuel Farjoun, "the average wage of an Israeli worker . . . adds up, together with fringe benefits, to earnings which are twice or three times those of an Arab worker from the Occupied Territories."[44]

The Histadrut has not acted to protect West Bank and Gaza workers from exploitation by the Israeli government. From its establishment in 1920, the Histadrut has systematically favored Jewish over Arab labor, while attempting to co-opt Arab labor without, however, fully integrating it.[45] After 1967, the Histadrut extended its activities to the areas that were formally annexed by Israel (the Golan Heights and East Jerusalem), but it has made no attempts formally to organize West Bank and Gaza workers. A memorandum issued by the secretary-general of the Histadrut, Yeruham Meshel, in the early 1980s sums up Histadrut policy toward workers from the Occupied Territories: "We have never attempted to organize these workers as Histadrut members in order to avoid the impression that we support the annexation of the administered territories. Nonetheless we have considered it our duty to grant full trade union protection to the West Bank Arabs working in Israel, and to ensure that they receive the same wages and social conditions as their Israeli Jewish and Arab colleagues."[46]

To receive this "protection," Palestinians pay a compulsory "organization fee" amounting to 1 percent of their wages to the Histadrut. This fee supposedly covers the cost of collective bargaining: Palestinian workers, who usually do not have individual contracts, automatically fall under the collective agreements negotiated by the Histadrut for each sector.[47] Although legally covered by these agreements, Palestinian workers face problems with enforcement, and few of the agreements have been translated into Arabic.[48]

Aside from Histadrut "protection," Palestinian workers are also eligible to receive protection from, and be members of, workers' committees on individual work sites in Israel. In 1983, the Israeli Department of Professional Unions issued a directive to the workers' committees in individual companies and plants to accept workers from the Occupied Territories in their ranks and grant them voting rights. These shop-floor committees are designed to investigate and channel workers' grievances about working conditions and wages.[49] There has, however, been strong grass-roots Jewish working-class pressure against including Palestinians on these committees, and in some cases Jewish workers have denied Palestinians even observer status on their committees.[50] In one example, striking West Bank workers employed by the Berman Bakery in West Jerusalem were denied Histadrut protection: "Though the workers concerned were legally employed through the Employment Service and though the factory has a Histadrut-affiliated workers' committee, the Histadrut local workers' council claimed that West Bankers' working conditions are not its concern."[51] In some plants Palestinians have set up their own workers' committees, but without effective backing from the Histadrut they have little leverage vis-à-vis their employers.[52] The absence of effective protection, in addition to Palestinian concerns that membership in the Histadrut could be interpreted as acceptance of the annexation of the Occupied Territories to Israel, was one of the reasons Palestinian activists began organizing these migrant workers in their own trade unions in the Occupied Territories after the mid-1970s.

Given the lack of effective recourse to trade-union protection, and the exploitation suffered after registration with the official labor exchanges, many Palestinian workers have circumvented the exchanges. They find work through labor contractors, or are hired directly by Israeli employers at one of the various "slave markets"—informal labor markets located at major road junctions leading into Israel from the West Bank and Gaza. This is especially true for construction workers since building activities tend to be less organized and smaller in scale than most agricultural and industrial projects. In 1989, only 40 percent of the workers from the Occupied Territories employed in Israel had work permits.[53] The risks are greater for undocumented workers, mostly because they can be arrested for working illegally, and also because they will be laid off first in times of recession. Labor statistics gathered during the recession that set in following the war between Israel and its neighbors in 1973 show that unemployment hit the undocumented workers first. These workers played the role, in other words, of a buffer for the Israeli workers in particular, and for the Israeli economy in general.[54] Because their position is inherently precarious, they cannot count on steady jobs or secure incomes. Their average net daily wages may exceed those of the documented workers, but, in the words of Farjoun, "it must be borne in mind that they do not enjoy even the few fringe benefits given to those who go through the labor exchanges, such as compensation for industrial accidents." In addition, "they are mostly hired for agricultural and other seasonal work, which implies a higher risk of unemployment during part of the year."[55]

Many Palestinian workers prefer to take the risks associated with being caught without a work permit rather than facing the perceived disadvantages of registering with the official labor exchanges; their wages are higher if they avoid the exchanges, and the government exercises less-effective control over their movements—for example, if they want to stay overnight across the Green Line without a permit. They also avoid security checks, which sift out any workers with prison records. Employing workers from the Occupied Territories illegally is also more profitable for the employers, who avoid providing for these workers' social and physical well-being. They are thus able to eliminate costs they would incur were they to hire Israeli workers enjoying trade-union protection.

If one accepts the average annual figure of 120,000 Palestinians from the Occupied Territories employed in Israel, and the official Israeli figure of 46,000 Palestinians employed through the labor exchanges, one can conclude that on average some 70,000 Palestinian workers from the Occupied Territories work in Israel without permits.[56]

The Histadrut has strongly opposed the phenomenon of undocumented Palestinian labor from the Occupied Territories, which, it claims, under-cuts Jewish labor. Mordechai Amster, a senior Histadrut official, said in 1983 that the building workers from the Occupied Territories would be the first to be fired if the depression in the construction sector continued: "They are not inhabitants of Israel and in every country with unemployment the foreign workers are the first to be dismissed."[57] The secretary-general of the Histadrut Construction Workers' Union said in 1984: "We have nothing against the 12,000 or so organized workers from the Occupied Territories sent by the employment agencies. They have the right to work. Our complaint is against unorganized [undocumented] labor."[58]

To sum up, Palestinians from the Occupied Territories, employed in lower-status jobs in Israel, have come to constitute a reserve army of labor in the Israeli economy. They have replaced Israeli Palestinians who have moved up the employment ladder into skilled occupations, which in turn have been abandoned by Jewish workers. A 1987 report of the International Labor Organization (ILO) states that "the great majority of Arab workers are employed under the least favourable conditions because of their lack of skills, or under conditions below the legal norm because their situation is irregular."[59] The Israeli preference for "local" workers has meant that Jewish workers take the better jobs, with more responsibility and higher wages, while Palestinians, especially those from the Occupied Territories, are relegated to performing menial tasks. According to Stanley Greenberg, the distinction between local and nonlocal workers "reflects a pattern of self-conscious development and urbanization that ensures the equation of local and Jewish labor."[60] The result, claims Greenberg, is that even though the Occupied Territories have been integrated "materially and ideologically" into Israel, "the 'green line' remains clearly drawn across the labor market,"[61] relegating Palestinians from the

Occupied Territories, in the words of Semyonov and Lewin-Epstein, to being the "hewers of wood and drawers of water of Israeli society,"[62] without rights and without protection.

Women's Labor

The level and specificity of the Israeli demand for unskilled and semi-skilled labor from the Occupied Territories has had three major effects in the West Bank and Gaza. First, it has prompted a brain drain of skilled and university-trained Palestinians abroad, mostly to the Persian Gulf, Western Europe, and the United States, because Israel's economic policy in the Occupied Territories did not allow for the development of industrial and financial sectors. In total, only about 20 percent of Palestinian high-school and university graduates are able to find work in their chosen fields in the West Bank every year. The remainder either find blue-collar work or emigrate. Only 30 percent of the men and 50 percent of the women ages ten to twenty-one in 1967 were present in the West Bank in 1984.[63]

Second, the daily flow of Palestinians to Israel has caused a scarcity of labor inside the Occupied Territories themselves, especially in agriculture and in the small industrial workshops. This has caused wages to rise. One of the results has been that many landowners can no longer afford to pay workers during the harvest season, and have been forced to abandon large-scale cultivation, thus contributing to the decline of agriculture in the West Bank.[64]

Third, the scarcity of labor in the Occupied Territories has opened job opportunities to an untapped sector of Palestinian society, women, who in the mid-1970s began to join the labor force. In migratory-labor economies, according to Susan Rockwell, "while remittances from laborers abroad have relieved some women of the necessity to work, the absence of family members has compelled others to assume greater workloads within the household or as wage earners."[65] At the same time, in those cases where a family cannot afford to send a man abroad for work, women may have to carry additional tasks to contribute to the income of a family suffering from the relative rise in prices as the families of migrants spend the remittances they receive from abroad.[66]

In the Occupied Territories, the reason for women's entry into the work force, aside from the aforementioned pull-factor of labor scarcity, lies in the imbalances caused by the integration of the West Bank and Gaza economies into the economy of Israel. According to Amal Samed, it was the relative decline of Palestinian wages resulting from inflation and the transfer of the Israeli price structure to the Occupied Territories that made it necessary for many women, and also for children, to look for wage labor to supplement the income of adult men—the traditional breadwinners—and "maintain a living income in the face of rising prices."[67] Few women work for fun or to increase their independence from their families (although this may result from their entry into the labor market). A survey conducted among women workers in Ramallah by one of the women's committees in the West Bank showed that at least 45 percent of those polled, but probably as many as 75 percent, were employed in wage labor because of financial need.[68] Susan Rockwell, who conducted a survey among 156 women workers in Gaza, reports that "Palestinian women said they worked because their families depended on their wages, and some earned the only income for the family. While some Palestinian women interviewed said that they enjoyed getting out of the house, factory work remains an undesirable interlude before marriage."[69] Randa Siniora, who conducted a parallel study in the West Bank, produced similar findings.[70]

Because of the continuing stigma attached to women working outside the home, only those who have no alternative—single, widowed, and divorced women—resort to this means of procuring a living. In Rockwell's words, in Gaza factories "the majority of [women] workers are single, and the turnover rate, due to early marriage, is high. Divorced and widowed women also work, but their number is few compared with single women. Married women rarely work: out of a sample of 156 Palestinian women, only one was married."[71]

Out of a total of 269,200 Palestinian workers in the Occupied Territories in 1986, at least 29,200 were women.[72] A considerable number of these women are employed across the Green Line, where they have taken jobs abandoned either by Israeli women or by Palestinian men: many working Israeli women have been drawn out of agriculture and the garment industry into the Israeli services sector after 1967; and many Palestinian male workers have been pulled into the construction sector. Palestinian women from the West Bank and Gaza tend to be concentrated, therefore, in seasonal agriculture (especially the citrus and tobacco harvests), the textile industry, and food processing.[73] Their numbers are unknown; most of this labor is irregular. One Ramallah unionist, who is also active in the women's movement, said that women from the Ramallah area

> began entering the labor force after 1967, and were involved in office work [in the Occupied Territories] and later simple factory work, like packing and labeling. They never really took part in the production process. So after five or even ten years, they still had not gained any experience or skills that would qualify them for other work. Women started going to work in Israel after 1975 when the economic situation [in the Occupied Territories] was worsening. These women had an interest in this because their own land was not producing enough.
>
> The women find work usually through social contacts in their village, not through the [Israeli] labor exchange. Many of the women don't have a work permit because of this. Not all bosses insist on their workers having a permit.

To facilitate the access of women to the Israeli workplace, employers took care of the transportation. The women [who work in agriculture] are usually picked up either by a contractor in a van or by [Israeli] Egged or Leshka buses. They leave around five or six in the morning and return twelve hours later. Transportation is not included in their monthly wage, which is about thirty to fifty dinars [approximately $90 to $150 before 1988]. Often they are paid for the amount of work they do, and in any case they are paid less than men. Several thirteen- and fourteen-year-old girls from Jalazon [refugee camp] are working in Israeli agriculture; their families are ashamed of admitting this. The women from the villages who work in Israel are usually older.

In the garment industry in Israel, the women earn between fifty and eighty dinars [approximately $150 to $240 before 1988]. Half the salary is paid in cash, the other half by check. When they quit their jobs, they receive compensation only on the basis of the check wage. Again, they don't get any work experience.[74]

Most women have been drawn into agriculture and the garment industry in Israel because there is a demand for unskilled labor in these sectors and because these are tasks that women had performed traditionally, though not for a wage. In that sense, according to Amal Samed, the women are skilled, not unskilled, even though the work is classified as unskilled, making it possible for employers to pay low wages.[75]

In the Occupied Territories themselves, most women are employed as teachers or secretaries, or in the garment industry. Recognizing that the way to reach more women was by employing them near their homes, Israeli textile and clothing companies have encouraged Palestinian entrepreneurs to produce for them through subcontracts, using women's labor in the Occupied Territories. In the 1980s, the garment industry in the Occupied Territories, producing clothes for Israeli companies, became the largest sector employing women. One unionist estimated that half the West Bank female labor force was employed in the garment industry.[76] Susan Rockwell found that in the Gaza Strip many factory owners "consider the pool of cheap female labor to be all that is keeping the outdated factories from going under in the face of Israeli competition. . . . Arab factory owners profit from societal stigmas that consider men to be the traditional breadwinners and that discourage women from working in Israel."[77]

Working conditions in the garment industry in the Occupied Territories have been a source of discontent, often articulated by the new generation of women's committees that have sought to organize women workers. A study by the WWC (now renamed the Federation of Palestinian Women's Action Committees, or FPWAC) among Ramallah workers in the late 1970s found that 95 percent of those interviewed had no work contracts, and that only about 50 percent were receiving the benefits to which they were entitled by law, such as paid sick leave, paid vacations, maternity leave, and workers' compensation.[78] Conditions also vary with the type of workshop. Flavia Pesa found that in the cottage industries in the villages and camps women are most exploited:

> The most common sewing workroom remains the home, and women are the primary work force. It is impossible to know or even estimate how many Palestinian women are involved in this form of home labour. The women contact only with the Arab hustler who delivers the cut material, picks up the work, sets pay rates, and is the middleman with the Tel Aviv manufacturers. His "cut" for his legwork is anywhere between 10 and 50 percent of the amount of the subcontract.[79]

In smaller workshops in the camps and villages, which have at most five machines, "women are hired according to unknown conditions and cannot bargain for better wages." In the larger factories, women usually have guaranteed wages, but rarely do they exceed 45 dinars per month (approximately $135 before 1988), compared with men in the same jobs, who may earn 110 dinars per month (approximately $300 before 1988).[80] Employers have been able to keep wages low because there is a ready supply of workers willing to take jobs vacated by others, and by claiming, with success, that women's work is temporary (in other words, until marriage) and that women do not have the same responsibilities as do men, who are usually families' main breadwinners.[81]

Few of the women employed in the garment industry are organized, either in labor unions or in women's committees, although specific recruitment drives have on occasion increased the latter's membership among working women. The main reason for this is the social control exerted by employers on workers, and by extension the pressures placed on women workers by their communities and families. According to Randa Siniora, "employers need not use force in order to control . . . workers. Instead, they continuously try to establish a paternalistic relationship with [them]. They try to convince them that they are in the position of their fathers at the workshop, and that they are their 'supporters' and 'protectors' at the workplace."[82] In addition, the method of recruitment plays a role in social control. Siniora reports that

> about 77% of women interviewed affirmed that they got their jobs through their female friends or relatives who were previously employed . . . at the same workshops where they are currently employed. About 17% of these women were close relatives to their employers. . . . This form of recruitment accompanied by the existence of an informal social relationship between the employer and the workers' families is strengthening the [employers'] control over the workforce. At the slightest disobedience or misbehaviour, employers will directly inform the worker's male supporters. . . . Women are forced

by their families to behave, since their misbehaviour will bring disrespect to
their families.[83]

Women working in the subcontracting sector have little leverage vis-à-
vis their employers in spite of their skills because of their limited geo-
graphical mobility and the fact that Israeli companies are under no legal
obligation to pay women employed in the Occupied Territories a minimum wage or fringe benefits. This underlines the vulnerability of the female workers, and the depth of their exploitation: their limited mobility
makes them fully dependent on the vicissitudes of the Israeli economy. In
either capacity, as wageworkers supplying all or part of their families' incomes, or as those cast in the less-visible roles of child rearing and performing household and agricultural tasks, women have, according to Amal
Samed, become the springboard for men's proletarianization: "The proletarianization of the Palestinian man tends to reduce the potential proletarianization of his wife."[84] Women's activities, be they at home or in the
wage sector, are part of a continuum in the cycle of capital accumulation
of which the Israeli economy is the chief beneficiary.[85] Thus women make
up the most exploited segment of the reserve army of Palestinian labor
that feeds the Israeli economy. At the same time, they constitute the un-
derclass of Palestinian society, an "invisible" proletariat.

Social Implications of Israel's Economic Policy in the Occupied Territories

One of the central features of the Israeli military occupation of the West
Bank and Gaza has been a gradual integration of the economy of the Occupied Territories into Israel's own. Researchers have described the result of this process as a type of "common market," but one in which one
participant has picked most of the fruits and borne the least burden at the
expense of the other. In the words of Baruch Kimmerling, "the biggest
beneficiary of this integration was the Israeli economy."[86] This "common
market" arrangement is clearly based on a colonial relationship, according
to Sheila Ryan, marked by three factors typical of colonialism: "the flood-
ing of the colony's market with the manufactures of the metropole, the
extraction of raw materials and the superexploitation of the colony's workers."[87] The result has been economic depression and blocked industrialization in the Occupied Territories. In the words of Meron Benvenisti,
"the economic environment of the Palestinian sector [the Occupied Terri-
tories] has been defined by us elsewhere as a curious combination of individual prosperity and communal stagnation, an auxiliary and subservient
sector of the Israeli economy, a source of cheap, unskilled labor and agricultural surpluses."[88]

The economic integration of the Occupied Territories into Israel lacks an attendant extension of political rights to the population of the Occupied Territories. To the contrary, an administrative system has developed through which the Israeli authorities exert full control over all aspects of social, cultural, political, and economic life in the West Bank and Gaza. Operating through a militarily staffed "civilian administration" and protected by a dual system of law,[89] the authorities have consistently advanced Israeli economic and political interests. Palestinians, says Brian Van Arkadie, "have not participated in the political process that has set the major economic policies affecting them or that has supervised the overall implementation of these policies."[90] As a result, "the poorer economies— lacking sovereignty, of course—have had no opportunity to use traditional policy instruments such as tariffs or exchange rate adjustments to serve their own economic objectives."[91] Exclusive Israeli control over the economy has also, according to Greenberg, "helped privilege the market position of the Jewish worker, foster ethnically-defined labor market hierarchies and segmentations, and restrict Palestinian proletarianization."[92]

The economic integration of the Occupied Territories, in the final analysis, amounts to their de facto political annexation by Israel. This has not happened by coincidence. The policy of the right-wing Likud has been to forestall the kind of "territorial compromise" advocated by some sectors in the Labor Party by stepping up the expansion of new Jewish settlements in the Occupied Territories and the "thickening" of existing ones. But it was the Labor Party that initiated the building of settlements, and it was also the Labor Party that promoted the economic integration of the Occupied Territories into Israel. If Labor had wanted to give up the Occupied Territories, it pursued the wrong economic policy from the beginning. In the mid-1970s Brian Van Arkadie noted that "no significant change in the political status of the Occupied Territories can now be seriously negotiated, or contemplated unilaterally by Israel, without attracting attention to its economic repercussions."[93] After twenty-three years of occupation it has become clear, as Meron Benvenisti has noted, that the occupation is not an economic burden to Israel, and that it may even be an economic asset.[94] The economic fruits accruing to Israel have helped perpetuate the occupation; today, from an economic point of view, there is no argument against the profitability of Israel's retaining the West Bank and Gaza.

But, as Baruch Kimmerling has pointed out, economic considerations are secondary. The primary considerations in continuing the military occupation were "political, emotional, social and/or stemmed from certain doctrines regarding national security."[95] Political considerations as well have prevented a de jure annexation of the Occupied Territories by Israel. In present-day Israel, the majority view appears to be that de jure annexation would be both dangerous and counterproductive. It is considered dangerous because the total Palestinian population of an enlarged Israel would amount to two-fifths or more of the total population; this demographic near-parity, it is feared, might be the prelude to a political revolt by the newly enfranchised Arab population against the dominant Jewish sector.[96] Formal annexation is seen as counterproductive, moreover, since the Palestinians could not be exploited as intensively if they had the same rights as Israeli citizens. Among those who oppose returning the Occupied Territories to Jordan and Egypt (or worse, permitting Palestinians to establish their own state) are Israeli employers in whose interest it is to continue to have access to a large supply of cheap labor, and Israeli workers who benefit from newly instituted basic minimum pay rates and from higher upward mobility as a result of the influx of Palestinian workers.[97] According to Avishai Ehrlich, the common Israeli interest in "permanently retaining the Arab labourer in the Jewish economy as a subordinate presupposes the open and formal institutionalisation of an unequal status to Arabs—discriminated, but tolerated."[98]

Thus the occupation is allowed to linger until the moment when a strong faction gains the upper hand in Israel that can succeed in implementing either an Israeli withdrawal from the Occupied Territories or a transfer of the Palestinian population to other countries. In the interim, the political status of Palestinians remains unresolved. This has facilitated their economic exploitation and has necessitated their oppression by the military authorities.

The process of economic integration accompanied by political oppression and segregation along national and ethnic lines has, naturally, shaped the perceptions of the occupied population. According to Benvenisti, Palestinians' "inability to bring any influence to bear on their economic situation has compounded their feelings of despair and their unyielding political posture."[99] The continuing attempt by significant sectors in the Israeli political system to annex the Occupied Territories outright as part of a supposed "Greater Israel," and the concomitant attempt to stifle any form of Palestinian self-expression, has encouraged strong and pervasive nationalist sentiments to surface in the Occupied Territories. The experience of the migrant workers is particularly significant in this respect.

One-tenth of the population of the Occupied Territories—more than 50 percent of the labor force—is directly involved in work in Israel. In reality, the number of people with experience in Israel is much higher as there is a constant turnover: young Palestinians, unable to find employment in the Occupied Territories themselves, seek work in Israel. At the same time, however, they remain on the lookout for jobs near their homes, first because that would save them time and expense, and second because it would allow them to stay in their own communities rather than the foreign society that is Israel. As soon as a job opens up near home, they will forsake their jobs in Israel, and return there only if forced to do so because of unemployment in the Occupied Territories. Few workers in their late twenties, therefore, have not had the experience of working at least once across the Green Line.

The lives of Palestinian families in the Occupied Territories are thus to a large extent shaped by their work experience in a different society. They have this in common with Turkish families, Moroccan families, Mexican families, Filipino families—in short, with people throughout the world who have seen their relatives disappear beyond frontiers in search of work in regional metropolises where demand for labor was high. The experience of Palestinians, however, differs significantly from that of most others. Salim Tamari lists four main differences: (1) the physical proximity of these workers to the Israeli workplace, which "allows them to continue their relationship . . . to their land, and to participate in village social life"; (2) the ambivalent class and ethnic identity of these workers, which derives from "the daily confrontation with . . . Israeli culture"; (3) the "preponderance of Palestinian village workers in . . . construction"; and (4) the lack of institutionalization of the recruitment process, and thus the higher degree of exploitation by contractors and employers.[100] In addition, Palestinians are living under conditions of military occupation; Israel's political control over the West Bank and Gaza Strip enables it to restrict the number and quality of the Palestinians' economic activities in the Occupied Territories, and to regulate the flow of Palestinians into its own economy, in a manner that West Germany, for example, is not able to do with its Turkish "guestworkers."

Objectively speaking, this is a casually and informally employed work force of itinerant day laborers and their families who live under a military occupation. The particular work experience of this population group, in addition to the realities of their daily lives in the Occupied Territories, has given rise to a particular consciousness and identity. Brian Van Arkadie, for example, has said, in reference to the Palestinian day laborer employed in Israel, that the worker "begins to see himself as exploited—vulnerable, and relegated to the bottom of the economic ladder."[101] Views of the occupier, and of the Israeli population generally, have been either stereotypical or unclear, but in either case they have been unambiguously hostile. Although contacts between Israelis and Palestinians abound, they tend to involve relations between workers and their bosses or contractors, or between occupier and occupied. According to Salim Tamari, most of the contacts of Palestinian peasant-workers employed in Israel,

both in going to work and on the construction site, happen to be with people from their own village, and often from their own clan. [In the villages west of

Ramallah,] buses transport villagers to their work site in Israel and bring
them back in the evening, thus reinforcing this village identity. . . . Despite
his deep penetration into the Israeli economy and his workable command of
Hebrew, the Arab peasant-worker's conception of Jewish society remains
that of a closed and undifferentiated mass.[102]

Ann Lesch cites an Israeli journalist who quotes a Palestinian commenting
on his perception of Israelis: "There are nice people among you, but we
hardly know them. We know the military governors, the soldiers who
conduct searches, merchants from the big towns in Israel, and the settlers
and members of Gush Emunim [the largest Israeli settler movement]."[103]

The experience of these workers in the Israeli workplace both encouraged organization—because of the flagrant violations of their rights and
the lack of protection from the Histadrut—and inhibited it because of military repression and sheer lack of time. For those who work in Israel it is
min al-farsha 'al al-warsha and *min al-warsha 'al al-farsha*—that is, from
bed to work, and from work back to bed. In addition, some Palestinians
have argued that the workers' ambivalent social status has militated
against their mobilization by union activists in the Occupied Territories,
but at the same time that it has brought about a particular brand of trade
unions. In the words of one Palestinian researcher: "This is not a proletariat but a hybridized form of wage-earners/peasants: they have peasant
values but they work in the metropolis. This creates a hybridization in
consciousness: they do not really know what they are. That is why their
membership [in trade unions] is unclear. Many members are not really
workers; most of the membership is politically oriented."[104] Given the
military repression, this also makes good sense: only those who already
had a good dose of nationalist consciousness were willing to risk their jobs
and join a union despite repression. These issues will be discussed at
length in chapter 4.

Two structural conditions account for the changed outlook on the part
of Palestinian women in the Occupied Territories that has led to their
politicization as women, and more particularly, as Palestinian women.
One is their increased access to education after 1967, and the other is their
partial entry into the labor force.[105] But other factors too account for shifting perceptions: the constant threat to home and family presented by the
occupier (in the form of arrests and house demolitions), the frequent absences of male breadwinners, male oppression within the family and in
the larger community (which is all the more difficult to accept given that
many men are not around very often), and later, as a result of women's
participation in the national movement, prison experience. Julie Peteet,
looking at the Middle East in general and at Palestinian women in Lebanon in particular, claims that "continuous crises, from which the domestic

sector is not immune, compel women to participate" in political movements.[106]

In the rural areas, the absence of men has pushed village women into those agricultural activities that were once the exclusive preserve of men. This had major ramifications for social relations in the villages, according to Salim Tamari:

> Women, old men, and children have assumed a greater role in the agricultural cycle, challenging and shattering the traditional sexual division of labour. The result is not a trend toward greater homogeneity in the worlds of men and women, but its opposite. Men bring in the outlook of the city, of the alien ideas of foreign lands, and of Israeli-Jewish society; women become the sole bearers of traditional culture and the preservers of peasant traditions.[107]

As such, women have played a key role in helping Palestinian society survive four decades of oppression and dispersion. Also significant is their influence over the education of their children, especially in those families where the male breadwinner is frequently absent. According to Peteet, the "socialization of children to be nationalists is widely recognized [among Palestinian women in the camps in Lebanon] as primarily the responsibility of women in the family. . . . Raising children in a militant, nationalist environment is considered a primary contribution to the struggle. Women refer to themselves as the producers of fighters."[108]

Other women are forced to find work in the towns, both in the Occupied Territories and in Israel. Amal Samed has argued that proletarianization in and of itself does not necessarily lead to a woman's liberation from the restrictive bonds of family and community. She has noted that the entry of Palestinian women into the labor force did not enhance their autonomy because the family appropriates the daughter's earnings, which are then "poured automatically into the family budget." The daughter's marriage may be postponed (in order to sustain the income), but she "has no opportunity to develop even a minimal amount of economic independence."[109] But this is not necessarily so. The very fact that the woman is bringing home an income means that she has leverage she previously did not have: she can (threaten to) refuse to give the money to the family; she can (threaten to) refuse to go to work. She does not have to carry out her threats; the mere use of the weapon of a threat means that she has more leeway in relation to those who seek to control her life than she did before. Moreover, at work she is exposed to women in similar situations who may form her first, still primitive, support group. On the next level, she may get in contact with union organizers, and she may be recruited, if not by a union, then (as is argued in detail in chapter 5) by one of the women's committees. In short, entry into the labor market and labor process entails an education of sorts, and it therefore has the potential of widening the margins of a woman's autonomy in her family and community; small though such a victory may be, it might be the first step on the road to political action. In the words of Linda Layne:

> Women's wage-earning may affect family patterns and change the role of women in society. Working women may gain economic independence and thereby escape the social control wielded by their male kin. They may be exposed to "non-traditional" influences and adopt new values as a result of the industrial experience. They may develop feminist solidarity and discover the power of collective action. And they may marry later and bear fewer children than their unemployed sisters.[110]

The importance here is the word "may." As Randa Siniora has shown, a number of factors continue to militate against the mobilization of women in political organizations in the West Bank. In the first place, the temporary nature of their employment "prevents them from developing [a] political, economic and social consciousness." Second, conditions in the workplace, through the transfer of patriarchal authority from the father to the boss, "do not differ dramatically from the ones existing at home," which also blocks any possible move toward greater independence, or even toward a sense of empowerment.[111] Logically, therefore, Siniora argues, those women from the Occupied Territories who work in Israel have a greater chance of developing a political and social consciousness, because although their employment is equally temporary, they have escaped the direct control of their families, they work in larger groups of Palestinian women, which broadens their horizons, and they are in direct contact with the Israeli employers who, in another form, are the occupiers of their land.[112]

Yet the importance of women's entry into the wage-labor force, even in the Occupied Territories themselves, should not be underestimated. One of the women's committees in the Occupied Territories published an article in one of its magazines emphasizing the impact of women's entry into the labor force on their social and political outlook, and on their actions. After 1967, the article suggested, "the Palestinian woman went out to work. Her national, class, and social awareness began to increase day by day. Eventually she was able to breach that imaginary obstacle that she always faced in society, and she proved that she was able to participate in the production process and in the building of the economy, which is a prerequisite for the liberation of women."[113] This in itself did not induce women to join the national struggle. A framework had to be provided conducive to their participation. This framework emerged in the Occupied Territories after 1970–71. The article explained: "In the 1970s, when the national movement gained in vigor, so did the women's movement, and Palestinian women martyrs fell on the road of sacrifice and struggle:

Lina Nabulsi, Taghrid al-Batma, Dalal al-Mughrabi, and Munaha al-Hourani. . . . Palestinian women were sensing the need to struggle to obtain their rights, so they began to form democratic women's organizations."[114]

Yet the limitations of such organizations should not be forgotten. According to Julie Peteet, "some women incorporated political activities into domestic life with little challenge to traditional definitions of female propriety and domains; for others, activism temporarily challenged the onset of married life and child-raising. For very few, however, did it pose a permanent alternative to domesticity."[115] It is in this context that we should see the emergence of a women's movement in the Occupied Territories in the 1970s.

Aside from changing conditions, and therefore values and perceptions, in classes and sectors of the population, other factors contributed to the emergence of a vigorous national movement in the Occupied Territories. One important consequence of the oppression of Palestinians across class lines was that economic actors who otherwise might have been in conflict with one another, such as workers and employers, have sought each other's company under the umbrella of nationalism. In the words of Sara Roy, who discusses the class structure in Gaza, it

> can be argued that although increasing economic integration with Israel has, on the one hand, reinforced many aspects of Gaza's pre-1967 class structure, it has, on the other hand, contributed to the development of a common political consciousness across classes despite clear political differences between those classes. The occupation, therefore, may on an economic level, support class divisions which on a political level, it has begun to bridge.[116]

In sum, by the mid-1970s a "human base" existed in the Occupied Territories, a population that—across the class spectrum—was economically exploited, politically disenfranchised, and culturally oppressed, and that was ready to be mobilized because of its experience of shared oppression. The economic policy pursued by the Israeli authorities, by discriminating against Palestinians collectively as a nation, made it possible for the various social actors in Palestinian society to unite in a common front against the occupation. Since the 1970s the main classes in Palestinian society, the workers (including migrant peasant-workers) and the petite bourgeoisie, of large traders and professionals, have joined in a nationalist alliance. The working class, such as it was, was to play a leading role in forging this alliance and cementing its mass base through its organizations, the trade unions and women's committees.

Chapter Three

THE POLITICAL CONTEXT

GIVEN AN EXPLOITED, disenfranchised, oppressed human base, the potential for mass mobilization exists. There has to be a force that can actualize this potential and give it structure, an ideology, concrete goals. This force must give expression to the grievances of the population and point the way toward a better future. In the Palestinian case, this role has been played, since the late 1960s, by the Palestine Liberation Organization, both inside and outside the Occupied Territories.

THE FIRST FIVE YEARS OF MILITARY OCCUPATION

The Palestinian National Movement and the PLO

Historically denied their national rights, the Palestinian people have continued to articulate nationalist demands whenever, wherever, and however they are able. Despite attempts by the successive occupying powers in the twentieth century—Britain, Jordan and Egypt, and Israel—to encourage non-nationalist forms of local leadership, organized nationalist sentiment has been the main driving force in Palestinian society in this century, except for short spells following major setbacks in 1948 and 1967. Thus, no study can be made of forms of mass mobilization in the Occupied Territories after 1967 outside the context of developments in the Palestinian national movement, both in and out of the Occupied Territories. The main articulator of Palestinian nationalist aspirations in the second half of the twentieth century has been the PLO.

The PLO was created by the Arab states at the first Arab Summit on 16 January 1964—not, however, as a vehicle for Palestinians' national liberation, but to be employed as an instrument of control over the increasingly restless Palestinians to protect the stability of the Arab governments. The PLO, according to Ibrahim Dakkak, was set up "as an envelope to contain the emerging non-conformity of the Palestinians."[1]

Despite its assigned role, the PLO provided an organizational framework whose utility soon became clear. Palestinian trade unions, women's groups, health committees, and student organizations were all set up under the aegis of the PLO. Arab control of the organization meant, however, that its activism during the first three years of its existence was limited to speeches by its chairperson, Ahmad Shuqeiri, in international forums. More important from a Palestinian perspective, therefore, was the creation of Fatah as a genuine Palestinian liberation movement in 1965. Fatah, as well as the Arab Nationalist Movement (ANM) and the (pro-Syrian) Ba'athists, carried out guerrilla attacks on Israeli targets, which, however limited in scope and military results, earned them growing legitimacy in the eyes of the Palestinian population whose allegiance they sought to win.

The 1967 war proved to be a watershed in the development of the Palestinian national movement as it demonstrated the bankruptcy of the Arab regimes, which convinced Palestinians that they were left to their own devices. The battle of Karameh in the spring of 1968 firmly established Fatah as a viable alternative to the Arab governments, and Fatah subsequently (at the fifth PNC meeting in Cairo in February 1969) succeeded in taking control of the PLO, which from then on headed the Palestinian nationalist movement. The PLO's goal was to liberate Palestine by means of armed struggle and set up a democratic state. Fatah and the newly emerged Popular Front for the Liberation of Palestine (PFLP, 1968) and Popular Democratic Front for the Liberation of Palestine (PDFLP, 1969; later the Democratic Front for the Liberation of Palestine, DFLP) agreed on the use of armed struggle, but the PFLP and PDFLP espoused as well the social transformation of Arab society in general and Palestinian society in particular as the "prerequisite for the liberation of Palestine," in keeping with their Marxist-Leninist ideology.[2]

If the 1967 war had catapulted the PLO to the fore as a liberation movement that had chosen armed struggle as a means to realize Palestinian aspirations, the war in Jordan in 1970–71 (which started with what is now known as "Black September" in September 1970) forced the PLO, which had been defeated by the Jordanian army, to redefine its goals and methods. Defeat had underlined the fact that the PLO would be unable to liberate Palestine by military means alone. The sights were lowered; there was still talk of "revolutionary armed struggle," but from 1970–71 on, the PLO began to move from the "democratic secular state" option to the two-state solution. Accordingly, although armed struggle was not abandoned, political and diplomatic struggle began to increase in importance as the PLO's methods of reaching its aims. The PFLP and DFLP also supported political struggle, which fit their agenda of social transformation.

Political Developments in the Occupied Territories

Following the defeat of the Arab armies in the 1967 war and the occupation of the West Bank and Gaza, the social and political infrastructure that had existed before the war was temporarily disrupted. During the first years of the military occupation there was little organizational activity on a mass level. This was so because (1) the existing trade unions in Gaza were outlawed, and those in the West Bank were systematically harassed (with many of their leaders arrested and some deported) by the military authorities; (2) Palestinians needed time to rearrange their lives, learn to cope with displacement, and readjust their hopes and expectations following the shattering experience of defeat; and (3) the prevailing perception among Palestinians during the early years of the occupation was that the occupation would be of short duration. Those who held this opinion were strengthened in their belief by official Israeli pronouncements suggesting that there might be a willingness on the Israeli side to "trade land for peace."

In the Gaza Strip a locally organized guerrilla war continued for three years before being brutally crushed by the Israeli army under Ariel Sharon. In the West Bank the leadership vacuum created by the war could not immediately be filled by any one group in particular. The West Bank branch of the Jordanian Communist Party (JCP) was the only group, according to Ann Lesch, that "had an underground structure that enabled its cadres to continue their activities under occupation but, even so, many of its leaders were still in Jordanian prisons and its actions were circumscribed."[3] The West Bank JCP, though part of the national movement, was not a member of the PLO; closely aligned with the Israeli Communist Party, it implicitly recognized the state of Israel and called for an Israeli withdrawal to the 1948 cease-fire lines through political, not military, struggle.[4] In other words, it propagated a two-state solution to be brought about by political struggle and negotiation, a program that at that time diverged widely from that of the PLO.

The traditional leadership in the West Bank, made up of mayors and village notables linked to the Jordanian regime, was fragmented after 1967 and had clearly lost its appeal among the masses of Palestinians. In its stead, local committees were formed to organize strikes and other forms of protest against the occupation, but in many cases the leaders of these committees were deported, and their impact therefore remained minimal. Such committees included the Islamic Committee, a committee of religious leaders based in Jerusalem, and the National Guidance Committee, which had branches in the main West Bank towns and which was controlled effectively by the JCP and the ANM.[5] These two committees, argues Dakkak, "were the first expression of the emergence of an independent Palestinian leadership inside Palestine."[6]

The war in Jordan in 1970–71 reinforced the trend toward self-organization in the Occupied Territories. In Lesch's words, the shock of defeat "jarred the residents into searching for new political strategies and more sophisticated political conceptions."[7] According to William Quandt, "West Bankers, who had long hoped for the end of the Israeli occupation, came to realize that outside forces could do little to bring this about. While continuing to hope for a political settlement, West Bank Palestinians also seemed to realize that the occupation would not end soon."[8] Thus a new perception emerged in the early 1970s, the perception that Palestinians would have to take their fate into their own hands and cease to rely on assistance, let alone liberation, from the outside;[9] they realized that there had to be a force that could counteract the actions of the occupier on a local level.

It had been apparent from the beginning of the military occupation that the occupier was not simply negligent in providing basic services to the population (which it is required to provide under article 43 of the 1907 Hague Regulations, which constitute international customary law and are therefore binding on Israel); it actually was seen to be disrupting the existing infrastructure.[10] In the words of Rita Giacaman, a lecturer at Bir Zeit University:

> The first ten years of occupation or so everybody worked very hard to inhibit the breakdown of the infrastructure—the economic, social, health, educational, and political infrastructures in the West Bank. It was clear to Palestinians that this attempt on the part of the Israeli military to break down the social and economic infrastructures really meant a fight for survival. That infrastructure, we all knew, was crucial for the reconstruction of Palestinian society in the future. We knew that much. We knew that the Israeli military was out to possess the land without us people. We knew that, too. What we didn't know was how to mobilize under occupation, when it was becoming practically impossible to move and do anything at the political or other levels without being subjugated to arrests or attacks from the Israeli military.[11]

It is in this context that we must see the efforts in the early 1970s, primarily of schoolchildren and college students, including young women, in West Bank towns like Ramallah and Nablus to clean streets and pave roads there as well as in the nearby villages and refugee camps. From street cleaning the teenagers moved on to mobilize volunteers' energies to address the problems caused by the atrophying social infrastructure. The children were encouraged by a number of their teachers. According to Lesch, "some young teachers and intellectuals in Jerusalem held informal study and discussion groups during the winter of 1970–71 in which they formulated and weighed ideas, groping for a way to articulate their nationalist beliefs."[12] One of the participants in these teachers' meetings was Munir Fasheh, who described the new activities as follows:

> Social action and community service became inspiring ideas among many Palestinians. A group of people, mainly teachers, started meeting in 1971 at the YWCA in East Jerusalem to discuss what we could do in light of the new

situation. The first outcome was the establishment of Nadi al-Ghad (Tomorrow's Club) at the YWCA; its main aim was to read books and articles and discuss them at a weekly meeting, as well as engage in some social and recreational activities. A year later, however, some members of the club, including myself, realized that discussion without action led to dead ends and to frustration. We decided to begin working in the community. . . . The discussion focused on what kinds of projects we wanted to engage in and how to go about them. The first projects were associated with the municipalities of [Ramallah and al-Bireh] but, soon after, we extended the work to villages and refugee camps in the Ramallah-Bireh area. The first projects included cleaning up a vegetable market in Bireh, paving a road in Ramallah, helping with the wheat harvest, constructing a school playground, and paving an alley in a nearby refugee camp.[13]

These community efforts received formal endorsements from educational institutions in 1972, and in 1973 Bir Zeit University included a "Community Work Program" in its curriculum, requiring students to spend a certain number of credit hours performing community work as part of their university careers. For example, a three-day olive-picking "vacation" has now become an institutionalized part of university life at BZU.[14] Such efforts, moreover, gave added impetus to the student movement emerging in the schools and universities.[15]

These developments in the urban centers had ramifications in the countryside as well, where socioeconomic changes (expanding education and the emergence of a migrant labor force) had already led to challenges to the traditional leadership and patterns of control. High-school students gave the impetus for the establishment of youth clubs and voluntary work committees. In a Ramallah-area village studied by Salim Tamari, commuter labor to Israel led to the "emergence of new cleavages in the village scene." Young people set up a Youth Association in the 1970s that has sought to improve the village's social and physical infrastructure. The issues addressed, according to Tamari, included "the establishment of an electricity cooperative, the building of a girls' preparatory school, and the exploitation of the village *waqf* [public, Muslim trust] land for development projects."[16] Reportedly controlled by the Communists, the association has held annual elections in which "various ideological trends vie for leadership." However, according to Tamari, Marxist politics were largely devoid of class content: it was the *patriotic* character of the association's activities that stood out. There was a generational conflict as well, in the form of a struggle against the older leadership in the village: "The Youth Association, or at least the radical elements within it, views the development of cooperative enterprises which undermine the patriarchal basis of village authority as both its objective and its *raison d'être*."[17]

Similarly, Rita Giacaman refers to popular mobilization in the 1970s as the main response to the occupation and the breakdown of the Occupied Territories' infrastructure:

> By the mid-seventies it was becoming very clear that there was a large sector that was still unmobilized even at the political level, and actually it was the women [who] discovered this fact. A women's movement emerged that was trying to go to the villages instead of expecting the villages to come to it. . . . That practical experience—the discovery of the villages—was the stepping-stone for the Palestinians under military rule that proved to be crucial in developing a new movement, which is a movement of committees, a popular movement.[18]

Thus the popular movement in the Occupied Territories was born, offering a dynamic combination of concrete services benefiting the community and a political context in which nationalist aspirations could be effectively expressed. What was still missing in the early and mid-1970s was the link between this movement, nascent and as yet disparate and unorganized, and the Palestinian national movement taking shape in the diaspora.

THE PLO AND THE POPULAR MOVEMENT IN THE OCCUPIED TERRITORIES

From the Outside to the Inside: Early Mobilization Efforts

From 1971–72 on, the PLO actively pursued a policy of political struggle in the Occupied Territories. For example, at the tenth PNC meeting in Cairo in April 1972 it openly called on activists to organize the masses, including in trade unions.[19] This new direction strengthened the nationalist inclinations of the new urban elites and made it possible for these elites to continue replacing the traditional village-based "notables" as leaders of the local Palestinian communities; it also gave the impetus for the setting up of new institutions and organizations loyal to the PLO.

These developments ran counter to Israeli interests, in particular Israel's wish to retain the Occupied Territories while supposedly permitting residents to run their own lives—Moshe Dayan's concept of "administrative autonomy." To carry out its plans in the Occupied Territories, Israel needed pliable Palestinian leaders. In an effort to take control over political life in the West Bank and forestall the emergence of a Palestinian nationalist leadership hostile to Israeli designs, the Israeli authorities in December 1971 decided to organize municipal elections in 1972. The results of the elections were not necessarily in Israel's favor, however. The mayors Israel had inherited from the period of Jordanian rule were generally conservative and pro-Jordanian or even pro-Israeli, but some had begun to adjust their positions as the likelihood of a return to the status quo ante started to dim; the occupation was harsh, and the Palestinian national movement was ascendant. The PLO called for a boycott of the elections, but local nationalist politicians, according to Ann Lesch, instead "urged the voters to 'resist' by reelecting the incumbents. . . . This pragmatic shift was supported—after the fact—by the PLO."[20] Thus some municipalities came or remained under the control of activist mayors, like Abd-al-Jawad Saleh in al-Bireh and Karim Khalaf in Ramallah.

In August 1973, Palestinians in the Occupied Territories established the Palestine National Front (PNF), a semiclandestine local leadership that emerged from the experience of (and frustration with) uncoordinated resistance activity during the first years of the occupation. In the words of Arabi Awad, one of the PNF's members who was deported by the military authorities in December 1973, "gradually, and especially after the September 1970 massacres in Jordan, the resistance organizations began to see how important unity was. . . . At the beginning of 1973, various forces actively began to establish such a Front. A program was written after consultations with a variety of trade union, student and women's groups and professional societies. Leaders of the Front were chosen from these groups and the Communist Party."[21] In a thirteen-point manifesto, the PNF asserted Palestinians' right to self-determination, and defined itself as "an inseparable part of the Palestinian national movement represented in the Palestine Liberation Organization."[22] The PNF saw its task as mobilizing support in the Occupied Territories for the positions of the PLO outside, whose charter it had adopted.[23] The PNF called for a boycott of Histadrut elections in Jerusalem in September 1973, which it saw as an Israeli attempt to legitimize the annexation of East Jerusalem. The boycott was reportedly successful.[24]

The Arab psychological victory in the 1973 October War enhanced the position of the PNF in the Occupied Territories. The PNF called on Palestinians not to pay Israeli taxes, which supported the Israeli war effort; it called on workers to stay away from their jobs in Israel; and it coordinated demonstrations.[25] In October 1974 the PNF sent a memorandum to Arab states meeting in Rabat that month, calling on them to recognize the PLO as the sole legitimate representative of the Palestinian people. Most important, the PNF acted as the framework for the national movement in the Occupied Territories, uniting all the movement's factions and mobilizing them around commonly accepted goals.

Even as the foundations were being laid for a nationalist movement in the Occupied Territories, a number of spectacular military operations enabled the PLO to ascend the world stage and gain legitimacy as the sole representative of the Palestinian population, both inside and outside the Occupied Territories. The Arab states explicitly recognized the PLO as such at the Rabat Conference in October 1974, while the world community of states extended implicit recognition of the pivotal role of the PLO by inviting PLO leader Yasser Arafat to address the United Nations General Assembly one month later. The PLO's efforts on the diplomatic front, as well as its military and administrative entrenchment in southern Lebanon, marked the start of the organization's transformation from a revolutionary liberation movement into "an embryonic quasi-state structure,"[26] according to some critics, or even a "quasi-Arab regime."[27] The most important consequence of this transformation was that the PLO reinforced its emphasis on political struggle in the Occupied Territories.

To thwart Israel's plans to achieve administrative autonomy, the PLO, according to Salim Tamari, "attempted to create solid loci of political power which would back the political demands of the PLO for independence and also act as barriers against compromises with an "autonomy" which would preserve the West Bank and Gaza under Israeli sovereignty."[28] At the initiative of the DFLP, the PLO adopted a transitional program, calling for the establishment of a "Palestinian national authority in any Palestinian areas liberated from Israeli control." This position later evolved into the two-state solution, which envisioned a Palestinian state in the West Bank and Gaza next to and at peace with Israel. As part of this strategy, the PLO encouraged local organizers to revive existing popular organizations such as trade unions and build new ones to serve as an infrastructure for a future Palestinian state, or, according to Tamari, "to prepare the Occupied Territories to receive the national authority."[29] In this effort, the PLO was well served by the Arab summit and United Nations resolutions in the autumn of 1974: according to Moshe Ma'oz, they "greatly enhanced PLO prestige and influence in the West Bank."[30]

The events of 1973–74 generated new energies and new ideas among activists in the West Bank and Gaza, especially among the young. The PNF provided the framework for the mass demonstrations that took place. Activity, according to two of the leaders of the PNF, Arabi Awwad and Jiryis Qawwas,

encompassed wide-scale mass struggles, in which the various mass organizations have taken part, including the labour and professional unions, the students' federation and the women's federation, and a number of other national bodies. This mass movement amounts to a popular uprising; it was the occasion for the deportation of the eight freedom fighters [including Awwad and Qawwas themselves], since when there has been a wave of mass struggle throughout the whole of the occupied territories, such as sit-ins, marches, and strikes in which schoolboys and schoolgirls and women's organizations have taken part. There have also been protests by municipal councils, chambers of commerce, and professional and labour unions. This activity has continued throughout the last six months, in spite of repression and intimidation.[31]

Activism was most pronounced in the towns, with schoolchildren forming
the vanguard. One Nablus activist, a woman who spent time in prison for
political work, recalls:

> In 1975 the issue of a Palestinian state was at its height, especially after the
> PLO had been admitted to the United Nations and Yasser Arafat made his
> famous speech at the U.N. It was as if the Palestinian Resistance Movement
> was newly activating itself, especially after the 1973 War. For me, it started
> with demonstrations at high school where many of the students were enthusi-
> astic and able to demonstrate against occupation. They arrested me because
> of membership in a political organization.[32]

A voluntary work committee, which included both boys and girls, was
formed in Nablus that year. All factions of the Palestinian movement were
involved—to the extent that schoolchildren had already asserted their
particular allegiance—but there was no clear sense of factions. This was a
period of ferment: the same children who one day cleaned up the older
quarters of town would the next day be demonstrating against the military
occupation. According to one of them: "In 1975 and 1976 it was the most
intense. . . . In 1976 . . . the whole West Bank was on strike for one year.
The number of girls demonstrating and being politically active was highly
accelerated at that time."[33] A factor that may have contributed to the
higher profile taken by women in the national movement is that women
for the first time participated in the municipal elections held in 1976. A
high-school girl said about the participation of girls in the demonstrations
that followed in the wake of the Camp David accords in 1978–79: "Though
the schools are divided between boys and girls, we demonstrate together. . . . We all know about politics because we are occupied and we
listen to news on the radio and read the newspapers. All of us are against
Camp David and the autonomy plan."[34]

Factionalism and the Popular Movement

Divisions in the Palestinian national movement were strongly reflected in
the movement in the Occupied Territories. One of the main local issues
was the role of the JCP, whose representation in the PNF was dispropor-
tionate to its weight in the overall national movement because of the JCP's
influence in popular organizations in the West Bank such as the trade
unions. Indeed, Fatah made a deliberate effort to alienate the JCP, and
although the PLO had endorsed the PNF as the PLO's political arm in the
Occupied Territories,[35] important currents in Fatah opposed the role of
the JCP in the PNF, and called for the establishment of an alternative
front free from Communist control.[36] In the event, the PNF faded as most
of its leaders were deported by the military authorities. The PLO, on the

other hand, began to focus its activities in the Occupied Territories on wresting control from Israel on the municipal level.

In April 1976 the military authorities for the second time organized municipal elections in the West Bank. The national movement, which had decided to support the elections, won overwhelmingly as pro-PLO candidates were reelected or swept into office in all the major towns except Bethlehem. The following period was marked by attempts by the municipalities to resist further Israeli efforts to integrate the infrastructure of the Occupied Territories into that of Israel. In addition, the nationalist mayors did not hesitate to articulate nationalist sentiments and express their support for the PLO.[37]

The victory of the nationalist forces in the Occupied Territories was offset the next year by the victory of the Likud bloc in the national Israeli elections in May. The Likud immediately stepped up the settlement drive and, following the visit to Israel by Egyptian president Anwar Sadat in November 1977, pushed a new autonomy plan, published in December. The Palestinians reacted with large-scale protest demonstrations, and nationalist leaders, including some of the mayors, began a series of meetings that culminated in the convening of the Jerusalem Conference to discuss the Camp David agreement of 1978. The conference condemned both the Israeli autonomy plan and the Camp David accords as contrary to Palestinian interests and Palestinians' right to self-determination. More important, participants in the conference established a new leadership group, the National Guidance Committee (NGC). Its executive committee, elected on 4 November 1978, consisted of six West Bank mayors, representatives from Gaza, and representatives from a number of mass organizations and national institutions in the Occupied Territories. The NGC decided to act in the open.[38]

The growing rift between the Fatah-dominated PLO and the JCP was highlighted by the composition of the NGC, which, though heavily influenced by the JCP, included a much larger number of more conservative figures in the national movement, unlike the earlier PNF. According to Ma'oz, the NGC "was initially established as a public political organ with the help of the Fath [sic] group in the PLO which had been concerned about the pro-Soviet character of the PNF."[39] Indeed, some of the more progressive mayors tried to revive the PNF in 1978–79 as a counterweight to the mainstream influence in the NGC, but the attempt faltered, and the authorities outlawed the new PNF in 1979.[40]

Taking the decisions of previous PNC meetings one step further, the NGC called for the establishment of a Palestinian state side by side with Israel. In the words of Tamari, "this fact is extremely important: the formation of the National Guidance Committee—militant, pro-PLO and popular, and at the same time willing to make territorial compromises with the state of Israel, with the aim of peaceful coexistence between the Israeli state and a future Palestinian state—has been the subject of the most ferocious attack by the Likud."[41] Of course, the Likud had its own agenda in the Occupied Territories, which it considered an integral part of "Greater Israel."[42] Since the NGC was set up to mobilize popular activities against the autonomy plan, it posed a direct threat to Likud's long-term plans in the Occupied Territories. The army therefore carried out mass arrests of grass-roots organizers, deported two of the mayors in 1980, and deposed the others (except Elias Freij, the pro-Jordanian mayor of Bethlehem) in March 1982, while formally banning the NGC.

Another reaction to the autonomy plan envisioned under the Camp David accords was the creation, at the Arab summit meeting in Baghdad in November 1978, of a fund to funnel money to the Occupied Territories to promote the steadfastness of the population. The fund was to be administered by a committee controlled jointly by Jordan, which had been trying to manipulate the municipalities in the West Bank through a selective funding policy,[43] and the PLO, which had made overtures to Jordan in 1977 for the first time since the massacre of Palestinians in Jordan in 1970–71. This committee was called the "Palestinian-Jordanian Joint Committee." It marked the first step in a growing cooperation between the PLO, or at least important currents inside the PLO (especially Fatah), and the Jordanian government regarding the fate of the Occupied Territories. This arrangement consequently became the focus of sharp criticism from nationalist leaders in the West Bank who had little faith in the intentions of the king of Jordan, and it led to splits in the national movement. The NGC sent a memorandum to the executive committee of the PLO following the Baghdad conference to put on record the committee's reservations concerning the arrangement.[44] The issue of Joint Committee funding was to become the main cause of contention in the national movement in the Occupied Territories in the late 1970s and early 1980s.

The national movement was basically divided into two ideological camps, with the PFLP, the DFLP, the JCP (renamed the Palestine Communist party, or PCP, in the early 1980s), and progressives in Fatah opposed to the conservative elements in Fatah and the Muslim Brothers, an Islamic fundamentalist organization. The basic causes of contention, according to Tamari, were the use of funding from the Arab countries, which amounted to $100 million to $150 million a year, and the form of struggle in the Occupied Territories: "The conservative forces tend to organize resistance along the lines of traditional institutions, such as municipal councils, professional unions, women's organizations, notables. The left, on the other hand, tries either to build new organizations or to radicalize the rank and file of existing organizations."[45] Tamari claims that the Joint

Committee was "overwhelmingly, or unduly, under Jordanian influence," and that Jordan was using money "to buttress pro-Jordanian forces in the West Bank": "Funds have been withheld quite often to penalize individuals, groups and sometimes whole cities who choose not to cooperate with Jordan in certain schemes, especially during periods when Jordan and the PLO are at odds."[46]

The conflict between the PLO and the PCP became increasingly bitter in the wake of Camp David, especially when Communists began defecting to Fatah and the DFLP because of disagreements over the PCP's rejection of armed struggle following a number of successful PLO-sponsored armed attacks on Israeli targets.[47] The PCP was wary of the PLO's alliance with the Arab governments that footed the bill to support the steadfastness of Palestinians under occupation, and Fatah saw the PCP as a competitor for control of the national movement in the Occupied Territories through its influence in the mass organizations. In turn, the PCP feared competition by Fatah and the other PLO groups in the popular movement, especially because Fatah was using Joint Committee money to increase its influence, for example by setting up rival organizations.[48]

The conflict between the various blocs in the national movement highlights the difficult relationship between the inside and outside wings of the national movement. The establishment of the PNF in 1973 marked the first occasion on which the inside dealt collectively with the outside to which it had pledged its allegiance.[49] By the late 1970s it was possible to say, in the words of Salim Tamari, that there had been "a certain change in the direction of increased importance of West Bank leadership in leading the struggle of the Palestinian people."[50] Ibrahim Dakkak, then a member of the NGC, remarked on the strains in this relationship: "People in the occupied territories have a central position because they are the people on the land. . . . But this also means that outsiders want to influence their decision-making."[51] A pro-Fatah activist in the West Bank said, characteristically, in 1985 that activists in the Occupied Territories "can often determine policy, but the large political issues remain in the hands of leaders outside the Occupied Territories"[52]—that is, in the hands of Fatah.

The Popular Movement in the 1980s

In the late 1970s the struggle between the inside and the outside turned into what has been referred to as a "war of the institutions." According to one local analyst, the PLO groups turned to the local organizations and institutions, which until then had been heavily influenced by the PCP, or set up alternative institutions of their own. The PCP tried to maintain its control over the mass organizations by clinging to the letter of the rules it had laid down to structure these organizations, and otherwise attempted to restrict the entry of activists whose ideology varied from its own. The result was that as soon as it became clear to the new organizers that they could not effectively penetrate an organization controlled by the Communists, they simply created a parallel structure with the same name. In the words of one local activist, "Especially Fatah went out of its way to create institutions, often only in name, and procure funding for them from the outside. Today Fatah has a grip on the national institutions and grass-roots organizations, but theirs is a bureaucratic structure sustained by external funding. When the funding stops, the structure will crumble."[53]

The popular movement meanwhile continued to develop, its recruitment activities most often spurred by competition with rival blocs. The voluntary work movement became factionalized after 1976, reflecting divisions in the national movement. The original committee continued under the name "Voluntary Work Committee 1976," while the rival blocs set up their own voluntary work committees. Some of the activists from these groups, graduating from school and college, became active in the trade-union and women's movements. Existing trade unions were infused with new life, while new ones were set up in trades where none existed. Moreover, unions began to organize the migrant labor force for the first time since workers had started crossing the Green Line into Israel in search of jobs. Women activists established women's committees that aimed to draw women out of their homes, teach them basic skills, and recruit them to the national movement. Professionals set up their own professional unions and, in the case of health professionals, a grass-roots movement of medical relief committees.

Like their precursors in colonial Africa and Asia, these organizations are aimed primarily at educating and providing basic services and protection to a population living in lawlessness and deprivation. By doing so they have sought to keep the Palestinian national heritage alive and provide fresh leadership to a community kept leaderless by the military authorities. More important, the aggregate of these organizations has come to constitute an infrastructure, possibly for the future Palestinian state, but at least for organized mass resistance to the military occupation. Because of the overwhelming impact of the occupation on Palestinian society, few of these organizations have hesitated to articulate or endorse nationalist positions, usually reflecting one of the four main trends in the Palestinian national movement headed by the PLO.

In each of these organizations and movements, individuals tend to identify with a particular political current in the national movement headed by the PLO, or else the organization itself has set itself apart from similar organizations, becoming for example the workers' branch of a particular current in the national movement. The four main branches of the popular movement in the Occupied Territories are:

1. The Youth Movement (Hareket al-Shabbibe), which takes its cue from Fatah (and which was outlawed by the military authorities in March 1988 for its alleged role in the popular uprising).
2. The Unity Bloc (Kutlet al-Wahda), which tends to hold political positions that reflect the program of the DFLP.
3. The Progressive Bloc (Kutlet al-Taqaddumiya), which is dominated by Communists.
4. The Action Front (Jabhat al-'Amal), whose political tenets reflect the program of the PFLP.[54]

Each of these movements is represented in the popular organizations, defining their political positions. Except for the Youth Movement, the four currents are not necessarily known by the above names, but are here categorized as such for the sake of convenience. One will find that organizations identifying themselves with, for example, the Unity Bloc will use the word "Unity" in their names, as in the case of the Workers' Unity Bloc (WUB) and the Student Unity Bloc, popular organizations whose nationalist, as opposed to tactical, work-related positions usually reflect the positions of the DFLP. These organizations have played an increasingly important role in setting the political agenda in the Occupied Territories while providing concrete services to the population. In the words of Sarah Graham-Brown: "The political organizations, unable to act in their own names, put forward their lines within various legalized entities. The municipalities were the most important until 1982, but now their destruction as democratic institutions is virtually complete. Unions, professional associations, student groups and local cultural and sports organizations have thus become arenas for political competition and mobilization."[55]

The 1980s were for the national movement essentially a period of recuperation from a series of setbacks suffered in the late 1970s (starting with the Camp David accords) and early 1980s (most notably the defeat in Lebanon). Israel made an unsuccessful attempt to create an alternative leadership to the PLO, called the Village Leagues, through which it hoped to control the local population.[56] For its part, Jordan's courtship of Fatah crystallized into a formal and highly controversial agreement in February 1985 whose main principle was the necessity of a peace settlement with Israel, to be brokered by the United States, which would return the West Bank to Jordan under some form of joint Jordanian-Palestinian control.[57] At the same time, Fatah promoted a new form of "media-leadership" in the Occupied Territories, including such personalities as Hanna Siniora and Fayez Abu Rahma, who stepped into the limelight to negotiate with individual Israelis outside the popular consensus (to the extent that such

consensus existed at that time). Political forces continued to be active in
the Occupied Territories, but a definite shift took place from the elites to
the masses, and from individual to collective endeavors. It was not until
the eighteenth meeting of the PNC in 1987 that the PLO's factions were
reconciled, at least on a formal level.

The eighteenth PNC meeting, held in Algiers from 20 April to 25 April
1987, was of great significance to Palestinians in the Occupied Territories
for two main reasons. First, contrary to the seventeenth meeting of the
PNC in Amman in 1984, which was organized and attended exclusively by
Fatah, all major factions of the PLO were present in Algiers, marking a
reconciliation of the Palestinian national movement after several years of
damaging discord. According to Rashid Khalidi,

> this PNC session was numbered the 18th. This apparently innocuous fact
> signified the reunification of the historic factions and leaderships of the mod-
> ern Palestinian national movement, after a split which lasted four years. It
> meant that all factions in attendance accepted the legitimacy of the 17th ses-
> sion in Amman, which many—notably the PFLP, the DFLP, and the Pales-
> tine Communist Party—had boycotted. Besides Fatah, these are the only
> independent mass-based Palestinian organizations with a developed political
> infrastructure in both the occupied territories and the diaspora.[58]

This reunification, which was in part inspired by the popular movement in the Occupied Territories, whose leaders had made several calls
for national unity in the months preceding the PNC meeting, resulted
in a glossing-over of the differences that thus far had divided popular
organizations.

The second significant development at the eighteenth PNC session was
the inclusion, for the first time in its history, of the Palestine Communist
Party in the PLO. PCP leader Suleiman al-Najjab was admitted to the
PLO's executive committee. This did not mean the PCP had suddenly
adopted armed struggle as a means of resisting the occupier of Palestinian
land, but rather that the PLO had moved so far toward explicitly recognizing Israel within its 1948 boundaries—a position traditionally adhered to
by the PCP—that the PCP was no longer out of bounds for the PLO. In
addition, according to Lisa Taraki, the admission of the PCP to the PLO
reflects "a reality to be faced" by the PLO—the reality of the PCP's
strength in the Occupied Territories.[59] It also reflects an abatement of the
acrimonious competition of the late 1970s and early 1980s, suggesting that
the various political groups had exhausted their pools of potential recruits,
and that unity could help cement the allegiance of the organizations' constituents, while continuing strife might demoralize them.

The reconciliation of the national movement and the inclusion of the
PCP in the PLO form the backdrop to the popular uprising in the Occu-

pied Territories that began in December 1987. The uprising produced its own new leadership group, the Unified National Leadership of the Uprising (UNLU), which was derived in large part from the leadership of those popular organizations and institutions that had been in gestation for over a decade and that by the late 1980s had reached maturity.

ISRAEL'S REPRESSION OF THE POPULAR MOVEMENT

The transition from mobilization to collective action is defined by the degree to which a movement succeeds, at the lowest cost possible, in asserting its power. In other words, the parameters of a mass movement are set, on the one hand, by the level of its organization and cohesion, and on the other, by the opposition it encounters. When Palestinian activists started building a broad-based popular movement in the Occupied Territories, they increasingly began to undermine the power of the occupying forces by outadministering them—by deploying mass organizations against the occupation. The Israeli military authorities have sought to counter this threat to their rule in the Occupied Territories, using a wide range of repressive measures.

Needless to say, Israeli repression preceded the Palestinian effort at institution building, as a military occupation is by nature repressive. In realizing its agenda of de facto annexation of the West Bank and Gaza, Israel faced the task of bringing an entire population to heel that was foreign and directly hostile to Israel's perceived intentions. The dialectic of repression and resistance in the Occupied Territories has therefore had a holistic quality: this has been a struggle not merely between two political actors, but between two populations. The rationale for army repression has therefore not been self-protection against individual acts of resistance, but attacks on the obstacle to integration of the Occupied Territories into Israel: the Palestinian population itself.[60]

The methods used to realize this objective have been twofold: (1) economic and administrative strangulation, so as to "spirit out" the population in the Herzlian sense; and (2) the type of collective punitive measures that by their nature affect everyone, whether directly through actual imprisonment, or indirectly by instilling fear, since everyone by definition is "guilty" of obstructing Israeli objectives. Repressive measures have been carried out on two levels: against the general population, and against its institutions and leadership.

The Israeli military occupation of the West Bank and Gaza constitutes a highly visible form of oppression. Military vehicles and foot patrols are ubiquitous, most families have had direct experience with the military authorities through the arrest of one of their children, shopkeepers and entrepreneurs face harsh taxation and other economic restrictions, settlements are scattered throughout the Occupied Territories housing heavily armed Israelis who on many occasions have carried out vigilante actions against the Palestinian population, and so forth.

Generally, the population in the Occupied Territories has been denied the right to freedom of expression. Political organizations are banned, and formal publications are subjected to strict censorship. By declaring the Occupied Territories a closed military area, the military authorities have effectively restricted the population's movement and made it contingent on acquisition of a permit, which is given only on proof of "good conduct." Curfews and economic punishments, like bans on marketing and exporting, are imposed on areas that challenge the occupation. All these punishments have been abundantly documented in the twenty-one years preceding the uprising and do not need elaboration here.[61]

To prevent organized resistance to the occupation, the Israeli authorities have attempted to stamp out any local organizing, whether political or not. Since the authorities have been singularly incapable of forestalling the emergence of a Palestinian civil society, they have singled out Palestinian institutions and popular organizations for specific repressive measures. On an administrative level this has entailed delegitimation by withholding permits, forcing organizations to operate informally, thereby reducing their rights and leverage under the law; and by temporarily closing institutions and offices, or banning organizations outright. On the level of membership, repression has consisted of harassment and intimidation in an effort to deter actual or potential activists from carrying out their work. On the level of leadership, repressive measures have included arrests and administrative punishments (those outside the judicial system), including town arrest, administrative detention, and deportation. All popular organizations have suffered from these measures since the beginning of the military occupation in 1967, particularly the student and labor movements.

Palestinian resistance to the occupation has never simply been an expression of opposition to foreign rule; it has also, and more importantly, been a method of survival. Hence the efforts of activists to build a popular movement. However, in light of Israel's enduring repression, the popular organizations were nurtured in an informal sphere of semilegality, with an amorphous, broad-based, and largely invisible leadership that was easily replaced if arrested or deported. Because the occupation had affected everyone from the very beginning, these organizations could gain a truly mass membership, rendering futile any attempts by the army to root them out.

This was the situation before the intifada. Subsequent events have shown that the strategy of institutional resistance was extremely well conceived. Although Israel's repression has increased manyfold since the beginning of the uprising, it has also become less effective in accomplishing Israel's long-term goal of bringing the population to heel.[62] Telling symbols of the Palestinians' success in devising an effective response to the occupation and everything it entails are the emergence and survival of the UNLU as a strong and legitimate local leadership, the formation of active popular committees in all localities, and the ability to maintain regular communication between the various levels of leadership both inside and outside the Occupied Territories.

Chapter Four

THE LABOR MOVEMENT

IN THIS CHAPTER the themes discussed in chapter 1 and the broad developments sketched in chapters 2 and 3 will be linked in a case study of one example—perhaps the most important one—of mass mobilization in the West Bank and Gaza after the mid-1970s: the labor movement. This is not to suggest that there was no labor movement in the Occupied Territories before the mid-1970s; to the contrary, Palestinian Communists had been actively organizing workers for decades, and the structures they created and the methods they applied in recruiting workers were important models for organizers in later years. But the Communist movement in the Occupied Territories had only limited appeal among the general population. In addition, the Communists rarely ventured outside the urban areas. When local pro-PLO activists decided to organize the masses, especially the workers, in the West Bank and Gaza in the mid-1970s, they were helped in their work by two main factors: the preexisting structures set up by the Communists and the Communists' limited constituency. Local activists sympathetic to the PLO program thus focused on exactly those workers who had not been recruited by the Communists: migrant workers and those sympathetic to other political currents. In the process, these activists mounted a serious challenge to Communist hegemony over the Palestinian labor movement in the Occupied Territories.

Several things happened as a result of the PLO's new interest in organizing workers:

1. A fierce competition ensued between Communists and militant nationalists for control of individual unions on the local level and over the General Federation on the national level. Political differences crystallized in the setting up of union blocs in the late 1970s and early 1980s, which vied with one another for the loyalty of workers, for the most part over political rather than unionist issues. This struggle led to a paralysis in the existing formal union structures: recruitment became more narrowly defined, union membership in the federation was restricted, and elections were postponed indefinitely. Labor organizing flourished, however. The nationalists, once they failed in their attempt to usurp the power of the Communists, started setting up their own parallel trade unions and, when these were barred from membership in the General Federation, their own parallel general federations.

2. In the process, the unions' agenda was modified. The Communists' emphasis had been on fighting for specific workers' rights in the classic

socialist tradition. They had organized workers to protect them against the exploitation of the owning class, and to work toward the establishment of a socialist state. This is not to say that Palestinian Communists did not address national questions; the Palestinian predicament had forced them to. But although they were nationalists like all Palestinians, theirs was in a sense a dual loyalty: to the Palestinian national movement on the one hand, and to the international socialist movement on the other. When the pro-PLO activists began to organize the workers, they emphasized the workers' national rights in addition to social rights. And when they addressed social issues, the motivation often was to keep a membership that was not satisfied to follow the call for the establishment of an elusive independent state alone. In the final analysis, the mix of national and social concerns has proven a dynamic one, giving the labor movement a mass following and propelling it to the forefront of the struggle for national liberation.

3. The dual emphasis on social and national rights had wide appeal among the people and thus led to an increase in unions and in union members. Workers were interested in joining unions to receive services to which they otherwise had no access, and to join a support group in a situation of national oppression. By becoming organized, they increased their collective power to fight exploitative employers and the repressive military occupation.

4. The rapid growth of the union movement necessitated a decentralization and democratization of the union organizations. The two most active union blocs evolved an elaborate structure that allowed for a large measure of worker participation on all levels of decision making. This made it possible for an entirely new level of cadres to be carefully groomed for national leadership.

5. As the union movement grew, and labor unions and other mass-based organizations geared up to outadminister the occupying power, the Israeli authorities responded with harsh repression, targeting especially the unions, their members, and their leaders. However, the democratic nature of the labor movement made it possible for young cadres to replace on short notice leaders imprisoned or deported by the authorities, who therefore could slow the process of mass mobilization, but could not control, let alone suppress, it.

Each of these issues will be duscussed in detail below.

THE COMMUNIST TRADITION IN THE PALESTINIAN LABOR MOVEMENT

The trade-union movement in Palestine had its beginnings during the first years of the British Mandate. Its emergence occurred in two important contexts: one, the Russian Revolution and the subsequent establishment of Communist parties in other countries; and two, Jewish immigration to Palestine. The Palestinian labor movement, like the Palestinian mass movement in later years in general, has since had two main strands: a socialist and a nationalist one. Nationalists and socialists at times set up their own labor organizations, and at other times competed within a single trade union for the support of the membership. But even for the socialist strand, the ultimate nationalist goal of establishing an independent Palestinian state remained paramount. Throughout Palestinian history in the twentieth century, though to a diminishing degree in the latter half of the century, the socioeconomic structure of Palestinian society with its peasant-based culture of traditions has played a significant restraining role on the effectiveness of these organizations.

During the period of British control of Palestine, workers were drawn from their villages to supplement the urban labor force at times of industrial growth. This was so especially during World War II. But the industrial work force, insofar as it existed, comprised primarily residents of the main coastal towns of Jaffa and Haifa. The membership of trade unions was therefore predominantly urban throughout the Mandate period. No serious attempts were made by trade unions to organize the migrant rural work force. Only in the 1940s did village-based workers employed in the coastal cities begin to join unions, and even then not to any great extent.

One of the first labor organizers was the PCP, which crystallized out of a number of Jewish socialist groups in 1923. The party, whose main tendency was anti-Zionist, remained almost exclusively Jewish until the late 1920s, and it therefore had considerable difficulty in attracting Arab workers to its trade-union branch, the Workers' Fraction. The influence of the PCP on the Arab population remained marginal until the 1940s. According to Korrie Hopstaken, "the majority of the Arab population felt threatened more by Zionist colonization than by 'normal' exploitation. People therefore reinforced their solidarity with the class that exploited them but which promised to lead the population in the struggle against the Zionist threat."[1]

The Jewish immigrants in Palestine set up their own institutions. Most prominent among these was the Histadrut, the General Federation of Jewish Labor that was established in 1920. Although the Histadrut did on occasion attempt to organize Arab workers, it never did so to any significant extent, and it usually did so in separate organizations within the general framework of the federation.[2]

Separate from the organizing efforts of Communists and in reaction to the exclusion of Arab workers from the Histadrut, Palestinian activists in Haifa set up the Palestinian Arab Workers' Society (PAWS) in 1925. Most of its members were railroad workers. Contrary to earlier labor organizations, which resembled guilds and included employers as members, the PAWS was the first real Arab trade union in Palestine.[3] The size and activities of the PAWS remained limited until 1929, when a nationalist fervor swept Palestine following a decade of Jewish immigration. The PAWS gained new members, opening branches in several other cities. In 1930 it convened the first Arab Workers' Congress. However, according to Musa Budeiri, the Arab labor movement "remained weak and divided" due to hostility in the ranks of the PAWS to Communist involvement and due to efforts by the supporters of the Mufti of Jerusalem to set up rival unions to compete for support among the working class for the nationalist goal.[4] Moreover, the unions set up by the Arab "notables" failed, according to Rachelle Taqqu, "to provide the leadership that the migrants missed. . . . [S]ince the bulk of Arab labor was employed outside the Arab economic sector, urban politicians were neither accustomed nor able to secure special favors for their supporters on a large scale."[5]

The Arab unions did grow, however, in the nationalist climate of the 1930s, in part because of the competition between the various factions in the national movement. As a result, their activities tended to be political rather than unionist in nature. According to Ann Lesch, "the labor societies were heavily politicized. Their expansion in the 1930s was used by the various political parties as a means to increase political mobilization and membership, rather than to redress specific labor grievances."[6] Thanks to the popular mobilization that took place in the early 1930s, trade unions played a fairly important role during the early stages of the Palestinian Revolt of 1936–39, when they tried to spread the general strike to as many sectors as possible. When the strike ended, however, the unions' influence waned as trade-union struggle was replaced by a more general nationalist struggle. Trade-union activity continued at a low level for the next few years.[7]

Mass activity experienced an upsurge during World War II, when large numbers of Arab workers were recruited to work in the British war industry. The PCP, which had been underground since the Revolt, resurfaced in 1942 and began to reactivate the labor movement. It operated inside PAWS unions and brought the PAWS increasingly under its influence. Haifa-based dissenters from the PCP, frustrated with the conservative character of the PAWS, split from the PCP in 1942, however, founding the Federation of Arab Trade Unions and Labor Societies (FATULS). The FATULS, following a "workerist" line, fought for the institution of a minimum wage and a social-insurance scheme, and other concrete improvements in the situation of workers.[8] The PAWS, by contrast, was primarily nationalist in orientation, calling in the first place for equality of wages between Arabs and Jews. The FATULS argued that only socialism could effectively weaken the imperialist stranglehold on Palestine, whereas the PAWS sought to address the issue of discrimination between the two national populations.[9] After 1945, the FATULS continued as the Arab Workers' Congress (AWC), which included several dissenting branches of the

PAWS. It gained considerable international recognition in the two years before the establishment of the state of Israel.[10]

The work of the Communists in laying the framework for popular mobilization during the Mandate period can hardly be overestimated. In the words of Joel Beinen, the PCP and its offshoot (1944), the National Liberation League (NLL), were "the first mass political parties with an ideological (as opposed to family) base of support," and they constituted "the only organized political force in the Arab community until the Arab Higher Committee was reorganized in 1946."[11] Through their influence on the labor movement in the Mandate period the Communists provided the infrastructure, as well as the organizational and bureaucratic skills, that ensured the continuity of the labor movement in the West Bank after 1948. NLL activists such as Fou'ad Nasser constituted the bridge between British and Jordanian rule, continuing their work in the West Bank despite the severe defeat suffered by the Palestinian nationalist movement in 1948.[12]

Jordan annexed the West Bank in April 1950; all trade-union activities in the West Bank fell thenceforth under Jordan's labor law. The surviving leadership of the AWC took the initiative to revive the labor movement, seizing control of existing workers' structures and establishing new ones. In 1950, for example, the Communists took control of the Workers' Association in Ramallah, and on 2 May organized a demonstration in front of the military headquarters. The association was promptly banned by the authorities, and the organizers were arrested.[13] Two years later, the Jordanian authorities outlawed the AWC, and labor activities remained subdued until after an intervention by the ILO and the decreeing of a new labor law (Law 35) in 1953.

On 18 January 1954, the Construction Workers' Union, with headquarters in Amman, was the first trade union to be established under the new law. Several more unions were set up in rapid succession, and on 25 July they federated into the General Federation of Trade Unions in Jordan (GFTU).[14]

From 1954 onward, the two main progressive currents in the West Bank, the Communists and the Ba'athists (Arab nationalists aligned with Syria), stepped up their efforts to organize a broad-based mass movement. The Communists, for example, founded the Democratic Youth Association, set up more trade unions, penetrated student and women's groups, and pushed for cultivators' associations, as in the village of Salfit. The Communists were routinely represented, alongside the Ba'ath, on the executive committee of the GFTU. By 1955 it had become clear that the Jordanian Communist Party, a successor to the PCP, was "the most highly organized body" in the West Bank.[15]

On 6 January 1956 the Construction Workers' Union in Amman moved its headquarters to Nablus in the West Bank, turning the Amman office into a branch.[16] This demonstrated the leading role played by West Bankers, as opposed to East Bankers, in popular mobilization in the kingdom of Jordan. The trade-union movement grew rapidly in the mid-1950s. Hani Hourani reports that in 1955 there were thirty-six trade unions in Jordan, twenty-five of which were affiliated with the GFTU.[17]

When King Hussein, after a short period of liberalization, outlawed all political parties in April 1957, he singled out the JCP. Despite this ban, however, the Communists were the only ones able to continue to organize the masses, because they had remained underground as a party all along, while the other parties never made an attempt to set up alternative structures. According to Helena Cobban, "those party activists who wanted to continue their work were then forced to do so underground, but in the event the only ones with enough sense of organisation to maintain their political infrastructure more or less intact over the following ten years were the few hundred Communists."[18]

Along with the political parties, trade unions were repressed after 1957. Some unions were banned outright. The total number of unions, which reached thirty-nine in 1957, declined to twenty-nine unions in 1959 and to sixteen in 1961. Membership also declined.[19] Only in the mid-1960s did the political climate improve. According to Hourani, the number of unions grew to forty and membership rose to twenty thousand.[20] The GFTU opened branches in Jerusalem and Nablus in 1965, an act that had proved financially prohibitive until that year.[21] Still, unions continued to face repression from the authorities. Although a new labor law was issued in 1965, providing a stable legal basis for unions, new legislation banned elections in all institutions unless the candidates had been approved by the authorities. In a crackdown on dissent, the Jordanian authorities arrested a great many activists, especially Communists and including unionists, in the period 1965–67. When Israel occupied the West Bank in June 1967, one oppressive ruler simply replaced another.

Union work, like all organized societal activity, was temporarily suspended following the Israeli occupation of the West Bank and Gaza in June 1967. In the West Bank, disruption was less severe than in Gaza, where a guerrilla war continued until the early 1970s. In Gaza, the military authorities outlawed all trade-union activities, and no labor organizing took place until 1979 when the ban was lifted, but even then little unionist activity occurred until 1986–87. In the West Bank, on the other hand, trade-union functions were resumed, to the extent possible, after a couple of years. The Communists, with the infrastructure they had created during earlier decades, should be credited for the revival of the unions. Significantly, it was two of the West Bank members of the executive committee of the GFTU in Amman, Adel Ghanem of Nablus (later to be the secretary-general of the revived GFTU in Nablus) and Muhammad Jadallah of Jerusalem, who carried their pre-1967 experience over to the period of military occupation, seeking to resurrect the unions they controlled before 1967 from the social ruins of the June War.

There had been twenty-four unions in the West Bank in June 1967, thirteen of which were in Jerusalem, which had been the area with the most union activity in Jordan after Amman, and six in Nablus. Ramallah, Bethlehem, Tulkarem, Jenin, and Hebron each had one union.[22] Although Jerusalem set out to be the center of union activity, repression by the Israeli authorities soon changed this situation. Jerusalem was formally incorporated into Israel at the end of June 1967, and the authorities made special efforts after that time to stifle any political or other organized activity by Palestinians in the city they considered the Israeli capital. As part of a policy to enforce the "reunification" of Jerusalem, the authorities encouraged East Jerusalem workers to join the Israeli trade-union federation, the Histadrut. This policy was resisted by Palestinian labor activists in Jerusalem, who attempted to revive their own unions. Repression reached its peak in 1969 as the authorities deported the secretary-general of the Jerusalem Electric Company Workers' Union, Michel Sindaha, imprisoned the secretary-general of the Hotel Workers' Union, Muhammad Jadallah, and carried out raids on a number of trade-union offices in East Jerusalem.

The activities of the Printing Press Workers' Union, which was founded in Jerusalem in 1954, were frozen following the unionists' refusal to turn to the Histadrut. According to one of its leaders, "any time we tried to revive the union, our people got arrested, deported, etc."[23] The general atmosphere of fear served to lessen union activity in the following period. The only three active unions left following this assault were the Electricity Company Workers' Union, the Augusta Victoria Hospital Workers' Union, and the Shoemakers' Union. At the same time, the Histadrut opened offices in East Jerusalem to recruit Palestinian workers from East Jerusalem employed in Israel.[24] As a result, the center of gravity of union activity in the West Bank moved from Jerusalem to Nablus.

On 10 January 1969, some of the West Bank members of the GFTU from the Jordanian period met in Nablus and elected a new executive committee of five. The secretary-general was Zaqariya Hamdan, who was deported by the military authorities three months later; he was replaced by Anwar Ya'ish.[25] In a second meeting, on 2 February 1969, more unions were admitted to the revived GFTU, which was officially renamed "The GFTU with its Center in Nablus."[26]

The military authorities in the West Bank employed the existing Jordanian labor law of 1965 to control the union movement. In fact, argue George Hazboun and Bassam al-Salhi, the Jordanian law served the purposes of the authorities to the extent that they saw no need to amend it until 1980, following the revival of the union movement, when Military

Order 825 was issued to change the content and spirit of article 83 of the labor law, governing union elections.[27]

One of the crucial steps taken by the West Bank trade unionists in this period was the decision to "freeze" the class struggle in response to Israel's policy of economic strangulaton and creeping annexation. In the words of Adel Ghanem, who later became the secretary-general of the GFTU:

> As unionists we believed in union struggle, but after 1967 we faced a new situation. We discovered that the danger from the occupation was greater than that from the capitalists. We were afraid that people would leave the West Bank [because of the economic situation]. So we wanted to help the national industries because this way we would also protect the workers. And so we decided to freeze the class struggle.[28]

In its activities the GFTU found itself sandwiched between the Israeli military occupation on the one hand and what remained of Jordanian institutional control (in the form of legal restrictions, funding, and the presence of Jordanian agents inside the unions) on the other. Relations between West Bank unions and unions in Jordan remained friendly until 1970. Then, after Black September, links between the unions on both banks were submitted to review. On 25 September 1970, the executive committee of the GFTU, convened in an emergency session to discuss the situation in Jordan, condemned King Hussein and launched a fund-raising campaign to help the Palestinians in Jordan who had been hurt by the army's crackdown.[29] In a later session, on 11 January 1974, the GFTU executive committee decided officially to sever its relationship with its counterpart in Jordan. By this time the October War had occurred, and Jordan's influence in the West Bank was waning as the PLO stepped into the international limelight. Later in 1974, after the Rabat Conference where the PLO was proclaimed the sole legitimate representative of the Palestinians, the GFTU, according to Hazboun and al-Salhi, was one of the first institutions in the Occupied Territories to declare itself in full support of the resolutions made by the Arab states in Rabat.[30]

Following this diplomatic defeat by Jordan, the Jordanian authorities attempted to recoup their loss of influence in the West Bank union movement by trying to split it. They supported the section within the GFTU headed by Mahmoud al-Sharbini (who had pro-Fatah leanings) and Shehadeh al-Minawi, and, among other tactics, they tried (in vain) to set up an alternative GFTU for the southern region through Sheikh Muhammad al-Ja'bari in Hebron.[31] In spite of these efforts to divide the union movement, the GFTU continued to organize sectors of the Palestinian working class in the West Bank, confining itself to the main towns and surrounding refugee camps. In 1974 it called on unionists in East Jerusalem to revive their unions, and admitted the Hotel Workers' Union and the Leather-work Industry Workers' Union into the federation even before they had been revived.[32] The Printing Press Workers' Union was revived in 1975: "The Israeli authorities could not prevent this," said one of the union's activists, "because of the general conditions that prevailed at that time: there was a lot of mass activity. So then they tried to obstruct union activities in an indirect way," a pattern followed throughout the 1980s as well.[33]

In 1976, the GFTU openly came out in support of the national movement in the West Bank by endorsing three unionists as candidates in the municipal elections: the Communists Adel Ghanem in Nablus and George Hazboun in Bethlehem, and the Ba'athist Mustafa Malhis in Jenin.[34] The results of the elections constituted a major victory for the national movement in the Occupied Territories. Hazboun was elected deputy mayor of Bethlehem.

There is no indication that the military authorities ever underestimated the potential power of the union movement, and they have therefore done much to impede the unions' normal functioning. Unionists were detained and deported throughout the 1970s, and the unions' membership, actual and potential, was harassed and threatened in an apparent attempt to prevent unions from gaining mass support. At least seven labor leaders were deported between 1969 and 1979, and an even larger number was placed under town arrest or in administrative detention.[35]

Despite military repression, however, the unions' membership continued to increase throughout the 1970s: from close to one thousand in 1967 to five thousand in 1970, to seven thousand in 1974, and to more than twelve thousand in 1979.[36] Yet unions remained small in size, and were confined to the main urban centers only—East Jerusalem, Nablus, Ramallah/al-Bireh, Jenin, Tulkarem, and Hebron. Generally speaking, the Communists were in full control of the institutions of the labor movement until the late 1970s, but by no means did they have the only voice. Their rivals included members of the (pro-Syrian) Ba'ath, and in the 1970s increasingly Fatah, the DFLP, and the PFLP as well. However, it was not until the PLO refocused its attention on the masses in the Occupied Territories in the mid- and late 1970s that these rivalries culminated in major confrontations.

PALESTINIAN NATIONALISM AND
THE REVIVAL OF THE LABOR MOVEMENT

By the middle of the 1970s a crucial coalescence took place that satisfied the main preconditions for mass mobilization against Israel's military occupation. First, a "human base" of economically exploited, politically disenfranchised, and culturally oppressed Palestinians existed; because of its shared experience of oppression, regardless of class, it was ready to be mobilized after a decade of military rule, as prospects of independence sponsored by the world community dimmed. Second, the PLO had gained sufficient power and legitimacy by the mid-1970s to take charge of organizational work in the Occupied Territories. The failure of elite-based resistance to the occupation underlined the need to organize the masses of the population in novel ways. The goal was to build an infrastructure of resistance that eventually would be capable of receiving and sustaining the "national authority."

The leftist factions in the PLO, the DFLP and the PFLP, were the first to turn to popular mobilization in the Occupied Territories. Local activists identifying with these organizations were in the forefront of the student movement, and then the voluntary work movement, the women's movement, and the labor movement. The method employed by these activists was to organize hitherto neglected sectors of the population, such as housewives and itinerant day laborers employed in Israel, offering services that otherwise did not exist. One observer has noted that "groups such as the DFLP had always talked about working 'inside,' but it is only after 1974 that they began to take their own words seriously, not only in terms of military struggle, but also political. How would they go about this? This had already been shown by the PCP: they had to focus on the workers, the students, the women, etc."[37]

To protect themselves against the repressive actions of the military, they built a network of organizations that operated informally, and fairly invisibly to the military authorities, among the masses of the population. Internal democracy, including regular elections, led to the emergence of a large group of trained cadres, which meant that if leaders were imprisoned or deported by the army, others could immediately take their place and carry on with the work. Many of the activists had themselves been detained in the 1970s, and had used their time in prison to work out strategies of mobilization within their own factions, while forging alliances with members of other factions. Interfactional networks created in detention usually proved unworkable outside prison, however.

Because attempts by one faction to organize the masses were seen by others as threats to their own popular support, a vigorous competition ensued that contributed to a rapid growth of the popular movement and tore apart whatever degree of national unity and cooperation existed among the three main factions of the PLO (Fatah, the DFLP, and the PFLP) and the PCP. Factionalism, therefore, was at once a dynamic and an extremely divisive element in the national movement in the Occupied Territories. The interfactional rivalries led to a veritable "war of the institutions" in the late 1970s and early 1980s, with activists vying for control of existing organizations, and splitting off to set up parallel organizations of their own if they failed. The massive infusions of money from the Arab states after the Baghdad Conference in 1978, most of which went to sup-

porters of Jordan and Fatah in the West Bank and Gaza, exacerbated existing rivalries and gave rise to a lot of the bitterness that has haunted the
four factions in the popular movement in the 1980s.

The four factions, identifying with their ideological counterparts in the
PLO outside the Occupied Territories, set up "blocs" or "movements" in
the West Bank and Gaza that served as umbrella organizations for grass-
roots activities. As noted above, although they do not exist formally, and
therefore do not have names, they can roughly be identified by the following labels: the "Youth Movement," which is close to Fatah; the "Progressive Bloc," aligned with the PCP; the "Unity Bloc," identified with the
DFLP; and the "Action Front," associated with the PFLP. The Unity Bloc
was the first to introduce a new and dynamic element to the national
movement by directing its energies toward organizing women and migrant day laborers. In 1978, Unity Bloc activists set up the WWC to lead
the women's movement, and the Workers' Unity Bloc (WUB) to address
the labor question.

The Workers' Unity Bloc: Organizing Migrant Labor

The WUB was the first union bloc seriously to target Palestinian workers
from the Occupied Territories employed across the Green Line, a task it
set about from its inception. Previously, workers employed in Israel had
been branded as "traitors" by certain factions in the Palestinian national
movement, especially the PFLP, and by the PCP as a *lumpenproletariat*
that, objectively speaking (from a Marxist perspective), could not be organized.[38] By the end of the 1970s, the attitude of most Palestinian activists toward these workers had changed, however, as it became clear that
work in Israel was the only means of survival for many Palestinian families, and that the organization of this labor force might have great nationalist potential. The WUB held, in the words of one of its leaders, that

> these workers form part of the Palestinian working class. But such as many
> other workers, most of them are not yet organized. . . . These are the most
> oppressed workers. . . . But there are trade unions that have set out to re-
> veal the oppression of these workers, this underemployed stratum of the
> working class. Objectively, this stratum can play a significant role in the na-
> tional movement and in the social struggle against the Israeli bourgeoisie.
> This is so because these workers play an important role in the Israeli econ-
> omy. A few years ago the Israelis carried out military operations in Hebron,
> and forbade everyone from leaving their houses. As a result several Israeli
> companies suffered serious financial losses. This demonstrates how depend-
> ent sectors of the Israeli economy are on Palestinian workers.[39]

One of the main problems the WUB and the other blocs faced in organizing workers employed in Israel was that they had no jurisdiction in Is-

rael, and therefore they could do little substantively to protect these workers. Yet the unions made special appeals to the migrant workers, trying to address at least rhetorically the specific situations in which they found themselves in Israel. The WUB, for example, set out to achieve the following goals, according to its program:

1. Equality in wages, rights, and working conditions for Arabs and Jews.
2. Transfer to the Palestinian unions of the funds that have accumulated in Israel from wage deductions, to be used for social insurance and health insurance programs in the Occupied Territories.
3. Exemption of Arab laborers from the Israeli tax law.
4. An end to oppression and national discrimination against Palestinian workers.
5. The right of Palestinian workers who are employed in Israeli enterprises to join their own unions in the Occupied Territories.[40]

The extent to which the WUB and others have succeeded in accomplishing these objectives will be discussed below.

The recruitment drive among migrant workers triggered by the organizing efforts of the WUB posed a serious challenge to the existing formal trade-union structure in the West Bank, which thus far had been controlled almost exclusively by the Communists. Trade-union elections used to be arranged, or, in the words of West Bank unionists, "settled in the tribal way," through prior negotiation and agreement sealed by an election in which the proposed candidates would be chosen by acclamation. The WUB was clearly not willing to go on this way because to do so was not in its interest. To gain representation in local trade unions and in the GFTU, the WUB therefore called for the reactivation of formal institutional procedures such as elections and proportional representation.

In response to the emergence of the WUB, which was the first labor "bloc" to identify politically with a particular faction in the PLO (the DFLP), the other political currents in the labor movement set up their own workers' blocs: pro-PCP activists established the Progressive Workers' Bloc (PWB) in 1979, and one year later pro-Fatah and pro-PFLP forces followed suit, setting up the Workers' Youth Movement (WYM) and the Progressive Unionist Action Front (PUAF), respectively. In addition, Ba'athists set up the Workers' Vanguard Bloc (WVB), which played a minor role in the labor movement in the early 1980s and had withered away by the time of the popular uprising in 1987.

The differences among these five blocs are based on four major factors:

1. Their ideology and their strategy of organizing workers. At issue here is mostly how much weight is given to unionist-social goals in proportion to nationalist-political ones.
2. How they perceive the military occupation and political conditions in the

Occupied Territories at any given time, especially with regard to the authorities' policy toward the union movement. Examples: the issue of registration of new unions; the Iron Fist policy of repression since 1985; the closure of union offices during the popular uprising.

3. How they perceive the tactical positions taken by the various currents in the Palestinian national movement at any given time. Examples: positions taken vis-à-vis the Camp David accords of 1978; the Hussein-Arafat agreement of February 1985; the "War of the Camps" in Lebanon in the spring of 1986; the opening of the United States–PLO dialogue in 1988.

4. How they seek to confront economic problems in Israel and the Occupied Territories, for example, rising unemployment and inflation in the mid-1980s.

The main challenge these activists confronted was how to provide those services and benefits to unions members that would ensure the latter's loyalty. The activists' main concern was the struggle for national liberation; they had little schooling in trade-union work. Yet they realized that in order to generate a committed constituency, they had to be able to offer more than a continuing struggle for the ever-elusive independent state. Taking their cue from the Communists, therefore, who had decades of experience in serious, though limited, union work, the new generation of union activists started to study the problems workers encountered in their places of work, and discussed methods of assisting them in securing their rights under the existing labor law. In the process they set up an elaborate support network for workers and their families, providing services that did not otherwise exist. The unions thus became part of a larger strategy of popular resistance to the occupation, with the aim of outadministering the military authorities. With this purpose in mind, the structure of the trade-union movement, and the process of reproduction, became crucially important.

The Structure of the Labor Movement

Before 1979, West Bank trade unions were established according to the Jordanian labor law of 1960. Under the law, any twenty or more workers in the same occupational sector or in the same workplace could set up their own trade union. They had to apply for a license from the authorities, who had to issue one if the union satisfied the conditions stipulated in the law. Unions, in turn, could establish labor federations, which in turn could affiliate with international union organizations.[41] After 1979, in the wake of renewed labor activity, the Israeli military authorities stopped giving licenses to new unions, although most applied for one. This has meant that the majority of West Bank unions has remained unlicensed.

Historically, trade unions in the West Bank were established first in the towns and only later, after the WUB began organizing migrant workers, in the villages. Workers from refugee camps usually joined unions in the nearest town. By 1987 there were over 130 unions in the West Bank, some more active than others. Most unions are small, not exceeding 250 members. This is partly due to the size of Palestinian enterprises: there are no large industries in the Occupied Territories. Some of the larger unions, such as the Construction and General Institutions Workers' Union (PWB) in Ramallah/al-Bireh, and the Hotel, Restaurant, and Cafe Workers' Union (WYM-WUB) in Jerusalem, have had an average of a thousand dues-paying members.

Unions have been organized by trade and by geographic location. Thus each major town has at least a construction workers' union, a textile workers' union, and a carpentry workers' union, which represent the main branches of Palestinian economic activity. The largest unions have often been the "general institutions" workers' unions, which are catch-all unions that have targeted the average itinerant West Bank worker who may be working on a construction site in Israel today, be unemployed tomorrow, and be loading and unloading trucks at the local vegetable market the day after tomorrow. The general institutions workers' unions are meant especially for West Bankers employed in Israel because of the irregularity of work in any particular trade there. They are often the first union to exist in a village, drawing in workers employed in all trades. Because the West Bank labor force is divided into a large number of small workshops and work sites, and is chronically only irregularly employed, unions established solely in a particular workplace are rare. They can be found in the largest companies and institutions, such as, for example, the Jerusalem Electric Company, Maqassed Hospital, and West Bank universities.

Unionized workers owe allegiance in the first place to their unions, to which they pay membership dues and which seek to protect their rights vis-à-vis employers. All card-carrying union members together have the right to sit and vote in the union's general assembly, which, according to each union's bylaws, meets annually or when called by the administrative committee or by one-fifth of the assembly's membership. The general assembly routinely elects an administrative (or executive) committee, consisting of seven to nine members, which governs the union for a specified period of time, usually no more than one or two years.[42]

Each union has a union council, which consists of the administrative officers of the union and its branches, and the members of the union's organizing committees located in the workplace or place of residence. The Council's task is to evaluate the union's work, and to make recommendations to the administrative committee. Unions' bylaws allow for the creation of an arbitration and supervision committee, which monitors the activities of the administrative committee and arbitrates disputes between members of the administrative committee and regular union members.[43]

Unions have other committees that are appointed by the administrative committee and chaired by one of its members. Such committees govern the union's finances, medical and health services, insurance and savings, social and cultural activities, voluntary work, and sports, among others. If a special problem presents itself, an ad hoc committee may be set up. Unions may have branches in other parts of the city or in the villages; these carry the same name as the parent union that controls them.[44]

Unions may elect members of their administrative committees to represent them in the GFTU's general assembly, according to each union's size.[45] The general assembly elects the GFTU council, which in turn holds biennial elections to the organization's executive committee. This committee, which consists of seven to thirteen members, in turn selects the GFTU general secretary and other officials.[46] The GFTU represents, defends, and directs the labor movement in the West Bank, and governs relations between and within individual unions.[47]

In addition to these formal structures, most workers identify with a particular workers' bloc, such as the Progressive Workers' Bloc or the Workers' Unity Bloc, just as they identify with particular factions in the Palestinian national movement. Not all union members are necessarily affiliated with a bloc, however. Those who are pay annual dues and elect their bloc's leaders in regular elections, according to the bloc's bylaws. The blocs direct a political struggle inside the union movement in the Occupied Territories. The WUB, for example, is organized as follows: It has tried to establish shop-floor or town-village "base units" of ten to twenty-five pro-WUB workers in every trade union; each base unit elects a secretariat. Within each union, the WUB has also tried to set up a "planning and decision-making committee for the bloc's activity in the union"; this committee maintains a secretariat for day-to-day affairs. Officials of these secretariats represent their union in the "district committees," which are geographically spread out through the West Bank and Gaza. On a national level, the WUB is governed by its general council, which is "composed of the representatives of WUB in the West Bank GFTU council, WUB representatives in union administrations, and WUB union secretariat secretaries and their deputies." The Council elects the eleven to fifteen members of the WUB Central Bureau, the highest WUB executive organ in the West Bank and Gaza.[48]

Since trade-union members may choose to join different union blocs, a trade union's administrative committee may comprise representatives of more than one bloc. The makeup of the committee is therefore important in determining which bloc or blocs control any particular union. If the committee is split between blocs, the internal balance of power determines which members are sent to represent the union in the GFTU.

Since 1984, some union blocs have also attempted to set up so-called trade federations, federations of which unions in the same trade can be members. This was done to decentralize the formal union structure and decrease the weight of the GFTU, which was split and then paralyzed after 1981. By 1985, only two blocs had established such federations: the WUB had six and the PWB had two.

The First Split in the Labor Movement

Within two years after the revival of the labor movement by grass-roots activists, the formal union structure succombed under the weight of rapidly increasing membership and bitter competition between union blocs. The WUB's focus on migrant workers and its appeal to the workers' nationalist emotions had helped it gain a large following in a relatively short time. In the beginning, the WUB concentrated on mobilizing workers, including those employed in the West Bank, at the grass-roots level, not directly threatening the position of the Communists who were represented by the PWB in the union apparatus. The WUB has pursued the following goals since its founding in 1978:

1. To form new unions, and integrate them into the GFTU.
2. To accept any new workers in the unions' ranks, including workers employed inside Israel.
3. To form professional federations for each profession or trade (for example, construction).
4. To set up branches of unions in villages and camps, and to open up unions to people from these areas.
5. To set up workers' committees in workplaces, even inside Israel.[49]

Using this strategy, however, the WUB soon began to pose a threat to the PWB's hegemony in individual unions as well as in the GFTU. The PWB had a considerable following within the urban working class and possessed the bureaucratic and union skills necessary to run workers' organizations effectively. In the late 1970s, the PWB's dominant role in the labor movement in the West Bank was reflected in the size of its membership, its control over most local unions, and its representation in the GFTU.

The pro-Fatah activists had failed in the 1970s to deploy Fatah's considerable human and financial resources in the Occupied Territories in the mass organizations. Fatah is essentially a bourgeois organization using the typical bourgeois methods of patronage and charismatic appeal to ensure the loyalty of the population. Fatah also controlled a number of formal institutions, such as charitable organizations, usually competing with pro-Jordanian elements. In the 1970s Fatah did have representatives in the labor movement, however, but they exerted no great control and at times acted in league with Jordan.

In response to the organizing efforts by the other nationalist groups at the end of the 1970s, pro-Fatah activists set up the WYM and began to make serious efforts to penetrate the trade unions in order not to lose control on the institutional level in the West Bank. In this it was helped greatly by the reputation and actual supremacy the Fatah leadership enjoyed in the diaspora, and by the considerable financial and institutional support offered by the Jordanian-Palestinian Joint Committee to those in the Occupied Territories who toed the Jordanian or mainstream Fatah line. The PWB was the WYM's main target (given Fatah's continuing uneasiness about the influential role played by the Communists in the PNF and the NGC, and the Communists' hegemony in the labor movement).

The PWB, in turn, attempted to resist the erosion of its popular base and its organizational hegemony. Countering the organizing efforts of the new nationalist blocs and the bullying of the WYM, the PWB began to use its organizational weight to close the GFTU to new unions and to close individual unions to new members. According to one observer, "elections used to be arranged beforehand, and this was an agreed procedure. But after 1979 this changed."[50] After 1979, every single meeting of the GFTU turned into a battle over numbers and representation. The first in a series of major confrontations took place early in the summer of 1981, when the WYM felt strong enough, not because of its membership, which was small, but because of its overall power in the national movement, to push for greater representation in the GFTU. The confrontations culminated in a formal split in the West Bank labor movement in August 1981.

In the spring of 1981, the West Bank unions were gearing up for the biennial GFTU elections due to be held later that year. The WUB's recruitment drive and the WYM's growing assertiveness led to an intense jockeying among the union blocs to increase their representation, through the unions they controlled, in the GFTU. The preelection period consequently featured efforts by all blocs to enhance their representation in individual unions, and to have new and yet unlicensed unions be admitted into the GFTU.

The struggle centered on the General Carpentry Workers' Union in Hebron, the Construction Workers' Union in Jerusalem, and the Construction and General Institutions Workers' Union in the village of Abu Dis near Jerusalem. In the first two unions, the WYM and the WUB, respectively, sought to challenge the supremacy of the PWB. In the third case, the WUB attempted to have its new and unlicensed union be granted membership in the GFTU. In response to the disputes that broke out in these unions, the council of the GFTU, acting as an intermediary, ruled that in the first two cases, the unions would be barred from participating in the GFTU council meeting scheduled for 29 May 1981 until the problems had been worked out by special committees set up by the unions' leadership.[51]

The GFTU council met on 29 May to pave the way for the elections. Contrary to the earlier council decisions, representatives from both the Jerusalem and the Hebron unions were present at the meeting. The WYM protested their presence, arguing that some of the Hebron union's members were not carpentry but construction workers, and did therefore not fulfill the conditions of membership in the union. A day-long and reportedly acrimonious debate ensued, and it was finally decided unanimously that the meeting be adjourned until 5 June.

The PWB, asserting its leadership role in the GFTU, chose to boycott the 5 June meeting, and arranged to meet instead on 12 June. The other four blocs—the WYM, the WUB, the PUAF, and the WVB—did meet on 5 June—forty-eight out of seventy-eight council members. A decision was taken that the GFTU elections would be held on 10 July.[52]

On 12 June, the PWB held its postponed GFTU meeting. Surprisingly, the WUB, which apparently hoped to benefit by switching alliances from the WYM to the PWB, was also present at the meeting. In the event, the PWB brokered agreements with the WUB, the PUAF, and the WVB to pull them to its side. The disputes in the Jerusalem and Hebron unions were settled amicably between the WUB and the PWB, and the Abu Dis union was admitted to the GFTU as a full member, as was a new PWB-controlled union. The three smaller blocs were all given representation on the GFTU's executive committee, which, however, remained firmly in control of the PWB. It was also decided that the GFTU elections would be held, not on 10 July, but on 7 August.[53]

On 7 August 1981, the GFTU, headed by Adel Ghanem, elected a new executive committee of thirteen members (an expansion of two compared with the previous committee). The WYM was absent from the meeting. In the local press it was later reported that "a total of 59 members from 16 labour unions were able to reach Nablus from various parts of the West Bank, but, unfortunately, 17 members from Jerusalem unions were [turned back] by the military authorities."[54]

The WYM justified its boycott of the elections by claiming that it had not been decided conclusively and unanimously which unions would be allowed to vote and which ones would not be.[55] In the event, all disputed unions were present and voted. In response the WYM sent a protest letter to the head of the election supervising committee, Saleh Abu 'Ida, declaring the elections illegal because there had been no quorum and because illegal unions had participated, and demanding that new elections be held.[56] WUB unionist Nabil Abu Seriya, newly elected to the GFTU's executive committee, stated during a public discussion on trade unions in the West Bank in Jerusalem on 16 August: "Although the election's result was not fair since I believe members from other unions should be represented in the executive committee, the elections are legal."[57] At the same meeting, WYM leader Shehadeh al-Minawi said that "some unions were given membership [in the GFTU] without having obtained official registration, and this is against the GFTU regulations."[58]

On 28 August the WYM held its own GFTU executive committee elections, thereby formalizing the split between the PWB-dominated GFTU and a new WYM-controlled GFTU. Each proceeded to claim that it was the sole representative of the Palestinian working class in the West Bank.

The unity in the labor movement in the West Bank came apart as a result of a power struggle between the PWB and the WYM, with the WUB, the PUAF, and the WVB, representing the leftist factions in the PLO, acting as swing votes. The struggle took the form of a fight over the right of representation of new unions in the GFTU and of new members in existing unions, but, as stated at the outset, the real reasons lie deeper. The WYM claims that the PWB initiated the split: Linked to the Communist countries of Eastern Europe, the PWB saw itself as the only authentic representative of the West Bank proletariat; fearing the growing strength of the competing union blocs, it attempted to close off the GFTU in 1981 to retain its historic control over the union movement.[59]

The PWB, on the other hand, argues that the WYM tried to gain control over the union movement on the claim that it should receive greater representation because of the relative strength of Fatah in the Palestinian national movement in 1980 and 1981. One PWB unionist said that the WYM's Shehada al-Minawi and Mahmoud al-Sharbini caused the split, claiming that they were the representatives of the PLO in the West Bank.[60] The head of the GFTU in 1981, Adel Ghanem, declared in an interview in 1985 that "the differences between the unions in the West Bank are not unionist but political in nature. In terms of unionist programs there is no difference between the various blocs. The reason for the split is Jordan and the Palestinian rightists, and the occupier is happy with this situation."[61] The PWB sees the WYM's motivation as unfair since Fatah's strength among the masses of the population has, in the PWB's view, nothing to do with the orientation of the organized labor movement inside the Occupied Territories.[62]

Both the WYM and the PWB asserted that they had majority support among workers in the West Bank. They each had their own method of calculating, however. The PWB counted its support through the biennial elections in local unions and the GFTU. The WYM, on the other hand, based its calculations on the relative support Fatah, or even the PLO in general, commanded in the West Bank, which is indeed very large.[63] The WYM deduced its numerical superiority among the working class from two premises: one, most West Bankers are workers, and two, most West Bankers support the "oneness of the PLO"—in other words, most West Bankers support the PLO, in particular Fatah.[64] Ergo the WYM, which identifies with Fatah, would receive most votes if all workers voted. The

PWB counters, however, that it alone has organized West Bank workers, and that most organized workers, who do in fact vote in union elections, demonstrate time and again that they support the PWB.

There is also an important monetary issue. The WYM is generally supported by the mainstream PLO, and has therefore received funding from the Palestinian-Jordanian Joint Committee, which was set up by the Arab states at the Baghdad Conference in 1978 to promote steadfastness in the Occupied Territories. After the 1981 split, the Joint Committee stipulated that one condition for receiving funding was that any proposal to the committee would have to be signed by Shehadeh al-Minawi, whom the committee recognized as the sole legitimate general secretary of the sole legitimate GFTU.[65] No unions affiliated with the PWB-controlled GFTU received Joint Committee funding after August 1981. Adel Ghanem has said that the WYM, which has done no serious labor organizing, survives only at the mercy of the Joint Committee, which has endowed it lavishly in the 1981–85 period. According to Ghanem, "if financial support from the outside were to be cut off, those who really are active on behalf of the workers [the PWB] will continue to be active, while the others [the WYM] will disappear."[66]

Since August 1981, two entirely separate General Federations of Trade Unions with identical names have been rivals, determined to lead the West Bank labor movement in their own particular ways. This was a momentous change, not merely on the formal level, but also in terms of policy. During the 1980s, the labor movement was gradually "nationalized" by the nationalist blocs. Even the PWB was forced, in the gathering nationalist momentum, to modify its tactics. It too began to organize migrant workers, and it more readily and more openly began to espouse national goals. Thus the roots for the streamlining of the modern Palestinian labor movement lie in this period. Yet the convulsions that started in the late 1970s did not end with the split in the labor movement in 1981. The early 1980s were fraught with conflict as the PWB faced further attacks on its hegemony in local unions and the GFTU from the side of the WUB, which stepped up its recruitment drive among migrant workers.

Trade Unions and the National Issue: The Alliance of Classes

The nationalist tendency of Palestinian trade unions is not an accident or a function of the influence of the PLO over the lives of Palestinians in the Occupied Territories. The programs of the unions clearly reflect the conditions under which they are forced to operate. Military occupation has provoked unions to articulate nationalist positions, not just because they see themselves as representative organs of an important sector of the population, the working class, but also because workers experience the occu-

pation in their everyday lives. According to the WUB, which in this respect does not differ from any of the other blocs:

> The Occupied Territories became annexed to the Israeli economy because it
> supplied cheap labour and constituted a consumer market for Israeli products
> preventing Arab commodities produced under severe competitive conditions
> from being sold. Consequently, the effects of the Israeli economic crisis (in-
> flation and high prices) were reflected in the Occupied Territories, leading
> to an intensive exploitation and oppression of the working class, particu-
> larly those working in Israeli enterprises. So the working class suffered the
> most from occupation policy. Hence it badly needs and fights for the end
> of occupation; it started to use its important role and influence amongst
> the ranks of the Palestinian people in the battle of liberation and national
> independence.[67]

A WUB official clarified her bloc's position as follows: "Our national goal
is to reconfirm the temporary program of the PLO, which is the right to
return, self-determination, and establishing an independent state on any
part of the national soil. Our class goal as a workers' bloc is to work toward
a socialist system where workers control the economy."[68] The secretary-
general of the GFTU-Ghanem, Adel Ghanem, made a similar statement
in an interview in 1985:

> This is a unique occupation. It wants to kick us out, while the British and
> French [as colonial powers] only sought to exploit. Lenin never imagined
> that a situation would arise where people would get together from every-
> where in the world and throw out another people. Lenin didn't consider that
> there would be a Jewish state, or that there would be an oil alliance between
> Saudi Arabia and the U.S. The situation here is worse than in South Africa,
> because there people are being exploited, but here they are being thrown
> out.[69]

On the level of individual unions, this PWB position has translated into
explicitly political statements, the following of which, from a unionist in
Hebron, is typical not only of the PWB but of all blocs:

> Our main work is union work, but we believe that workers cannot get their
> rights as long as there is no independent Palestinian state, i.e., one that is not
> affiliated with Jordan. That is why we are also involved in politics. Our an-
> swer to the Israelis, who claim that we are political organizations, is that the
> workers' issue cannot be separated from politics, from the occupation. The
> bourgeoisie wants the King [of Jordan] to come [and take control of the West
> Bank], but the workers do not believe in such a solution.[70]

The nationalist tendency of the unions led to a "freezing" of the class
struggle and the creation of a "national alliance" between the workers and
the entrepreneurial class in the Occupied Territories. The Municipality

and General Institutions Workers' Union (WYM) in Nablus, for example, issued a statement in 1985 accusing the Israeli occupation of causing economic problems that affect all Palestinians, workers *and* employers. It then went on to proclaim the need for employers to recognize that workers play a crucial role in national economic development, and that employers should therefore "carry their national responsibility" to work together with workers and employees to develop their enterprises and institutions. The statement called on workers to increase production, and ended by stating: "Let us all, workers and employers, work together to realize the aim of our Palestinian people: the liberation of the land."[71] The WUB has similarly stressed the need for an "alliance of classes," considering that the occupation has distorted the Palestinian social structure, erasing the clear dividing lines between the two main social protagonists while accentuating national oppression. But it has emphasized at the same time that within this alliance, responsibilities must be shared equally. In the words of one WUB official:

> The Israeli economic policy is aimed at weakening the Palestinian economy by putting restrictions and clamping taxes on Palestinian enterprises. So workers have begun to compromise their own rights to protect the national industry, and therefore the national bourgeoisie. For instance, they gave up the thirteenth month pay. The WUB believes that there can to some extent be negotiations with the national bourgeoisie. There can be compromise, but not to the extent that everything will be loaded onto the workers' backs.[72]

All three of the leftist blocs, the PWB, the WUB, and the PUAF, have cooperated with employers, agreeing to resolve labor disputes peacefully. But they have insisted that this should not be done at the cost of the workers, and that the workers should not be made to carry the full burden of this national alliance. There is, in the words of a PWB unionist, a "red line" that cannot be overstepped by employers.[73] The location of this "red line" is contingent on political and economic conditions at any particular time, and is negotiable. At the same time, its very existence is significant, as it demonstrates the considerable power the labor movement acquired inside the Palestinian national movement in the Occupied Territories in the 1980s.

The political character of some of the activities and many of the official pronouncements of the union movement in the Occupied Territories is not unique in today's world. Nor is the occurrence of splits between unions for political rather than unionist reasons a rare phenomenon. In fact, the union movement in the Occupied Territories is essentially similar to union movements in other countries, and there are clear parallels with the colonial period in Africa and elsewhere. The everyday impact of the military occupation, however, has made for a particularly pronounced tendency to place national goals before social ones on the unionist agenda.

This is not a characteristic only of the trade unions, but also of other popular organizations in the Occupied Territories. Nationalism has proved a powerful magnet, attracting large sectors of the population. Yet this can in and of itself hardly account for the growth of the union movement in the 1980s. The tangible services offered by unions to their members is the second, equally important element that helps explain the rapid development of grass-roots organizations in the Occupied Territories during the second decade of Israel's military occupation.

Counterpoint: The Antinationalist Alliance of the Joint Committee and the Palestinian Enterpreneurial Class

Because of their work at the grass roots of Palestinian society, organizing workers by offering them tangible services and mobilizing them under the banner of Palestinian nationalism, trade unions in the West Bank helped lay the foundation for an infrastructure of resistance to the established forms of control in the late 1970s and early 1980s. This infrastructure was elaborated in the 1980s, and proved its worth in the intifada at the end of the decade, which was the first sustained and organized attempt by the Palestinian population to shake off Israeli rule since 1967. Institutional power in the Occupied Territories, however, was not exercised by the Israeli occupation authorities only. There was also Jordan, the ruling power from 1948 until June 1967, which retained its claim to the West Bank throughout the first twenty-one years of the military occupation, to relinquish it only in the face of failure at the height of the intifada, in July 1988.

Because Jordan has had no direct access to the levers of power in the West Bank since 1967, it has attempted to sustain its claim to the territory through local municipalities and Palestinian institutions. Before 1967, most of these institutions were charitable societies. Their leaders' loyalties were divided between Jordan and Palestinian nationalism, especially after the ascendancy of the PLO in the mid-1960s. Jordan exercised control through funding and by backing pro-Jordanian personalities, and its internal intelligence service was there to take care of nationalist "troublemakers." This policy was continued after 1967, to the extent possible, and with diminishing effectiveness as the occupation wore on.

The Jordanian regime has used a number of stratagems in its attempt to gain legitimacy in the eyes of the Palestinian population. Most importantly, it has consistently tried to forge an alliance with the Palestinian bourgeoisie outside Palestine, and with the mainstream Palestinian national movement, most notably Fatah (or certain factions in Fatah), in the West Bank and Gaza. Fatah had an interest in such an alliance because it faced a growing challenge to its control over the population from the side of the leftist factions in the PLO and the PCP, who were busy organizing the masses rather than buying their loyalty, the traditional Fatah approach in claiming popular legitimacy. At times of conflicts and splits in the national movement, Jordan and Fatah teamed up against the PFLP, the DFLP, and the PCP. This was most commonly done through Jordan's remaining institutional levers: control of funding, much of which was procured from other Arab states and the Palestinian bourgeoisie in the Persian Gulf and channeled through Jordan; and ties with the Palestinian merchant and entrepreneurial classes in the Occupied Territories. At times, these efforts at reasserting Jordanian control crystallized into a veritable antinationalist alliance of Jordan with Palestinian elites, constituting a powerful counterpoint to the grass-roots work of Palestinian activists and the "national alliance of classes." These countervailing alliances, added to the repression carried out by the Israeli military, have set the parameters of mass mobilization in the Occupied Territories in the 1980s.

The resurgent trade-union movement was caught in the middle of this battle in the late 1970s, especially because unions were chronically short of money to provide real services to their members. Most unions collect money from workers' membership dues and from sales and similar activities, but the amounts involved are puny. For example, union members pay membership dues of perhaps one or two Jordanian dinars (approximately three to six dollars before 1989) per year, in addition to an initial admission fee of perhaps twenty-five fils (approximately seventy-five cents) and the costs of a union card, fifteen fils (approximately forty-five cents).[74] Unions also receive donations from nonmembers on occasion, and sometimes members who have received compensation from their employers after a successful action by the union donate a percentage to the union. Sales revenues from bazaars and exhibits also accrue to the union. Some unions have succeeded in initiating projects that generate money for the union, such as the WUB's printers' cooperative in Shu'fat. Finally, national institutions in the West Bank have occasionally sponsored specific union projects, as have foreign funders, such as the British organization War on Want.

The creation of the Palestinian-Jordanian Joint Committee at the Baghdad Conference in 1978 proved a windfall to the trade unions, as indeed it did for all Palestinian institutions and organizations in the Occupied Territories. However, the issue of funding was from the outset thoroughly politicized, as it favored projects sponsored primarily by pro-Jordanian figures or conservative forces in Fatah. Soon the Joint Committee's manipulations in the Occupied Territories had discredited those who accepted these monies, and the Joint Committee had become a dirty word—except to the privileged few who were able to build expensive villas for themselves—by the time the funding dried up in the mid-1980s.

The GFTU in the West Bank, and its affiliated unions, were among the regular recipients of Joint Committee money after 1978. When the split occurred in 1981, precipitated by the WYM's attempt to gain control over the union movement, Joint Committee money was probably a factor in the internal debates that took place. After the WYM had set up its own GFTU, it was recognized by the Joint Committee as being the sole legitimate representative of the Palestinian working class in the West Bank. Subsequent to the split, any union applying for money for specific projects from the Joint Committee was forced to obtain the signature of the GFTU-WYM's secretary-general, Shehadeh al-Minawi, at the bottom of the application. Because of the refusal of the four other blocs to do so, only the GFTU-WYM and affiliated unions received Joint Committee money after 1981. The secretary-general of the GFTU-Ghanem, Adel Ghanem, summed up his federation's predicament as follows: "Our financial resources depend on our membership. In the past we used to get a lot of financial support, but after the split we have not received any more money."[75] A PWB official in Ramallah said:

Since the establishment of the Joint Committee, our union has received money only twice, each time a thousand dinars [three thousand dollars]. The current restriction on Joint Committee funding was imposed for political reasons after the 1981 split. There are now two conditions for receiving aid from them: (1) Minawi has to sign the papers, and (2) the union has to agree with the Joint Committee's political stands, such as the Hussein-Arafat agreement [of February 1985], the seventeenth PNC [of November 1984, organized and attended only by Fatah], and the new Jordanian policy vis-à-vis the West Bank, the so-called Second Camp David. Of course we reject all of this. Our principles are not for sale. We are committed to the hopes of our people to create an independent Palestinian state. Most of the workers reject the Joint Committee's policy because it runs contrary to their interests. The Joint Committee's policies won't change things, except on the face of it: the workers will still be controlled by the same class but it is of a different [Jordanian] nationality.[76]

WYM-affiliated unions received annual sums of money from the Joint Committee after 1981, in addition to funding for specific projects and causes. Unionists of the Hotel, Restaurants, and Cafe Workers' Union (WYM) in Jerusalem, for example, claim that the union received three thousand dinars annually in the years 1979–1983. Unionists said that because of the recession in the Persian Gulf, funding was then cut in half. The union received fifteen hundred dinars in 1984 and 1985 each.[77] The Shoemakers' Union (WYM) in Hebron has reported receiving between a thousand and fifteen hundred dinars annually from the committee.[78] The Municipality and General Institutions Workers' Union (WYM) in Nablus managed to procure Joint Committee support for those employees of the Nablus Municipality, who went on strike after the dismissal by the Israeli military of the mayor and municipal council in 1982, who were members of the union.[79]

Minawi's own GFTU-WYM used Joint Committee funding to construct a new building for itself and six of its Nablus-based affiliated unions in the heart of Nablus, a stone's throw from the old GFTU building abandoned by the WYM after the 1981 split and still occupied by the GFTU-Ghanem and some of its affiliated unions. I can say from personal experience that the building is clearly used for certain occasions and fills up at such times, but that generally only a handful of unionists and workers are present. The WYM-controlled unions in Hebron similarly used Joint Committee funds to build a new union headquarters in the center of town, which had to be unlocked by the unionists for my interview with them to take place.

The issue of Joint Committee money has clearly exacerbated the problems that existed between the GFTU-Ghanem and the GFTU-WYM after 1981. Adel Ghanem has accused the Committee of "only supporting capitalists, who invest the money elsewhere, for instance in Europe," following his appeal to the committee to finance cooperative societies in the West Bank as a way of addressing the problem of unemployment.[80] A WUB leader, a member of the executive committee of the Printing Press Workers' Union in Jerusalem, reported the following experience:

> Our political position does create problems because although we are legally registered in Jordan, we do not receive *Sumud* [Joint Committee] money. The Shabbibeh [the WYM] tried to take advantage of this by running in our union's elections last time in the hope of luring workers away from us with promises of money from Jordan. They would point at us [the WUB] and say that we couldn't get any money, and that the workers should therefore vote for them instead. But the workers are very conscious. They didn't vote for Shabbibeh.[81]

The Palestinian entrepreneurial class has been divided in its loyalty between the "national alliance of classes" and the Jordan-sponsored antinationalist alliance. Clearly, a number of West Bank employers support the leftist factions of the PLO; when labor problems occur, they can usually be solved via the mediation of unionists of the same political persuasion. However, labor activists have reported many attempts by employers to thwart union efforts to carry out their tasks of organizing and defending workers. In the words of a Ramallah unionist:

> The owners always try to prevent workers from joining the unions. Once they find out that a worker has joined, for example, they may fire him. They also discourage workers from joining by telling them that the unions cannot do anything for them. They also try to keep us from meeting with workers. The owner of the Tako [tissue paper] factory [in Ramallah] called the police on us,

back in 1973. The owner of Silvana [sweets factory in Ramallah] has bought a big truck with which he picks up workers from their homes. [Many Silvana workers are women from the Jalazon refugee camp.] In the afternoon this truck will refuse to drop women off in Ramallah if they live outside Ramallah on the pretext of wishing to protect them. During lunch time, the workers have to remain inside a fenced-in area. In order to establish contacts the union therefore has to work through messengers, messages thrown over the fence, etc. The manager started to check the workers' bags when they leave the factory to look for union pamphlets after such pamphlets had been distributed at the factory a few years ago.[82]

If they cannot prevent workers from joining a union, employers can play one union bloc against another thanks to the split that broke the movement in 1981. A WUB official said: "Factory owners have taken advantage of the split by refusing to recognize particular blocs. They will make workers sign a form claiming that they are a member of a certain bloc, and then when a union linked to a different bloc comes in, they refuse to recognize it."[83]

Some West Bank trade unions, especially those affiliated to the WYM, maintain close links with employers, and it has been alleged that in some cases employers have doubled as union officials. This may explain the reluctance of some unions to engage employers in labor disputes. One Hebron unionist, for example, has charged that the Carpentry Workshop Workers' Union (WYM) in Hebron, the Workshop Owners' Union in Jerusalem, and the Textile Workers' Union in Hebron are all controlled by workshop owners. (Obviously, in the case of the Jerusalem union, the name says it all.) The secretary-general of the Hebron Spinning Workers' Union, for example, Samara Natsheh, is said to own a local spinning factory.[84] The secretary-general of the GFTU-WYM (until 1987), Shehadeh al-Minawi, who himself is a pharmacist, responded to this particular charge by saying that although Natsheh indeed did own the factory in question, he had not been in its possession at the time of his election to the union post, and he would now not be eligible for reelection.[85] In another example, the management of the sesame seed oil factory in Nablus has been accused of having a representative in one of the local general institutions workers' unions.[86] There have also been suggestions that the secretary-general of the GFTU-Ghanem, Adel Ghanem, owns a factory in Nablus.

Even if a union is not directly compromised by a clear overlap between the union's leadership and workshop owners, some unions have gone out of their way to back employers in labor disputes. One suspects that the nationalist reasons offered are not always genuine, but rather serve as a cover for a close alliance between union officials and the local entrepreneurial class. The head of the Shoemakers' Union (WYM) in Hebron, for example, readily admitted his union's support of employers on certain issues: "In 1979 the military authorities put a 15 percent [value-added] tax on workshop owners. Some workers wanted to sue the owners because the latter were unable to pay out wages due to the tax hike. The union came out on the side of the owners because we thought that this way we would better support the workers." Exactly how, he did not divulge.[87]

The Joint Committee has also entered the fray, siding repeatedly with employers against certain unions, or against workers in general. More than once employers have used the Joint Committee as leverage against workers' demands for higher wages and strike threats. One important case concerned the Nuseibeh tiles and stone-cutting company in al-Bireh. According to a WUB unionist:

Nuseibeh received funding from the Joint Committee in 1981 to employ a hundred workers. He began with hiring only forty and then, after pressure from the national movement, he employed another twelve. He keeps receiving money on the claim that he does in fact have a hundred workers. The WUB opposed Nuseibeh, because it thought that he was taking undue advantage of the workers. Nuseibeh also called in the police once to throw out the union delegation that was visiting the company. He clearly went out of bounds with the national movement on that occasion. Later, when workers formed a committee inside the company to negotiate with Nuseibeh about wages and safety, he refused to talk with them. The workers then struck for a week. Nuseibeh in response closed down the plant for a month, fired all the workers, and hired new ones. Now the factory is closed once again, but Nuseibeh does not care since he receives money from the Joint Committee.[88]

In another case in 1985,

a worker got injured in the Silvana [sweets] factory in Ramallah. The manager fired him. Then the other workers organized themselves, and demanded from the manager that their colleague be reinstated and that his medical costs be paid. But the company refused, arguing that the workers would then have to strike but that this would not matter, because [he said] "we get our money from the Joint Committee." The owners of the Star [chemicals] factory [in Ramallah] used the same argument once when the workers there were considering a strike.[89]

The actions of the Joint Committee strengthened the hand of Palestinian entrepreneurs in the 1980s, and complicated the work of trade unions in settling labor disputes. The committee's effective demise in 1985 helped clear the way for the partial reconciliation that took place in the PLO at the eighteenth PNC session in 1987, and made possible at least some degree of coordination among West Bank trade unions after the beginning of the uprising.

FACTIONALISM AND EXPANSION: THE 1980s

In the period following the fateful split in 1981, unity was not restored in the Palestinian labor movement. Except for one failed attempt in 1984, when representatives of both federations met to resolve their differences, the two sides were resigned to being formally apart. The GFTU controlled by the WYM (the GFTU-WYM) continued to hold elections in which only representatives from WYM-controlled unions participated. Fighting continued, however, inside the GFTU controlled by the PWB (the GFTU-Ghanem, which included the PWB, the WUB, the PUAF, and the WVB), effectively freezing its activities throughout the 1981–85 period. The main protagonists were the PWB, which tried to preserve its hegemony inside the GFTU-Ghanem, and an insurgent WUB challenging the PWB's control.

Parallel and Cardboard Unions

After 1981, the WUB and the WYM, each for its own reasons, began to set up as many new unions as possible. One WUB unionist clarified his bloc's policy in an interview in 1986: "Whenever there is a union controlled by another bloc, we will set up a parallel union."[90] From 1981 on, the WUB in fact accelerated its recruitment of workers, establishing unions in trades where none had previously existed and creating "parallel" unions (unions bearing the same name) to existing ones when a rival bloc resisted the WUB's attempt to inflate the union's membership with its own new recruits, many of whom were employed across the Green Line in Israel. The WUB was singularly successful in this effort: if in 1981 it controlled nine unions in the GFTU-Ghanem, by the end of 1985 it claimed to control at least fifty-five, many of them new unions, and said it was aiming to control seventy by the end of 1986.[91] Most of these unions were not recognized by the PWB as legal (formally registered) or even legitimate unions, and they were thus denied representation in the GFTU-Ghanem.

Today unions bearing the same name in the same West Bank town abound. The following is an incomplete but indicative list. Hebron has two Electricity Workers' unions (WUB and WYM), two Blacksmiths' unions (WUB and WYM), two Woodworkers' unions (PWB and WYM), two Textile Workers' unions (PWB and WYM), and two Carpentry Workers' unions (PWB and WYM).[92] Nablus has two Construction Workers' unions (PWB and WUB), two General Institutions Workers' unions (WUB and PWB), three Textile Workers' unions (PWB, WVB, and WUB), two Municipality and General Institutions Workers' unions (PWB and WYM), and two Blacksmiths' unions (PWB and WUB).[93] The twin cities of Ramallah and al-Bireh have two Construction and General Institutions Workers' unions (PWB and WUB), among others.[94]

Besides parallel unions, some blocs (especially the WYM) also set up what are often referred to as "cardboard" unions, unions that exist on paper but have no membership other than the twenty-odd individuals necessary to sign the official papers in accordance with the law. The raison d'être of cardboard unions was twofold: they could receive funding from the Joint Committee (this was especially true for those who accepted the signature of the secretary-general of the GFTU-WYM), and they could increase the representation of the bloc to which the union belonged in the GFTU vis-à-vis the other blocs (in the GFTU-Ghanem). By the mid-eighties, cardboard unions had outlived their usefulness as the three main union blocs (PWB, WUB, and WYM) had isolated themselves in their own exclusive GFTUs, and Joint Committee and other Jordanian-sponsored funding had begun to dry up.

All blocs other than the WUB, which prides itself in having initiated the union race, have condemned the creation of parallel and cardboard unions, even blocs such as the WYM that were themselves accused of joining in the practice. Shehadeh al-Minawi, for example, described the post-1981 period as follows:

> As we were working hard for workers, the others started setting up parallel unions, which have no license either from Jordan or from Israel. Then they also established cardboard unions by paying a union registration for thirty workers who perhaps were already members in another union. We [the GFTU-WYM] don't have any such unions, but they [the GFTU-Ghanem] have about a hundred such unions, which is impossible. In the 1981 elections we had sixteen out of the twenty-four unions, and they had eight, and now they have a hundred! Let's join all Carpentry Workers' unions into one and then hold new elections in the general council of the GFTU![95]

The GFTU-WYM itself grew from sixteen to forty-two affiliated unions in the span of four years. A PWB unionist gave his bloc's version of how this had come about. Note the varying opinions on the number of unions each bloc supposedly had in the GFTU in 1981:

> Minawi had seven unions in the GFTU [in 1981], and Ghanem had twenty. From this moment a race began to set up new unions, like unions for cassette-sellers, bread-carriers, and so on, which is clearly ridiculous, just for the sake of being able to say that they [the GFTU-WYM] were justified in setting up their own GFTU. After that, it seems that not only the Shabbibeh [the WYM] had learned this method, but that the WUB picked up on this spirit as well![96]

In 1983, the GFTU-WYM claimed to have forty-two affiliated unions, and the GFTU-Ghanem twenty-nine. In the latter, the unions were divided among the various blocs as follows: the PWB had ten; the WUB had nine;

the WVB had four; the PUAF had one; and five unions were shared among blocs.

The proliferation of unions, genuine or not, placed tremendous pressures on the GFTU-Ghanem, and in particular on the bloc that controlled it, the PWB. After 1983, the GFTU-Ghanem began to block entry of any new unions to the federation. In the words of 'Ali Abu Hilal, leader of the WUB: "If all new unions had been admitted, not only would Ghanem [the GFTU-Ghanem] exceed Minawi [the GFTU-WYM], but the WUB would exceed the PWB [inside the GFTU-Ghanem]. This is so also because the balance of power in some unions has shifted from the PWB to the WUB." Abu Hilal cited as examples of "seizure" by the WUB the Construction Workers' Union in Jerusalem, which until 1981 had been controlled by the PWB but which fell under shared control of the PWB and the WUB in elections held that year, and finally went to the WUB in the 1983 elections; and the Hotel, Restaurant, and Cafe Workers' Union in Jerusalem, also a traditional PWB domain, which came under shared PWB-WUB control in elections in 1981, and then fell to joint WUB-WYM control in elections held in 1983.[97] Abu Hilal explained the situation in the union movement as follows:

> There are two main problems: internal democracy, and the national role of the GFTU in the face of the occupation, i.e., the unions' right to organize under the law of the occupying power. Because of the expansion of the working class, especially after 1979, there was an urgent need to organize workers in the trade unions that had already been established, and to found new unions in the trades that had not yet been organized. In 1981 the WUB put together a program to organize the workers, including those employed inside Israel, because we realized that in order to improve the social conditions of the working class, it was essential to *organize* the working class. This contradicted the interests of the two parties in the conflict: the occupation, which is opposed to the organizing of workers employed in Israel in unions in the West Bank; and the PWB, which is opportunistic.[98]

Recruitment and Union Work

Despite the momentary proliferation of cardboard unions after 1981, real recruitment of workers and real union work did take place. The PWB and the WUB were the most active. How do West Bank unions recruit new members? The secretary-general of the GFTU-Ghanem, Adel Ghanem, has made a useful distinction between workers who support the concept of trade unions, workers who face a specific problem and come to the union for help, and workers who are not aware of or have no faith in trade-union activity.[99] There are no real obstacles to recruiting workers in the first two categories; problems arise only after induction into the union when harassment and intimidation by the army and Shin Bet (Israel's internal intelligence service) discourages some workers from continuing affiliation. However, a strong activist approach is required to recruit workers from the third category, especially migrant workers, who are unaware of the existence of trade unions and their activities, or who have little faith in unions' effectiveness. Typically, union activists and other union members distribute information about union work and workers' rights to relatives at home or colleagues at work. An official of the Construction and General Institutions Workers' Union (PWB) in Ramallah/al-Bireh described his union's recruitment strategy as follows:

> Sixty percent of our union's members work in Israel. We visit them in their villages, not at their work. Every week there are three or four visits by an executive committee member of this union to the villages. They explain to workers what their rights are: equality of wages between Arabs and Jews, fair insurance, etc. Any nonmembers are then encouraged to join. We offer them services: a lawyer in case of a conflict at work; health services; and cultural activities, including discussions and seminars at the union office.[100]

Alternatively, union activists make the rounds on the "slave markets" where day workers hire themselves out to Israeli contractors. More often than not, however, a worker is pulled into a union by a friend or relative who is already a member. In such cases, the personal tie tends to be more important than the ideological leanings of the bloc that controls the local union, especially for younger workers who may not have yet defined their political affiliations within the national movement. At the same time, though, politics may play a dominant role in a worker's choice of union, and it is quite common for entire families or groups of friends to adhere to a particular current in the national movement.[101]

It should be clear, however, that aside from personal ties or political loyalties, a union's activities play a major part in attracting new workers and keeping them as committed members. A base requirement for all unions is to provide a location where a worker can socialize with friends and relax. Any West Bank trade union worth its salt must have at least a small recreation area with a Ping-Pong table and backgammon boards, as well as a small cafeteria. Unionists give lectures in these locations and organize general discussions that serve to educate workers about their rights and reinforce their identity as Palestinian workers living under foreign rule. Beyond that, what counts are the tangible benefits a union can provide. The WUB, for example, claims that it has managed to attract workers through its unions' activities. In the case of the Printing Press Workers' Union in Jerusalem, the following strategy was followed:

> The first thing we did was to organize all the workers in the Arab sector [East Jerusalem]. We visited them in their places of work and encouraged them to

join. The main benefit for them was that the union would represent them and their demands. Our second activity was to organize cultural events, meetings and lectures on workers' rights, labor law, and the benefits for a worker of having a union. Our third activity was to improve working conditions and obtain benefits such as holidays, and to try to get [collective] agreements between workers and employers. We succeeded in two or three workplaces in this. Our fourth activity was to organize a monthly consumer bazaar for workers in our union building, where we sell food, clothes, etc., at lower than store prices. Finally, we set up a cooperative society for printing workers in Shu'fat. We have bought machines and other equipment, and have set up our own presses so that unemployed workers can find work there. The profits from the printing press will go to our health-insurance fund.[102]

The thrust of trade-union activity has been directed toward improving the conditions of workers who are employed in the West Bank itself. This is so obviously because migrant workers, the majority of whom live in villages, tend to be difficult to reach and because West Bank unions have no direct access to Israeli workplaces. Whereas unions can negotiate collective contracts with Palestinian employers, they can do little more for itinerant day laborers than provide health insurance and legal aid on an individual basis, and educate these workers about their rights under Israeli labor law and ILO conventions.

To give a typical example of a West Bank union's activities on behalf of its membership, the Construction and General Institutions Workers' Union (WUB) in Hebron has the following to offer:

1. Medical services from a doctor affiliated with the union for a token fee, and medicine at cost-price; other affiliated doctors offer a 50 percent reduction in cost for medical care on display of the union card; the union also provides assistance in case of hospitalization, maternity, etc.
2. Food, clothes, and other products at cost-price through the monthly bazaar. These goods are procured from local factories.
3. Literacy classes every evening and English classes according to demand.
4. Legal services from the lawyer or legal consultant affiliated with the union in case of labor disputes.
5. Regular lectures about workers' rights.
6. Sports and folklore events.
7. Organized tours for leisure and education.[103]

A WUB-controlled union in Nablus has made an arrangement with local hospitals for its membership, and sponsors visits by a mobile clinic to Nablus-area villages. It also organizes voluntary work by members in the community to raise the union's profile.[104] The Municipality and General Institutions Workers' Union (WYM) in Nablus has a health insurance plan for its members: the doctor affiliated with the union asks only half a dinar (approximately $1.50 before 1989) for a regular visit, and sells medicine at reduced cost. The union organizes seminars on a variety of subjects in cooperation with teachers from Al-Najah University, of which the union's secretary-general is a graduate.[105]

The main accomplishment of West Bank unions appears to be the provision of medical services to workers. The unions have thereby filled the gap created by the absence of a national health plan in the Occupied Territories. In addition, legal services and consumer bazaars play a similar role in improving the quality of life for workers and their families by reducing the cost of living which, given intermittent devaluations of either the Israeli or Jordanian currency, has on occasion been unbearably high, as during the economic recession in the mid-1980s.

Collective Bargaining and Labor Disputes

Another area in which unions have proven active and fairly successful is collective bargaining, if that is the right word. I am not aware of a single contract as of 1990 that applies to an entire industrial sector throughout the West Bank. The prime reasons for this are, in all likelihood, the rivalry between the GFTUs and the inability therefore of any one GFTU to assert authority on a nationwide level (like the Histadrut in Israel), and the absence of a Palestinian government, including a labor ministry, that could legislate and enforce labor laws. In the words of one labor organizer, "the role of the unions is to negotiate collective agreements with employers. But we cannot enforce them because there is no government. If we had a Palestinian state, we would be able to do this."[106]

Most common, therefore, are contracts negotiated by local unions with individual employers, which may then be extended, through further negotiations, with other employers in the same town and sector. Most active unions have negotiated such contracts. An official of the General Carpentry Workers' Union (PWB) in Hebron, for example, said:

> We succeeded in negotiating collective contracts for the carpentry workers with the workshop owners. This has increased the security of the workers, because on the basis of the contract a worker, if injured, has more legal support if necessary. The contracts also serve the interests of the owners, because workers cannot just walk out before the contract expires. In the beginning the owners did not understand this and they were therefore opposed to the union, but now they are quite satisfied.[107]

Normal union demands include fixed working hours, tying wages to the cost of living, paying wages in Jordanian dinars rather than in the unstable Israeli currency (before the collapse of the dinar in 1988–89), paid holidays, special days like May Day, Women's Day, and Palestinian national days off, workers' compensation, sick leave, and work safety.[108] The issue of compensation has become significant in recent years because of the deteriorating economic situation in the Occupied Territories, which has forced a number of the smaller workshops to lay off their workers and close their doors.

One of the problems unionists face in negotiating collective contracts is that the Jordanian labor law of 1965, which is the only labor law applicable in the West Bank, is outdated, and therefore rarely reflects the needs of workers. Employers have used this against workers, and it usually takes intervention by unions backed by prominent members of the Palestinian community to reach agreement with employers on (justified) demands that reflect the socioeconomic realities of the 1980s. Again, a Palestinian government would be able to address such problems by canceling all Jordanian laws and issuing new legislation in the independent Palestinian state. In the absence of an alternative, however, unions often used the Jordanian labor law as a basis for negotiations, at least until the intifada.

To compound the problem, the Israeli military authorities have transferred the powers of the Jordanian Department of Social Affairs, which under the law is responsible for the monitoring and enforcement of basic economic rights, to a labor inspector. This inspector is an employee of the Israeli Civil Administration, which itself is a branch of the military government in the West Bank. Palestinian unions have been hesitant to ask the labor inspector to intervene in labor disputes, and since the beginning of the intifada the labor inspectors, as indeed most Israeli officials and institutions in the Occupied Territories, have been boycotted.

In the absence of collective contracts, or in cases where they exist but are violated by an employer, a union will resort to action on behalf of its members, or on request from nonunionized workers. In almost all cases of dispute between an employer and its workers, a third party will be called on to mediate. This is not necessarily a union; it could be the head of a local institution or a member of the municipal board, or a committee of these. But concomitant with the growth of the labor movement, unions have become the logical source of help for workers with individual or collective grievances.

The secretary-general of the Construction and General Institutions Workers' Union (PWB) in Ramallah/al-Bireh explained his union's strategy vis-à-vis employers as follows:

> We visit workers in their places of work. The old Jordanian law applies there. We organize workers' committees in the workplace to defend the workers' rights as stipulated in the Jordanian law. When a conflict occurs, for instance demands for a salary increase, an eight-hour working day, an annual holiday,

or safety at work, we will adopt the case. Officially the labor inspector, an Israeli, is responsible for [monitoring] minimum wages, etc., but we do not go to him. The union is also fighting for rights that are not mentioned in the law, which is old and leaves much to the discretion of the minister of social affairs. The union has done a study of the law's weaknesses. When these new changes are applied in the workplace, like the May 1 holiday, they become custom, and therefore tantamount to law.[109]

One rather typical case of negotiations between a union and an employer took place in Nablus in November 1985. Workers in the Nabil Arafat garment workshop threatened a strike action against their employer because of low wages, poor working conditions, and inequality between workers (some getting paid per piece, others on a monthly basis). After two weeks of talks between the owner and officials of the local Textile Workers' Union (PWB), the problem was resolved satisfactorily without a strike.[110]

Another illustrative example of negotiations between a union and an employer occurred at the time of a visit to the Textile Workers' Union in Nablus. During an interview with the secretary-general of the union, two employers walked into the office to argue about a case involving two of their workers, members of the union, who had quit and were demanding severance pay covering fifty-two Fridays of piecework. One of the employers claimed that the workers were not really employed by him but by an Israeli, via a subcontract. "That is not true," the unionist responded. "You are the subcontractor, so that means that you are their employer." Typically, further discussion concerning the matter was postponed for two days, a tactic designed to give the employers time to think the matter over, with a measured threat of union action if they refused to comply with the demands.[111]

If, however, no bargain can be struck between a union and an employer in a labor dispute, the aggrieved worker or workers may take the employer to court. In the words of a Nablus unionist: "When there are problems between the workers and their boss, our union will try to settle the problem peacefully. If this does not work, we go to a lawyer."[112] Most unions have relations with one or more local lawyers, usually of the same political persuasion, who will litigate in a local civil court on behalf of the union's workers. This strategy may bear fruit but, as will be shown below, in many cases it does not, and when it does, the actual benefits are not necessarily clear.

Rarely do workers go to a lawyer directly. Legal fees are prohibitive. 'Adnan Natsheh, then head of the WUB, said during a panel discussion in 1986: "Many lawyers are commercially motivated. Many will not take a case if there is not a lot of money involved."[113] A Nablus unionist described the predicament of a worker seeking his rights as follows:

Workers come to the union to improve their conditions. They do not have money to hire a lawyer, so the union's lawyer will go to court on the worker's behalf. But in many cases the courts do not issue a decision, with no reasons given. There are not enough judges. They will tell you that they have a lot of cases. Then if you go to the labor inspector at the Israeli labor office, he tells you to go to the labor court in Tel Aviv. He says this for political reasons, and to show international organizations that there are labor problems in the West Bank. Palestinian workers refuse to go to an Israeli court [for local matters]. Some workers would rather lose their compensation than go to an Israeli court.

Sometimes a worker who has gone to a local court will win compensation—in [unstable Israeli] shekels. The owner will appeal the decision, and the case continues for a while. Eventually there is nothing left of the compensation. For example, a woman named Bahya worked in a local institution for fifteen years. She then decided to quit, but she was not given severance pay. According to Jordanian labor law, she is entitled to nine months' wages. Her case has been in court for two years now. The union failed to solve the problem because the owner flatly refused to give compensation.[114]

A Ramallah unionist described the following problems the union encounters when it takes an employer to one of the local civil courts:

According to Jordanian law, there should be a labor court in the West Bank, but so far none has been established. In the civil courts we run up against a number of difficulties. It takes a long time before a case is heard; this itself is against the law. In some cases it may take up to two years. In the second place, it is difficult to prove the rights of workers in court. A worker has no particular right until the court approves it. The law is weak and outdated. It has not kept up with social and economic changes. Most of the cases the union handles involve arbitrary dismissals and the employers' refusal to pay compensation. We win approximately 95 percent of the cases. The real problem is that so many workers won't come to the union or go to court, especially women for whom it traditionally has been a shame to appear in court. Even men sometimes feel that it is a shame. Once a union member who had been asked to testify on behalf of a friend of his refused to do so for that reason.[115]

Because of such problems, every effort is made to reach a settlement out of court. The employer has an interest in this as well, since it does not serve his position in the local community to be known as one who treats workers unfairly. A Hebron unionist gave an example dating from 1982 when workers at the 'Awni Khayyat shoemaking workshop threatened to walk out because of conditions in the shop. "When the workers quit and were not compensated, the union intervened through its lawyer, who managed to get JD 1,000 for each of the three workers out of it without going to court. The employer preferred not to go to court." And then, as if to justify the role of the union under occupation, he added: "The union does not play the game of the occupiers by closing down the workshop for them, because we do not want to lose three jobs. But if the owner is rich, we do not compromise on the rights of the worker."[116]

It is usually only individual workers who, through their unions, will take their employers to court. In many cases, the threat of legal action alone is sufficient to induce an employer to talk with the union and reach an equitable settlement. When labor problems erupt in a workplace between workers collectively, or significant groups of workers, and the boss, and mediation by trade unions or local notables has failed, workers, supported by their union or unions, may resort to strikes.

Strikes are not the preferred method of labor dispute settlement in the Occupied Territories. Unionists are generally reluctant to blame employers for low wages or the dismissal of workers. Before anything else, an accusing finger is pointed at the military occupation, which has stymied economic development, forcing employers to trim their enterprises to the bone in order successfully to withstand competition from Israeli firms marketing the same products. The class struggle was officially "frozen" by West Bank unions for explicitly nationalist motives at the beginning of the occupation. It is "unfrozen" only in exceptional cases where an employer is seen to be unnecessarily unfair and exploitative, especially if the employer has close links to the Jordanian regime—in other words, if he is not a nationalist.

Union-backed strikes against Palestinian employers are also rare because, in the words of a labor organizer in Jenin, "unions are still few and small, and [most] could not carry out a successful strike if they wanted to."[117] Employers are doubtless aware of the unions' weakness, and have taken advantage of it, often using bullying tactics. A unionist in Nablus said:

> Strikes against Palestinian employers are not common. They are difficult to organize. Especially in the general institutions where workers get paid very little there are problems. There too strikes are rare. . . . In 1985 a strike was threatened at Golden Sweets in Nablus when workers were getting together signatures for their demand to have working conditions improved. The owners fired the five organizers. The others were too scared to strike.[118]

In many cases, workers will start a strike spontaneously and then receive support from a local union. Usually, smaller actions like a one-hour work stoppage or a one-day strike will precede a full strike. The following are examples of some important strikes that took place in local institutions in the 1980s.

In 1981, the Hotel, Restaurant, and Cafe Workers' Union (PWB) in

Jerusalem initiated a strike at St. George's Hostel. The strikers' demands
included a wage increase, tying wages to the dollar (because of the rapid
devaluation of the Israeli currency), and the management's recognition of
the union as the workers' representative. Unionists claim that the Palestinian-Jordanian Joint Committee tried to interfere by paying the hostel's
owner enough money to last out the strike. But the workers had some
success. They received a small raise, and wages were indeed tied to the
dollar. The union, however, was not recognized.[119]

An important strike took place at the Jerusalem Electric Company
(JEC), with two thousand employees the single largest private employer
in the Occupied Territories, in 1979. The JEC, which has been threatened with extinction through Israeli government efforts to reduce its concession from all of Jerusalem to only the city's Arab neighborhoods, has
been under predominantly Jordanian tutelage through its chairman (in
1979), the pro-Jordanian mayor of Bethlehem, Elias Freij, and the funding channeled through the Palestinian-Jordanian Joint Committee. The
strike lasted sixteen days. According to Simon Taggert, the union's members considered that this "was the largest and most important strike since
1948 in that it won support from both sides of the Green Line."[120] A leader
of the Construction and General Institutions Workers' Union in Ramallah/
al-Bireh, whose members joined the pickets, said:

> This was an important strike for two reasons. First because the JEC is a
> crucial company for the services it provides; and secondly because of the
> attempt by the Joint Committee to break the strike through [company chair-
> man] Elias Freij. The Joint Committee tried to change the entire staff of the
> company. Freij was willing to sell the company to the Israelis. Today's prob-
> lems in the company stem from that period. The workers demanded that
> their wage, paid out in shekels, be tied to the dinar, and that the company not
> be sold to the Israelis. They won on both counts. The strike was a success
> because there was great solidarity among the people in the West Bank. Our
> union provided food and clothes for the striking workers.[121]

In June 1986, another strike occurred at the troubled company. Having
fended off several attempts by the Israeli Electric Company, its creditor,
to seize the JEC's assets, the JEC was forced to come to an agreement
with the IEC following a court ruling on 1 June. According to the agreement, all JEC expenditures would have to be approved by the IEC's lawyer. The JEC's workers' wages were not included in the agreement, and
the IEC refused to sanction payment of the JEC's workers' May wages.
The workers went on strike 1 June. A statement issued by the JEC Workers' Union read: "We are not the slaves of the Israeli company working for
no salaries. We demand not charity from them but rather our rights." At

the same time, the JEC union promised to stand by the company in its efforts to survive Israeli attempts at takeover, but condemned any form of bargaining between Jordan and Israel over the company's future. Workers were paid their May salaries on 5 June, and they ended their strike.[122] The union's victories during these years, while important in strengthening its own position, proved hollow as continuing Israeli efforts to squeeze out the company finally bore fruit. In December 1987, only days before the outbreak of the intifada, the JEC's concession was indeed reduced to Jerusalem's Arab neighborhoods, while the company continued to be heavily indebted to the IEC, which supplies the JEC with the bulk of its power.

In May 1985 a strike took place at the *Al-Quds* daily newspaper in East Jerusalem. This was an important strike because, according to an official of the local Printing Press Workers' Union (WUB), "there has been a general trend among employers to lower wages, and this was the first real response from workers." All sixty-two of the paper's workers struck for five days after the paper's owner decided to calculate workers' wages, calculated in dinars but paid in Israeli shekels, according to the official rather than the black-market rate of the dinar, as had been the custom. This meant a decline of one-third in the real wages received by the paper's workers. Forty-two of the workers were members of the Printing Press Workers' Union, which backed the strikers, supported by a number of local organizations and institutions. The owner of *Al-Quds* in the end bowed to pressure, as the workers managed to paralyze the paper's production. "In five days they had their demands satisfied," the unionist declared, "and no one lost his job because of the strike. There are no similar success stories preceding this strike. This goes to show how much stronger and more conscious workers have become. It shows the development of the union movement here. It was a victory for all workers. It was an example, and it set a precedent."[123]

Finally, a strike lasting a little over three months took place at Bir Zeit University in the summer of 1986. The university was facing financial difficulties and decided to fire all employees, only to rehire them at lower salaries. The university's branch of the Union of Employees of Private Institutions of Higher Education launched a strike in June, protesting the action and demanding contracts at full salaries, as well as an effort on the part of university officials to intensify and diversify fund-raising. Eventually a compromise was reached whereby the university signed contracts at full salaries starting in 1986, and the employees agreed to a temporary reduction in pay, donating 15 to 20 percent of their salaries in the academic year 1986–87 to the university. The employees' opinions are divided on whether this accomplishment was a success.[124]

Labor Action in the Israeli Workplace

Taking action against an employer is even more difficult for Palestinians from the West Bank and Gaza employed in Israel than it is for their colleagues who work in the Occupied Territories. Although Palestinian workers employed in Israel are in theory covered by collective contracts negotiated by the Israeli trade-union federation, the Histadrut, in reality they cannot pursue their demands because they cannot organize. Not only are they not members of the Histadrut; in most cases they are also effectively excluded from the Histadrut-controlled shop-floor workers' committees. If they try to organize informally, among themselves, they must do so surreptitiously because they have no effective recourse even when an employer fires them summarily, while the Israeli secret police, the Shin Bet, keeps an eye on potential "troublemakers."

The problem is compounded because the Israeli authorities, who have made life difficult for unions in the Occupied Territories, maintain that workers from the Occupied Territories who are employed in Israel are protected by the Histadrut. Said one Palestinian union activist: "Every Israeli company has a security person who keeps a file on every Palestinian worker. If there is trouble, the worker can easily be fired."[125] In a later interview he added:

> It is generally known that Israeli bosses try to prevent Palestinian workers from organizing on the shop floor or in unions at home. There are many kinds of punishment, like refusing to pay health insurance or to give annual benefits at anniversaries. Those who play the boss's game receive higher benefits. Actual punishment is only carried out by the Israeli authorities: they detain activists for interrogation and beat them.[126]

Another unionist enumerated the following problems West Bank unions face in protecting workers employed in Israel:

> We advise these workers about their rights and we provide them with medical insurance, but we cannot talk with the owners. Also a [Palestinian] lawyer cannot help. There are now ideas of putting together a group of Israeli lawyers to intervene on the Palestinian workers' behalf, because there are a lot of cases. You see, you cannot bring an Israeli employer to court in Nablus: we are under Jordanian law here. Theoretically a worker with a permit who has been fired by his Israeli employer can go to the Histadrut for recourse, but it is known that the Histadrut does not help Arab workers.[127]

Organizing workers employed across the Green Line in Israel and providing the necessary backup for labor strikes have proven almost insurmountable tasks for West Bank unions. In the words of one unionist:

In the first place, many strikes fail because Palestinian and Israeli workers work next to each other, and the latter do not want to strike with the Arabs. And Palestinians do not join strikes organized by Jews. Secondly, the Palestinian workers in one workplace come from different areas in the Occupied Territories, so there is no geographic unity, which makes organizing them very difficult. In addition, workers are committed to different unions and blocs. Even within one bloc there is little communication between, say, Jenin and Ramallah. Finally, there is no unity in the demands of Jewish and Arab workers. Our union has not tried to encourage these workers to be active because they are too hard to organize.[128]

Another unionist cited high unemployment as a main obstacle in organizing workers employed in Israel. "In addition," he said, "the black labor market undercuts the possibility of strikes. Jamil al-'Amla of the [collaborationist] Hebron Village Leagues buses hundreds of workers to Israel daily, and handles the wages for the Israeli contractors. His control over the workers also makes strikes difficult."[129]

WUB-affiliated unions have made it a priority to support and organize workers employed across the Green Line. WUB officials claim that they have directed union members to set up Palestinians-only workers' committees in Israeli workplaces, and to negotiate with employers through these committees. WUB leader 'Ali Abu Hilal claimed in 1985, a few months before he was deported to Jordan by the Israeli military authorities, that his bloc had established "many such committees in Israel." He gave as examples a committee at the Berman bakery in West Jerusalem, a committee at a poultry factory in West Jerusalem that in 1984 succeeded in negotiating higher wages and fixed work hours, and a committee at the Shalom Hotel in West Jerusalem. This last committee was formed after the hotel management had fired a number of Palestinian workers in 1980. The committee demanded that these workers be reinstated. Although this demand was not satisfied, the dismissed workers were given severance pay. "We considered this a victory of sorts."[130]

Both the WUB and the PWB have at times pursued legal means in their attempt to protect West Bank workers employed in Israel. As with labor disputes in the West Bank, seeking legal recourse against Israeli employers is complicated and costly. In addition, the role of unions is less direct. According to a WUB unionist from Ya'bad in the Jenin area: "The WUB has worked on many cases via its lawyer through the Jenin court. Here in the West Bank we can go to court. For cases in Israel the union acts as a go-between for workers with a [Israeli] lawyer," since West Bank lawyers are not permitted to practice in Israeli courts.[131]

One of the most salient problems for Palestinians seeking redress for violations suffered in the Israeli workplace is the scarcity of lawyers trained in labor law. In cases involving Palestinians from the Occupied Territories, the fact that the complainants are not citizens of Israel complicates matters, as it is not always clear which laws apply. Few lawyers are willing and able to take up such tangled issues as the right of an undocumented worker from Nablus to receive workers' compensation from an Israeli construction company, like the Histadrut's subsidiary Solel Boneh, that employed him in the settlement of Ariel in the West Bank, building the houses of Jewish settlers whose very presence in the Occupied Territories, according to international law, is illegal. In all of Israel there may be only fifteen lawyers (including Palestinian Israelis) who are schooled in labor law, and even they are often at odds on specific legal issues concerning workers from the Occupied Territories.[132] One of the Israeli lawyers, Amos Givon, speaking at a panel in Jerusalem in 1986, listed several problems, paraphrased as follows:

> Some West Bankers go via the labor exchanges, some do not. Regardless, there are no written laws for workers from the Occupied Territories. And even when there are, they are not enforced. There is a tendency not to write anything down. . . . In the labor court, where several cases are now pending, there is a hesitancy to set precedents. The economic consequences would be disastrous for Israel, and the court is therefore cooperating with the state, or at least being very careful not to work against it.[133]

In addition, he said, "the choice of judges in the labor courts is manipulated in case of complaints from workers from the Occupied Territories." However, Givon remarked, the court faces a possible dilemma created by the law: "The court cannot decide against a [Palestinian] worker from Deheisheh [refugee camp] because it would then also have to decide against a [Jewish] worker from [the Jewish settlement of] Kiryat Arba. The court cannot differentiate between Arabs and Jews because it cannot afford to be openly racist." Givon therefore saw a real opportunity for workers and unions in setting a precedent: "It is like a domino effect." Unions should start on this issue very hard: they could start the domino."[134]

If Palestinian workers feel they have not received a fair hearing in a labor court, they can appeal to the Israeli High Court of Justice, which sits in West Jerusalem. There are advantages to such a course of action, according to Givon: "Most labor dispute cases go to the labor courts, but the High Court is much more courageous in its decisions and has more prestige. In the labor courts political considerations prevail, but in the High Court you could ask, for example: 'Why is it that the labor exchanges do not use any written forms?' As a lawyer I would suggest pursuing such a course of action."[135] Some of these proposed methods of legal action remain highly problematic for the vast majority of Palestinian workers. Trade unionist 'Adnan al-Natsheh, who succeeded 'Ali Abu Hilal as leader of the WUB after the latter was deported to Jordan by the army, explained:

West Bank lawyers cannot go to the High Court, and many Palestinian workers do not believe that they can find an Israeli lawyer who will go against an Israeli court. Then, many cannot afford to sue, because such lawyers are very expensive. This is true for the unions as well, so lawsuits are rare, but the unions are swamped with cases since all the workers have problems. The decision to sue the state is taken by the union, not by the lawyer, but the only way to do it is via a lawyer.[136]

The military authorities have also tried to thwart lawsuits brought by unions against Israeli employers on behalf of union members, presumably to undercut unions' credibility among West Bank workers. One union organizer recounted: "One of our lawyers is Walid Fahoum [a Palestinian Israeli]. In 1983 Fahoum worked on one of our cases. After the case he was summoned to the military headquarters in Bet El [in the West Bank], intimidated, and told not to take any more cases for West Bank unions."[137]

Nevertheless, successful cases of legal action involving Palestinian workers from the Occupied Territories and Israeli employers exist. For example, in 1983 the Peres Pingad construction company in Jerusalem

suddenly changed the way in which they paid workers their wages. It used to come through the post office, which gave you evidence of receipt. But now they began paying their workers directly, thereby changing the contracts from annual to daily. Our union sent a memo to the [Israeli] labor inspector in the West Bank through [GFTU secretary-general] Adel Ghanem, and the GFTU also put an ad in the paper and hired [an Israeli] lawyer, Felicia Langer. The owners felt threatened by this, because they feared a scandal. So they reverted to the old method of payment, and also raised the workers' wages. No court case was necessary.[138]

In another successful example of labor litigation, a Palestinian worker from Ramallah employed in the Israeli settlement of Bet El sued his employer, the Peres Mohandissim construction company, who had laid him off without compensation in 1986. The worker's union, the Construction and General Institutions Workers' Union (PWB) in Ramallah/al-Bireh, hired a lawyer, Jawad Boulos (a Palestinian Israeli). This was all that was needed. Before the matter could be brought to court, a settlement was reached, and the worker received compensation.[139]

Although strike action by Palestinians in Israel is far from frequent, workers resort to strikes much more readily today than in the past. Several factors account for this: the length of the occupation and the growing familiarity of Palestinians with Israeli society; the obvious injustices that prevail in the Israeli workplace and the Palestinians' heightened awareness, thanks to educational efforts by West Bank trade unions, of what exactly their rights are under the law; a rising interest among progressive groups and parties in Israel like the Israeli Communist Party, which has made public its position on the rights of Palestinian workers and has encouraged lawyers in its circle to take on cases; and last but not least the growing strength of the unions in the West Bank and their interest in organizing itinerant day laborers, which means providing them with tangible benefits.

When strikes are organized, they tend to be short. This must be attributed to Israeli repression (the dismissal or arrest of strike leaders) and workers' lack of legal protection, as well as to West Bank unions' inability to sustain a longer strike for lack of a strike fund.[140] One-day strikes marking a particular commemorative event such as Land Day or Partition Day are common. The Construction and General Institutions Workers' Union (WUB) in Abu Dis, for example, organized a strike for all workers employed on building sites in the nearby Jewish settlement of Ma'ale Adumim on Land Day in 1984.[141] The Israeli invasions of Lebanon in 1978 and 1982 also sparked workers' strikes, called by the Palestinian national leadership and by local institutions.[142] During the intifada there have been repeated absences of workers from their jobs across the Green Line.

The following are examples of strikes carried out by Palestinian workers, sometimes aided by West Bank unions, in Israel. They highlight the particular roles played by the Israeli secret police, the Histadrut, and Palestinian trade unions, respectively.

In 1981, a Palestinian worker attempted to organize his Arab colleagues at the Berman Bakery in West Jerusalem. He managed to set up a workers' committee but was arrested after the owner called the police. He was dismissed after his release, although he had worked at the bakery for ten years.[143]

In 1983, Palestinian workers at the Mahadrin citrus-packing company in Netanya struck for a day on advice of their West Bank union to demand payment of their wages on the first rather than on the fifteenth of the month to avoid erosion of their wages as a result of hyperinflation. The Histadrut tried to intervene, but the Palestinian workers refused to deal with it. The strike succeeded. A worker from Ya'bad in the Jenin area was fired from the same factory on a separate occasion when he refused to recognize the Histadrut-installed workers' committee and tried to represent the West Bank workers directly.[144]

In September 1984, some of the Palestinian workers employed at the Holy Land West Hotel in West Jerusalem went to the Hotel, Restaurant, and Cafe Workers' Union (WUB-WYM) in East Jerusalem, saying that they planned to strike to demand better food and a better work schedule. The union encouraged them and explained that they could legally strike for eight hours according to Israeli law. The workers began the strike, and after four hours the manager reportedly conceded to the demands.[145]

In September 1985, an Israeli security guard employed at the Diplomat Hotel in West Jerusalem reportedly cursed Palestinian employees following a Palestinian resistance attack on Israeli settlers that had taken place in Hebron the day before. The workers got angry, a shuffle ensued, and in the melee the guard was injured. The quarrel then erupted into a major fight, and four Palestinian workers were fired. Their colleagues at the hotel spontaneously declared a solidarity strike. The management, aided by the Histadrut, responded by declaring the strike illegal. In the end, the fired workers failed in their attempt to be reinstated, but their striking colleagues, as a compromise of sorts, were retained despite a clear threat that they too would be dismissed.[146]

In early 1986, West Bank workers doing overtime at the Berman Bakery in West Jerusalem struck once they discovered that the management had been systematically underpaying them. A researcher at Hebrew University who studied the workers' pay slips concluded the following:

> In October 1985, Yussuf, who lives in a refugee camp a short distance from Jerusalem's Gilo neighborhood [sic; Gilo is a Jewish settlement on Palestinian land annexed by Israel in 1967] and works night shifts at one of the city's big bakeries [the Berman Bakery], earned a net monthly salary of NIS 136.6 (just over $90). His pay slip, prepared by the State Employment Service, shows that on the first eight hours of each shift, Yussuf grossed just above the legal minimum for industrial workers. But he was paid 20 per cent below the minimum for overtime hours! Had Yussuf earned what was due to him under the legally binding collective agreement for the bakery industry, the cost to his employer would have risen at least threefold.[147]

Finally, Palestinian workers employed in a factory in Bnei Brak threatened to go on strike after their manager, who was highly unpopular, refused to recognize their spokesperson as their representative. Following the threat, the manager fired those he suspected of being behind the action. One of the dismissed workers, who had had a work permit for a year, went to the Histadrut to get assistance in claiming severance pay. The Histadrut told him he would need a lawyer, but advised him not to pursue the matter since the lawyer's fee would far exceed the compensation he might hope to receive.[148]

ISRAEL'S REPRESSION
OF THE PALESTINIAN LABOR MOVEMENT

In their attempt to implement the Israeli project of annexation of the Occupied Territories, the military authorities had to stamp out any form of resistance to Israeli rule. The attack focused on the leadership and structure of Palestinian society because they contained the nucleus for nationalist resistance and provided a possible stepping-stone to a Palestinian state. Repression widened in the 1980s to include the cadres of the growing popular movement, as well as the movement's organizations, especially the trade unions. It is likely that trade unions were singled out, along with student committees, because of their nationalist outlook and potential mass base.

There is no simple way to classify military repression of the labor movement, or to explain why some unions or blocs were targeted rather than others, or to explain the timing of particular repressive measures. Repression has appeared at times arbitrary, perhaps reflecting the personal approach of local Shin Bet agents, who, for example, through their control over files, had unusual prerogatives in determining which activists should be deported or placed in administrative detention or otherwise be restricted. Chronologically, it seems sensible to suggest that during the early years of popular organizing, the military focused on stifling a nascent movement by delegitimizing activists, denying registration to new unions, and deterring actual and potential members through harassment and intimidation. In later years, as the labor movement reached a certain size and level of maturity despite, and in part because of, military repression, the army resorted to more visible tactics aimed at debilitating a thriving movement by closing unions and jailing or deporting those who were seen as the main organizers.

Interference in Unions' Formal Structures

The presence of the military in the Occupied Territories is pervasive, affecting all facets of daily life. One of the chief mechanisms of control employed by the military is the permit system. The population is required to obtain permits for just about any social, economic, or cultural activity, and such permits are routinely refused if the applicant has a record of political activity. When, therefore, activists set out to revive the labor movement in the late 1970s through a mass recruitment campaign especially aimed at itinerant day laborers, they were confronted almost immediately by a refusal on the part of the military authorities to register new trade unions. In the 1970s, only five unions received registration in addition to the twenty-six that existed (at least in name) in the West Bank in 1967. Since 1979, however, no new unions have been licensed, according to the ILO, which quotes West Bank unionists.[149] This has not deterred union organizers. At least eighty unlicensed unions have come into existence in the West Bank in the 1980s. In 1986 alone, some thirty-one applications for registration were submitted to the military authorities; according to the ILO, none was accepted.[150]

Although unions can carry out their work even without a license, specific problems may arise related to their formal standing. The issue of licensing has been used in interbloc fighting as a way of keeping hostile unions out of the GFTU. It has enabled the military authorities to claim that West Bank unions are not real trade unions at all but fronts for the PLO. It has also made it difficult for unions to represent their members in negotiations with employers or in court.[151]

One important union that has been affected by the authorities' refusal to recognize new trade unions is the General Committee of Government School Teachers (GCGST) in the West Bank, a trade union set up in 1981 by Palestinian teachers employed by the Israeli government in public schools in the West Bank. That year the union carried out a strike lasting a hundred days to give force to its demand for higher wages in the face of wage erosion as a result of the continuing and rapid devaluation of the Israeli shekel. The strike resulted in minor improvements; the military authorities have tried to get rid of the unlicensed union ever since. According to a report in the local press, "the Israeli officer in charge of education has bent over backward to break the GCGSTWB. Virtually all known leaders have been transferred to new schools long distances from their homes, fired, or forced into early retirement."[152] One of the union's founding members commented on the military authorities' attempt to break the union: "We have requested increases in our salaries in every possible way. All our written requests are ignored, and when we ask to establish any kind of collective representative body, we are not allowed."[153]

In East Jerusalem, which was annexed by Israel in 1967 but is considered part of the West Bank by Palestinians, the authorities tried to block the development of Palestinian unions. Those who wanted union protection were told to join the Histadrut. The Israeli Federation maintains an office in East Jerusalem, and workers employed in municipal services have had no choice other than to become Histadrut members. But the Histadrut's poor record with regard to the protection of the rights of Palestinian workers prompted many workers to turn to the few Palestinian unions that emerged despite official warnings and repression. In the words of one unionist:

> The authorities tried to stop the unions' development [in the early 1970s].
> There was no official policy, but unofficially a lot was done to suppress them.
> The authorities invited all union leaders to a place in West Jerusalem and told
> them that they had the choice to either join the Histadrut or go to prison. The
> unions who disagreed with them were closed down. They would be accused
> of being linked to the PLO, of being covers for the PLO.[154]

Today, East Jerusalem counts a number of active unions, including the Hotel, Restaurant, and Cafe Workers' Union, the Printing Press Workers' Union, the Drivers' Union, the Maqassed Hospital Workers' Union, and the Jerusalem Electric Company Workers' Union.

The military authorities have also acted through their agents in the Pal-

estinian community to contain the growing union movement. Some
unions report having been denied hook-ups to basic services like electricity in those municipalities that have a mayor who is a collaborator. The
head of the regional WUB office in Jenin, for example, claimed that Jenin
mayor Lahlouh refused to provide the office with water and electricity as
long as the unionists did not have a license. But, said the union organizer,
"we had requested a permit from the Israeli labor office a long time ago,
and we never received an answer."[155]

The most significant intervention made by the military in the trade
unions' formal structure occurred in 1980. That year, the authorities issued Military Order 825, which amends article 83 of the Jordanian labor
law of 1960. Article 83 concerns elections to the executive committee of a
trade union and reads:

> (a) No persons other than workers or those employed full-time by a trade
> union can be elected to its executive committee.
> (b) No person convicted of a felony punishable by more than three years'
> imprisonment or of offenses involving public disgrace can be a member of the
> executive committee of the union.[156]

Military Order 825 changed article 83(b) as follows:

> (b) In addition to clause (a), none of the persons mentioned below shall be
> allowed to be members in the Union's Administrative Committee:
>   i. any person convicted in a competent court in the Area or in Israel of
> committing a crime punishable by five years or more;
>   ii. any person convicted in a competent court in the Area or in Israel of
> committing a crime against honor.

Military Order 825 also added clauses to the original law, including:

> (c) The Union shall present to the responsible person at least thirty days
> before the election a list of candidates for membership in the Administrative
> Committee. The responsible person may strike out from the said list the
> name of any candidate proved to the responsible person's satisfaction not to
> fulfill the rules of clauses (a)–(b) above.[157]

By changing "felony" into "crime," and therefore leaving room to include
political offenses that were not included in the Jordanian law, the military
authorities tried to reduce sharply the number of those who could run for
election to a union's administrative committee. Many Palestinians have
served prison terms for political ("security") offenses, and the existing military legislation allows for severe penalties. For example, Military Order
101 (1967), the "Order Regarding Prohibition of Acts of Incitement and
Hostile Propaganda," which covers offenses such as, for example, possession and distribution of illegal materials, raising the Palestinian flag, and

membership in an illegal organization, allows for a maximum penalty of ten years in prison.[158] Military Order 378 (1970), the "Order Concerning Security Regulations," which covers more serious offenses such as possession of firearms and attacks on members of the Israeli armed forces, allows for a maximum penalty of life imprisonment (and, theoretically, the death penalty).[159] By thus changing the existing law and taking power to eliminate undesirable candidates for administrative posts, the authorities tried to take control of union elections. By 1980, however, West Bank unions had already grown so strong that they were able to ignore the order, and they have held elections since then without notifying the army or submitting lists of candidates to the military's scrutiny.

Harassment and Intimidation

Even without an official permit and without water and electricity, and in spite of military orders designed to restrict union elections, a trade union can function relatively normally as a trade union. There are many ways in which such restrictions can be circumvented. But one essential ingredient unions cannot do without is a steady membership of workers. One of the tactics of the military authorities against the unions has therefore been to deter actual and potential union membership through a policy of harassment and intimidation. One common practice involves harassing, and sometimes beating, workers inside a union office or at the outside door as they enter. On 28 October 1985, for example, soldiers were posted outside the entrance of the Construction and General Institutions Workers' Union (PWB) in Ramallah/al-Bireh, allowing no one to enter the building without first being photographed.[160] Once a person's photo is on file, he or she can be summoned to military headquarters and questioned by a Shin Bet officer. Several unions report that members have been questioned about their activities in the union. In addition, regular break-ins by soldiers of union offices have a potentially deterrent effect, especially when those present in the office are detained, usually for a period of from a few hours to a couple of days, and threatened with worse trouble if they are seen near the union office again. The cumulative effect of such measures is that they create fear. For many workers it is simply not worth the trouble.

The military does not need a search warrant to enter union premises. Typically, soldiers enter a union office, line up those inside, arrest a number of them, confiscate union materials, and later bring the main union organizers to trial for "possession of prohibited publications." Such publications have included union calendars, pamphlets from international trade union federations, and the union's own bylaws. According to Military Order 101 (1967), no publications can be brought in, sold, printed, or kept in someone's possession in the West Bank unless a permit has been obtained for them. Since it is impossible for purely practical reasons to obtain a permit for every single book, magazine, pamphlet, or other piece of printed material that is brought into or printed in the West Bank, few Palestinians have permits for the publications in their possession. It is equally impossible for the military authorities to enforce Military Order 101. The problem, however, is one of selective enforcement. There is no easier pretext for bringing a unionist to trial than his or her possession of illegal publications confiscated during a raid. In fact, the conviction justifies the raid, which itself served to deter the union from being too active.

To give just one example, the military authorities informed a Qalqiliya unionist, Feisal Hindi, on 10 July 1987 that he would be charged for having published materials without a permit. The materials included information on labor laws, the workers' right to certain benefits, and other information, mostly provided by the Histadrut and the Israeli government. Hindi's crime, it appears, was not so much publishing materials that are at any rate freely available in Israel, but being a unionist.[161]

Again fairly typically, the army raided the regional WUB office in Jenin in December 1984 and April 1985, and confiscated everything. The second time, seventeen workers were detained for a few hours and questioned about their activities. The bloc's regional leader at that time, Walid Nazzal from Qabatiya, was initially placed under town arrest, and later deported to Jordan. His successor said: "The Israelis used the files they confiscated during the break-in to call in union members individually and to intimidate them. The father of one of our members drives a taxi to the bridge [at the border with Jordan]. The authorities revoked his permit and asked him questions about his son."[162] The army raided the same office a third time on 12 February 1987. According to the Palestinian human rights organization Al-Haq, "soldiers and police carrying out the raid assaulted one union official, threatened union leaders with detention, destroyed several displays in the office, and confiscated office supplies, publications, and documents, including the union's membership lists and pamphlets prepared by Al-Haq on workers' rights."[163]

Detentions and Restrictions on Movement

Increasingly in the 1980s, the army began targeting individual union activists. The most common method of intimidation has been direct and indirect threats. Many unionists report having been summoned to military headquarters where they were interrogated about their activities and told not to continue with their union work. Short-term detentions without charge are frequent. A Ramallah unionist reported that three members of the executive committee of the local Construction and General Institutions Workers' Union (PWB) had been called in by the military authorities for questioning on separate occasions during the spring of 1986. A fourth member was detained for eighteen days (the maximum amount of time a person can be detained without having to be brought before a military judge), and then released.[164] One union organizer said that he had been detained eleven times over a period of several years, each time for eighteen days. He was never charged or tried.[165] Another unionist spent two years in administrative detention in the late 1970s, again without charge or trial.[166]

The purpose of these arrests may be to disrupt temporarily particular actions by unionists, or to prevent union action on Palestinian commemorative days like Land Day. On 19 April 1987 the army broke up a meeting of the WUB's central bureau at the Textile Workers' Union in Ramallah. They jailed eight of the ten union leaders present, releasing them after ten days without charges. That month, several other members of the WUB's central bureau were either in administrative detention or under town arrest, and the WUB was therefore effectively without its leadership for ten days.[167]

At other times, unionists have been convicted of "membership in an illegal organization." Research of 1983 military court records shows that Palestinians accused of membership in an "illegal organization" received stiffer sentences if it turned out that they were also active in the labor movement.[168]

Individual leaders have been barred from entering union offices or from engaging in unionist activity for certain periods. This again shows that the military is less concerned with illegalities (for which they could charge a person) than with union organizing itself. In November 1987, fifteen unionists of the Construction and General Institutions Workers' Union (WUB) in the village of Deir al-Ghussoun in the West Bank were forced by the military authorities to sign statements agreeing not to engage in unionist activity for a period of six months. The union office was closed for the same period. The unionists later claimed that the army informed them verbally that they were not permitted to educate workers about their rights, find lawyers for workers in case of labor disputes, or solicit blood for workers injured at work, as they had been doing. They were also told that they would face administrative punishments such as deportation and administrative detention if they violated the ban. The apparent pretext for the army's action was a poster in the union office protesting a recent house demolition in the village and denouncing the "Zionist occupation."[169]

To prevent West Bank unionists from establishing international contacts and speaking out against Israeli abuses at public forums outside the country, the army has on many occasions forbidden organizers to travel. For example, in 1986 'Adnan Dagher, the secretary-general of the Construction and General Institutions Workers' Union (PWB) in Ramallah/al-Bireh, was unable to obtain a laissez-passer, a travel document that would have allowed him to leave the country via Ben-Gurion Airport. In the past he had also been turned back by the Israeli authorities at the border crossing with Jordan, so with both his options closed, he was effectively barred from travel.[170] Many unionists report similar problems; Shaher Sa'ad, the secretary-general of the GFTU-WYM (from 1987 on), was not given permission to leave the country to attend a labor conference in Great Britain in November 1987 to which he had been invited by a British trade union.[171]

Finally, the army has frequently imposed temporary closure orders on meeting halls to prevent union gatherings. On 4 July 1985, for example, the police in East Jerusalem closed down Al-Hakawati Theater for twenty-four hours to prevent the annual WUB conference, which was scheduled to take place on 5 July. A sit-in staged by unionists and supporters outside the theater on 5 July was broken up by Israeli paramilitary border guards. Three Palestinians were reportedly beaten and arrested.[172] On 1 May 1987, the authorities closed down Cinema Al-Hamra in East Jerusalem for twelve hours to prevent WUB members from celebrating May Day. The High Court overturned the order later that day, but by then most union members had already gone home.[173] The next day, the authorities closed Al-Hakawati a second time for twelve hours to prevent the PUAF's celebration of May Day.[174]

The cumulative effects of such repressive actions have been minimal so far as union organizers are concerned. Activists appear to have been hardened, not weakened, by repression. The effect on unions' membership is not clear. Palestinian trade unions in the West Bank experienced enormous growth in the 1980s, but it is likely that they would have grown even faster in the absence of military repression.

THE LABOR MOVEMENT BEFORE THE UPRISING

In the years following the split in 1981, West Bank trade unions stepped up unionist work and escalated recruitment efforts, despite attempts by the military authorities to stifle the movement. There was an unmistakable growth in union membership in the 1980s. This was due in part to the tapping of new sectors of the labor force, sectors that had previously been taboo to organizers, such as workers employed in Israel. In part it is due to the explicit nationalist ideology of the new union leadership, which attracted young working Palestinians who found in trade unions vehicles for expressing and discussing their experiences of discrimination in the Israeli workplace and oppression under military occupation. Unions cemented their growing support among the working population by providing tangible services to their members.

Reliable figures on union membership in the 1980s are not available. Although most trade unions do keep files, union leaders are reluctant to show them to outsiders; in the past, confiscation of union files by the military has led to harassment of union members. Furthermore, many labor organizers prefer to keep things as informal as possible, and therefore do not maintain formal membership lists. Especially since the intifada, a number of unions appear to have stopped keeping union records.[175] Even the files themselves cannot necessarily be trusted, nor can the membership figures quoted by union leaders. The issue of size of membership became highly politicized in the 1980s because of the struggle between the various union blocs for hegemony in the West Bank labor movement. The stated size of a union's membership will determine both the amount of financial support that can be obtained from funders, like the Joint Committee, and the size of the union's representation in the GFTU. The 1981 split in the labor movement, as well as the split in 1985 (discussed below), occurred against the backdrop of irreconcilable differences of opinion about the size and legitimacy of certain unions. It has often happened that a union's secretary-general quotes a certain membership figure for his or her union, which is then promptly discounted by a unionist from a rival bloc across town who holds that the union in question has in fact no constituency at all.

From the wildly varying figures provided by the leaders of the three largest union blocs in the West Bank it is clear that at least two of the blocs have artificially inflated their own membership counts, assuming for a moment that no bloc would deliberately understate its own size. Adel Ghanem, secretary-general of the GFTU-PWB, estimated in December 1985 that between 17,000 and 18,000 West Bankers were unionized at that time, about 12 percent of the West Bank labor force of 150,000.[176] Shehadeh al-Minawi, secretary-general of the rival GFTU-WYM, claimed that his GFTU-affiliated unions had a total membership of 35,000, or 24 percent of the labor force.[177] Finally, 'Adnan al-Natsheh, the leader of the WUB, declared in a public forum in April 1986 that 35 to 40 percent of West Bank workers were organized in unions.[178]

What is immediately clear is that the three men made their calculations according to different criteria. Ghanem, for example, does not recognize the GFTU-Minawi, nor WUB unions that have been refused admission to the GFTU-Ghanem, and his figure therefore reflects membership in the unions that are formally affiliated with the GFTU-Ghanem only. The Ghanem unions have generally kept files. Al-Natsheh, by contrast, does not accept formal affiliation as a criterion for legitimacy, and therefore includes more unions in his count, excluding only "cardboard" unions that have a phantom membership. The WUB has been the most informal of the three blocs in its recruitment strategy, so al-Natsheh's figure is particularly difficult to verify. Al-Minawi's estimate is clearly the least trustworthy of the three; many of the unions affiliated with his GFTU are "cardboard" unions. His calculation may be based on the amount of support the GFTU-WYM is able to drum up from pro-Fatah forces in the West Bank on occasions like May Day celebrations.

None of these three figures can be accepted as reliable. Ghanem's PWB is the most worker-oriented of the three main blocs, but it adheres to a very narrow definition of a worker. In the PWB's view, itinerant day laborers are not really members of the proletariat but a sort of hybrid lumpen element that one day may make the crossover from peasantry to proletariat. In addition, in order to ward off the WUB insurgency and WYM powermongering in the GFTU, the PWB cannot afford to count WUB and WYM adherents as legitimate workers. The WYM, on the other hand, will refer to any worker who supports Fatah as a WYM member, and in fact a number of these workers may have formally joined WYM unions. But these unions have few activities and offer few services. It is rather more likely that their members' adherence to the bloc stems from considerations of political loyalty and patronage alone; the bloc has been particularly well-endowed financially. The WUB, finally, clearly has a large following, especially among day laborers in villages who work in Israel. But exact figures are almost impossible to ascertain, and the WUB too has an interest in overstating its own size.

It seems fair to say that some 20 percent of the West Bank labor force is organized in trade unions. These are workers who have paid membership dues in any of the trade unions that have been set up, whether or not they are affiliated to any of the GFTUs. Not all of these workers will participate in union activities, but they will probably take advantage of a union's health plan. This is the narrow count, indicating union membership rather than general support for the labor movement. On national occasions, or on May Day when unions hold large celebrations, nonmembers are likely to turn up to join in events. Their participation is likely to be based on identification with the political faction the labor bloc represents in the national movement. They may not even be workers, and they may also show up for events sponsored by, for example, the parallel women's organization. The line between unionism and nationalism is a fine one, if it exists at all. This is precisely what explains the success, such as it is, of the labor movement in the West Bank in the 1980s.

The Second Split in the Labor Movement

The rapid growth and increasing assertiveness of the WUB caused severe strains in the GFTU-Ghanem after 1981, leading to a virtual paralysis in the federation's activities, including elections. The GFTU continued to exist on a formal level, but in practice it was no longer capable of leading the Palestinian working class. This role devolved to the four constituent union blocs (PWB, WUB, PUAF, and WVB) separately, highlighting the level of politicization of union organizing in the 1980s. Each bloc from 1981 on went its own way, recruiting new members and organizing its own activities. Several attempts were made to reactivate the GFTU-Ghanem, or even to reunite the two GFTUs, but the political differences and ensuing bitterness were so severe that all these efforts came to naught. Worse, they produced a second split in the labor movement in 1985, which formalized what basically had become a reality in the four years after the 1981 split. What is crucial is therefore the timing of the split, only one month after the Israeli military authorities launched their Iron Fist policy in the Occupied Territories.

On 3 June 1985, the WUB issued an appeal to reactivate the GFTU. This was not the first such appeal issued by one of the blocs, but this time it set the stage for important events that followed three months later. The WUB noted in its appeal that the various organs of the GFTU, such as the federation council and the executive committee, had not been meeting routinely, as required by GFTU bylaws. The WUB referred to the worsening economic situation in the West Bank as justification for convening an emergency meeting of the GFTU's executive committee to discuss the federation's reactivation. The WUB made a number of suggestions that it said would ensure the success of the meeting, most importantly (to the WUB) the need to admit parallel unions to the GFTU on the principle of proportional representation.

The PWB favored the reactivation of the GFTU, but not on the WUB's conditions, which did not serve the PWB's interests. By 1985, the WUB was much larger than it had been in 1981; to admit WUB unions into the GFTU-Ghanem would for the PWB be tantamount to surrendering its control over the federation. On 11 July, the PWB organized a meeting, attended only by representatives of its own bloc, the small PUAF, and the diminutive WVB. They reached agreement that the GFTU-Ghanem should be reactivated, but without the WUB, turning the quadrupartite into a tripartite federation.

Coincidentally, Israeli Defense Minister Yitzhak Rabin launched his Iron Fist policy at the beginning of August, reviving and intensifying such administrative punishments as deportation and administrative detention. The military authorities targeted the popular movement in the Occupied Territories in particular, and focused on hard-core activists, especially from the DFLP and the PFLP, as well as a number of Fatah supporters. Among trade unionists, the WUB was hardest hit—fairly reflecting its militant role in the workers' struggle in the 1980s. Within a month, eight WUB leaders were in administrative detention, including four members of the bloc's central bureau, and one, Walid Nazzal from Qabatiya, who was also a member of the central bureau, was in jail pending his deportation. In addition, the news agency Al-Manar and the weekly newspaper *Al-Darb*, both of which closely identified with the WUB's political line, were shut down by the military. By the end of October a total of thirteen top WUB leaders were in administrative detention, including eight members of its central bureau (and including the WUB's second-in-command Muhammad al-Labadi), Nazzal had been expelled to Jordan, and WUB leader 'Ali Abu Hilal was in prison appealing a deportation order.[179] Thus with ten of its members out of commission, the WUB's seventeen-member central bureau had effectively been decapitated after three months of Rabin's Iron Fist.

On 6 September 1985, the GFTU-Ghanem met in session and reactivated itself by appointing a new executive committee. Contrary to the agreement reached with the PUAF and WVB on 11 July, only representatives of the PWB were present. Thus, rather than reactivating the GFTU-Ghanem, the PWB in effect established its own exclusive GFTU (the GFTU-PWB), using technical arguments to exclude its three partners from the alliance. The Israeli military authorities, as always uncannily adroit at exploiting divisions in Palestinian society, promptly lifted restrictions on the PWB's second-in-command, George Hazboun, who had been under town arrest in Bethlehem for several years.

The WUB, PUAF, and WVB, which were outraged by the PWB's preemptive move, protested instantaneously and unanimously. Just one day after the PWB announcement of its action, the PUAF published a lengthy statement in the daily *Al-Mithaq* denouncing the appointment of a new executive committee in the GFTU-Ghanem. Blaming the split in 1981 on Shehadeh al-Minawi's WYM, the PUAF accused the PWB of creating a far more dangerous split by turning "the legitimate GFTU into a working office of the PWB."[180] On 6 October, the WUB, PUAF, and WVB issued a joint declaration, urging the PWB to reverse its action, which they considered "a deadly blow to the national unity in the GFTU and a violation of its rules and structure."[181]

In an interview three months later, Ghanem defended the PWB's move as follows:

> Each bloc wants its own men in. So they set up new unions of their own. Why don't they support the existing ones? You cannot have parallel unions. The union movement must be for the workers. To the workers, the unions are their bread. If the unions were to collaborate with Israel, the workers would fight the unions. . . . In our GFTU we have four blocs. The other three said that we ought to divide the federation equally: that we should each receive one-fourth; that the federation is like a table with four legs, each of which provides support in equal measure. But we said that we wanted it done democratically, and that if they wanted to create a split, they could go to hell.[182]

In a second interview a month later, Ghanem added that in his view there could be no unity in the GFTU until the other blocs acknowledged "their true size."[183]

The crisis was not resolved. To the contrary, the WUB was not prepared to wait until unity was achieved before resuming its own activities on the federation level. A WUB leader explained in December:

> The WUB is trying to achieve unity by promoting democratic methods, and therefore a democratic atmosphere, and by denouncing selfishness of individual blocs. If there is a democratic atmosphere, unity may be restored in the GFTU-Ghanem, and after that in the entire GFTU [including the WYM]. . . . The WUB considers itself part of the first, original GFTU [prior to the split in 1981]. Al-Minawi set up the second GFTU. Then Ghanem created the third GFTU. The WUB, the PUAF, and the WVB want to reactivate the first federation, but the efforts have now been frozen because of the measures taken against 'Ali Abu Hilal and the al-Labadis. But as soon as the first federation has been reactivated, the other blocs will be encouraged to join.[184]

By January 1986, the WUB had recovered from the blows dealt by the army's Iron Fist and reactivated what the WUB considered the "first, original GFTU" by electing a nine-member executive committee consisting exclusively of WUB unionists. It used, according to established practice, the GFTU's stamp and letterhead, and henceforth referred to itself, as did the GFTU-PWB and the GFTU-WYM, as the one and only GFTU. The secretary-general of this third GFTU (the GFTU-WUB) was 'Azmi Sandouqa, with 'Amneh Rimawi as his deputy, the first woman to serve at the leadership level of the Palestinian labor movement. Rimawi explained the move as follows: "The creation of the GFTU is an intermediate step. We could say that our federation is open to the other blocs, but they won't come. So therefore an agreement will have to be reached among the [three] federations."[185] This agreement was not soon to come. The PUAF went its own way after 1985, at times aligning itself loosely with the GFTU-PWB. The decline of the fourth bloc, the WVB, as a credible political and unionist force in the West Bank was accelerated by the institutionalization of the break-up of the GFTU-Ghanem, and it soon disappeared from the scene in all but name.

Rabin's Iron Fist

Yitzhak Rabin's Iron Fist policy had more than a catalytic effect on the paralysis of the labor movement. It put popular organizations on the defensive for the next two years, but not without considerable damage to Israel's continued control over the Occupied Territories, as the uprising was to show in 1987.

The military authorities announced the Iron Fist in response to pressures by Israel's right wing, and especially the settler movement, to take harsher measures against the Palestinian population following the controversial release by the Israeli authorities in May 1985 of 1,150 Palestinian political prisoners in exchange for three Israeli soldiers held by Palestinian forces in Lebanon. According to the arrangement negotiated with the PFLP-General Command, who had captured the Israelis, some six hundred of these prisoners were permitted to return to their homes in the West Bank and Gaza. This infuriated Israeli settlers, who at once started a heated campaign to have Palestinians punished, demanding the death penalty and mass expulsions.[186] At the end of July the government gave signs of bowing to these pressures, and during the first week of August Rabin revived some of the administrative punishments that had been used sparingly during seven years of Likud rule, such as deportation and administrative detention, while intensifying others, such as house demolitions and closure of newspapers and institutions.

Most of these administrative punishments are effected through the Defense (Emergency) Regulations 1945, a legacy from the period of Britain's colonial rule. Revoked by Britain on the eve of its departure from Palestine in May 1948, they were revived by the Israeli authorities in 1967.[187] The regulations grant sweeping powers to the military commander of the West Bank (and Gaza), who can order the arrest, detention, or deportation of anyone without formal charges or trial. Even though no formal charges are required, military spokespersons routinely quote undefined "security concerns" when issuing such orders, accusing Palestinian activists of "incitement" and "membership in illegal organizations." Administrative detention orders, which are issued under a separate military order that finds its origin in the regulations, and other restrictions imposed under the regulations are usually for six-month periods, but can be renewed indefinitely. No judicial court proceedings are involved, and appeal procedures are very limited.[188]

On 5 August, one day after Rabin announced the new policy, the *Jerusalem Post*, apparently acting on good information, intimated that the policy's chief targets would be "West Bank Arabs in student, professional and municipal groups, ranging from trade unionists to lawyers to members of student-union executives."[189] Palestinian popular organizations, the emerging infrastructure of resistance to Israel's rule, were indeed the target of repression, as the following two years were to show.

Since August 1985, scores of trade unionists from the four main blocs have spent time in administrative detention or under town arrest, or have been restricted in other ways. The General Committee of Government School Teachers (GCGST) in the West Bank, in a statement on 1 August 1987, protested the summary dismissal on 1 June of its member Fadwa al-Labadi from her job as a teacher "after serving twenty-one years, without being charged or ever appearing before a civil or military court." Al-Labadi had been placed under town arrest in her village of Abu Dis for six months in February 1987; the order was renewed for another six-month period in August. The GCGST also protested the town arrest order issued against its member Malek Marmash from the Nablus area, who was restricted to his place of residence for six months on 5 July 1987.[190]

In its annual report for 1987, Amnesty International noted that it had "received the names of 66 people, mostly students and trade unionists, who during 1986 were restricted to their home towns or villages."[191] Amnesty added:

> Majid al-Labadi, a trade unionist from Al-Bireh, spent one year under a restriction order imposed in October 1984 confining him to his home town, then six months in administrative detention. In July 1986 he was served with another six-month restriction order. According to the authorities he was a leading activist in the Democratic Front for the Liberation of Palestine (DFLP—a faction of the PLO which had been involved in acts of violence) and had previous convictions for recruiting others to the organization. Amnesty International expressed concern that he had been restricted and detained for over two years without full reasons being given when it had not been shown that he had used or advocated violence.[192]

One increasingly frequent method of union repression in 1986 and 1987 was the closure of union offices by order of the military commander of the central region. Two PUAF union offices in Nablus were closed in the beginning of March 1986 for a period of six months. The order was later renewed for six months for one of the unions, and for a year for the other. The headquarters of the GFTU-WYM in Nablus were shut for one month on 24 August 1986. The headquarters of the GFTU-WUB in Nablus were ordered closed for a year on 20 October 1986. The Construction and General Institutions Workers' Union (WUB) in Ya'bad was shut for a year on 9 October 1986.[193] A cooperative printing press run by the Printing Press Workers' Union (WUB) in Shu'fat was shut for six months in July 1987.[194] The office of the Construction and General Institutions Workers' Union (WUB) in the village of Deir al-Ghussoun was shut down for six months in November 1987.[195]

At the end of 1986, the Palestine Trade Union Federation (PTUF), the pro-Fatah labor branch of the PLO based in Tunis, submitted a complaint against the Israeli government to the ILO Committee on Freedom of Association.[196] The complaint, Case No. 1390, which was endorsed by the World Confederation of Labour in Prague, of which the PTUF is an affiliate, focused on several military break-ins and closures of trade unions, as well as deportations and restrictions imposed on trade unionists, in the

West Bank and Gaza. The Committee on Freedom of Association ruled on the matter in 1987, asking approval for the following recommendations from the ILO's governing body: (1) that the Israeli authorities respect the inviolability of union premises, and (2) that the authorities "ensure that such actions as house arrest or the expulsion of trade unionists are accompanied by the necessary judicial guarantees and, in addition, . . . ensure that such measures are not employed in such a manner as to restrict trade union rights or constitute interference in the activities of the trade union organisations."[197] It was a victory for the Palestinian unions, but in the absence of effective enforcement mechanisms, the importance of the ruling lay mostly in its being a precedent, the first such ruling by an ILO committee concerning Palestinian trade-union rights. (A second ruling involving Gaza unions is discussed below.)

The Israeli military authorities are on record as not opposing trade-union activity in the Occupied Territories, that is to say, in their words, "legitimate" trade-union activity, whereas they do outlaw trade-union activity that in their view is "hostile" to Israel. The legal advisor to the military government in the West Bank stated in a letter to the Palestinian human-rights organization Al-Haq in December 1986:

> The Commander of the Israel Defense Forces in the area and the authorities under his command do not consider organized activities within the framework of legal [registered] unions, whose objectives are to improve the welfare of the workers of the area in particular and of the population in general, to be illegal as long as these activities fall within the unions' objectives [what is presumably meant are union bylaws].
>
> When enough evidence is available to the commander of the area or to any authority empowered by law or by security legislation that there are hostile activities in a professional union or a labor federation that could endanger the security of the area, the safety of the Israel Defense Forces, the general order, or proper administration, this commander or authority should take the necessary preventive and administrative measures, such as restriction orders, administrative detention orders, or closure orders, to stop such activities.[198]

The stated policy of the authorities to protect the right of association and to allow "legitimate" trade unions is belied both by measures the army has taken against unionists who were clearly engaged in unionist activity (for example, confiscation of materials on workers' rights, interference in union elections, and barring unionists from performing explicitly unionist activities) without charge or trial, and by repression of the union movement generally, which has made any form of labor organizing extremely difficult and hazardous to the organizers.

The standard argument advanced by the authorities against Palestinian trade unions is that they are fronts for factions of the PLO. The PLO is an outlawed organization in the Occupied Territories. Since PLO "members" do not walk around with membership cards in their pockets, however, it is sometimes difficult to convict people on the basis of this charge. The authorities do not need to resort to the PLO argument to crack down on union activity, however. Historically they have banned any nationalist expression and interfered with any organized activity by Palestinians in the Occupied Territories, labeling such expressions and activities a threat to Israel's security. The word "security" has a very wide meaning in the official Israeli vocabulary, and seems to refer generally to Israeli "interests."[199] Nationalist expressions and organized activity by Palestinians run directly counter to Israeli interests in the Occupied Territories, and are therefore labeled threats to Israeli security.

Even if there is a legitimate security concern, the military is under no legal obligation to explain itself. Evidence is routinely declared classified, and is disclosed in administrative review sessions to the military judge only, never to the defendants and their lawyers. For example, despite repeated requests by Al-Haq to be informed of the authorities' justification for the one-month closure of the GFTU-WYM in Nablus in August 1985 (referred to above), the military authorities refused to state the grounds for the closure other than that it was done to "maintain security." In a letter to Al-Haq, the military legal advisor added that the "activity which took place in that [trade union] federation is as far removed from the activities in which a professional union should be involved as East is from West."[200] Needless to say, no evidence was presented. In this case, as in countless others, the military has proven entirely unaccountable for its actions.

Trade unions received some international support for their position in 1987 when the ILO observed in its annual report on the conditions of workers in the Occupied Territories that Palestinian trade unions were not political structures but indeed legitimate trade unions:

> In the past, the Israeli authorities have on a number of occasions expressed the opinion that the activities of trade unionists in the occupied territories were concerned with political matters rather than trade union issues and that their meetings were devoted to discussions that could not be considered as trade union business. The Director-General's representatives were struck by the fact that, contrary to the many fears expressed by the Israeli authorities, no questions of a political nature were raised during their talks; the trade unionists they met confined themselves to matters relating to the difficulties involved in carrying out trade union activities aimed at promoting and defending the interests of Arab workers.[201]

The cumulative effect of Israel's repression of the Palestinian labor movement in the West Bank, escalated after the announcement of the Iron Fist policy in 1985, has been very limited in terms of protecting Israeli interests. Indeed it can be argued that repression has backfired. It forced trade unions and other organizations to pursue more informal methods of organizing that in the short term made effective work difficult but in the long term ensured their survival. It also meant that second-level cadres who otherwise might not have assumed leadership positions were groomed in relatively short periods of time whenever the army imprisoned or deported the unions' leadership. The base of trained cadres was therefore large and accustomed to working surreptitiously, skills that unionists put to excellent use during the uprising that began in December 1987.

Labor Organizing before the Uprising

The period following the creation of the GFTU-WUB in January 1986 was marked by continuing persecution by the military of union activists, especially members of the WUB, and a normalization of the new situation in the labor movement. Elections were held in individual unions, in union blocs, and in the three general federations.

By March 1986, most of the unionists who had been placed in administrative detention in the summer and fall of 1985 had come out of prison, either because their six-month terms had ended or because they had been reduced to four or in some cases to three months following a quasi-judicial review. The months of April, May, and June were a period of relative calm. Then in July and the following months, the military authorities reverted to their old, pre–Iron Fist tactic of placing activists under town arrest for (renewable) periods of six months. Soon most of the WUB unionists who had been in administrative detention were now confined by military order to their towns of residence. But the policy of administrative detention was not ended. In October, the army placed Mahmoud Ziyadeh, who had just become the WUB's new secretary-general following elections, succeeding 'Adnan al-Natsheh (who himself had replaced the deported 'Ali Abu Hilal), in administrative detention for six months.

In the face of rising tensions in the Occupied Territories in the spring of 1987 the authorities intensified the use of administrative detention, again targeting the most militant among the popular organizers. In the labor movement in the 1980s, these were WUB activists. Arrests were doubtless related to the large demonstrations that took place throughout the Occupied Territories between December 1986 and May 1987, as well as to the eighteenth PNC meeting that was convened in Algiers in April 1987. PWB unionist George Hazboun, an outspoken member of the trade-union movement as well as of the Bethlehem community, was issued a four-month administrative detention order in May, possibly in anticipation of the flood of foreign journalists who were expected to appear in June for the twentieth anniversary of the occupation, or as a punishment for the new role accorded to the PCP in the PLO during the PNC meeting.[202]

The reconciliation of the various factions of the PLO in Algiers, and the inclusion for the first time in its history of the PCP in the PLO, resulted in a glossing-over of the most glaring differences that divided the various union blocs. Tacit alliances sprang up between the WYM and the WUB on the one hand, and between the PWB and the PUAF on the other, and mutual criticism became muted. The deputy secretary-general of the GFTU-PWB, George Hazboun, and the deputy secretary-general of the GFTU-WYM, Ghassan Ayyoub, published statements in the local press at the time of the PNC session to present the positions of their respective blocs. They condemned the absence of unity in the usual hackneyed language, but carefully refrained from identifying specific culprits, contrary to previous practice.[203]

The PCP's admission to the PLO augured well for moves toward formal unity in the labor movement, but there were no immediate signs of impending reconciliation. To the contrary, even as the members of the PNC were deliberating in Algiers, the PWB held elections in the GFTU-PWB, including once again only members of the PWB. A new executive committee came to office on 25 April; for the first time it included a woman, Samar Hawash from Nablus.

The importance of the PNC session is that from April 1987 on, even if union leaders could not see eye to eye on issues related to the union movement (such as reunification), they were able to debate political matters. This had great ramifications for the period that followed: during the intifada, only months later, resistance activity could be coordinated by the four factions of the PLO jointly, and union organizers, with their labor constituencies, their years of leadership experience, and their stature as former detainees, took a prominent role. However—because of continuing paralysis in the formal organizations of the labor movement—unionists could not talk to their rivals from other blocs as representatives of their own union bloc. They could only talk to each other as representatives of political factions, which had become possible following the formal reconciliation in Algiers. Because the nationalist role of trade unions took precedence over their unionist functions during the early months of the uprising, union leaders were able jointly to coordinate daily events in the new organizations of the uprising, the popular and neighborhood committees, and the strike forces, as well as in the UNLU, which counted several unionists among its members.

In the summer of 1987, another event furthered moves toward reconciliation, however slow, in the labor movement. In a surprise announcement at a meeting on 30 July, Shehadeh al-Minawi offered his resignation as secretary-general of the GFTU-WYM. Local newspapers suggested at the time that al-Minawi had failed to get himself nominated for reelection in the GFTU by his own union.[204] Financial improprieties were also alleged.[205] The resignation was accepted by the federation's executive committee, which chose the treasurer, Shaher Sa'ad, to replace al-Minawi. The apparent coup was seen by observers as a move by Palestinian nationalists against the pro-Jordanian current in the GFTU-WYM, and should probably be assessed in the context of the eighteenth PNC meeting during which the PLO's Jordanian option (embodied in the Jordan-Fatah agreement of February 1985) was decisively pushed to the sidelines. A Nablus activist, interviewed coincidentally at the beginning of July before the putsch, offered the following assessment of al-Minawi's role in the national movement: "Throughout the 1970s al-Minawi was suspect in Fatah eyes because he was seen as pro-Jordanian. [WYM member Mahmoud] al-Sharbini was the Fatah-card, and he was supposed to push out al-Minawi. But al-Minawi 'went Fatah,' and so he was accepted. But until today is he is not called upon by people in Nablus because they do not see him as a Fatah personality. His influence is therefore limited. Why is he still heading the WYM? Probably because they don't have anyone to replace him."[206] That is, not until July 1987.

In short, by the late 1980s a modus vivendi had come about between the various union blocs in the West Bank. In less than a decade, the character of the labor movement had undergone a dramatic transformation. From a relatively small, urban-based movement organized on the basis of a socialist program (with some nationalist features), it had grown into a mass movement organized primarily on the basis of a program of national liberation, which had relegated most of the social concerns to the second plan. The movement's new orientation gave strength to the overall national movement in the Occupied Territories, making possible the sustained support unions provided to the popular uprising that began in December 1987.

The Revival of the Labor Movement in the Gaza Strip

Unlike in the West Bank, trade-union activity in the Gaza Strip has been negligible throughout the twentieth century. Considered an economic backwater, Gaza did not attract the attention of union organizers active in the coastal area during the Mandate period, and after 1948, the Egyptian authorities prevented the Palestinian refugees from organizing. After 1967, when many Gazans found work inside Israel, efforts to unionize workers were immediately suppressed by the Israeli military authorities.

Repression has been worse in Gaza than in the West Bank during the military occupation; the military considered Gaza, one of the most densely populated areas in the world, a powder keg that might explode were local organizers given an opportunity to light the fuse. In the end, Israel could not prevent a conflagration in Gaza, as the uprising has proven.

During the British Mandate, activists made several attempts to establish union branches in the Gaza Strip, but the area's agrarian economy inhibited the emergence of a large labor movement. The southern branch of the AWC was the only group that reached down to Gaza.[207] After 1948 it took a full sixteen years before the labor movement, such as it was, could be revived. Inspired by the establishment of the PLO in Jerusalem that same year, nine Gaza workers formed an executive committee of the General Union of Palestinian Workers (GUPW) in July.[208] The GUPW held its first general conference in Gaza in 1965. The GUPW later became the PTUF, a PLO umbrella organization with branches in Arab and several Western countries that has sought to represent the interests of Palestinian workers in the diaspora.[209]

When the GUPW pursued affiliation with the GFTU in Amman, it met with a good deal of opposition. The GFTU, which was controlled by pro-Jordanian forces despite a strong Palestinian Communist influence, declared that it was particularly unhappy about the way in which the GUPW had been set up, and stipulated two conditions for the GUPW's admission: (1) that the GUPW be established on the basis of a decision of member unions (according to the Jordanian labor law), and (2) that the GUPW's headquarters in Gaza be of a temporary nature, until such time as an independent Palestinian state was established. According to Hazboun and al-Salhi, the GFTU used these conditions as a way to stymie the GUPW's development because of strong Jordanian fears that the PLO might come to pose a threat to Jordan's hegemony in the West Bank.[210] Seven unions joined the GUPW in the three years before June 1967.

Virtually no union activity took place in Gaza during the first two decades of Israel's occupation. The seven unions were closed down by the Israeli military authorities when they took control of the Gaza Strip. Despite repeated appeals by unionists to the Israeli authorities to allow them to reopen, the unions remained closed until 1979. Then pressures exerted by the ILO brought partial success. Although the unions were allowed to reopen, they were prohibited from holding elections or recruiting new members without obtaining prior permission from the army. In effect this has meant that Gaza trade unions have operated only minimally from 1979 on. The local branches in Khan Yunis and other locations were not permitted to reopen at all. The head of the federation was Muhammad al-Darabi, who was not a worker but the owner of a factory employing Palestinian workers in the Israeli industrial settlement of Erez just inside the border of the Gaza Strip. Described as a collaborator by Gaza unionists, he was acceptable to the Israeli authorities, and for years represented the Gaza federation to the outside, including to the rare visitor, such as the ILO's annual delegation.[211]

In its 1985 report on the situation of workers in the Occupied Territories, the ILO stated with regard to Gaza:

> The membership of the unions belonging to the Gaza Trade Union Federation has not changed and, with fewer than 500 members, still represents 1 percent of all the workers employed in Gaza. This shows how trade-union activity in this territory is as problematic as ever. Some measures have been taken in response to the numerous demands made by the federation concerning in particular the acquisition of a site on which to build offices, the grant of financial facilities and authorisation to transfer funds. But permission has still not been given by the authorities to accept new members, which is of course an indispensable measure both to improve the federation's financial position and to make progress towards achieving the effective exercise of trade union rights in Gaza. There is no doubt that the perpetuation of this situation can only undermine the federation's credibility with the workers which is already compromised according to several of the people with whom the mission spoke who questioned the representativity of its executive bodies.[212]

Early in 1986, younger activists within the trade unions, some of whom took their cue from the WUB in the West Bank while others identified with the program of the Communist Party, managed to sideline Darabi, not deposing him but effectively taking over his role as the federation's chief representative. They also submitted a list of demands to the Israeli authorities, including the demand to hold elections, to be permitted to have a telephone, and to be allowed to organize cultural and sports-related activities.

The authorities responded to the list of demands by intimidating and detaining several of the WUB-backed activists.[213] But processes had been set in motion that changed the character of the Gaza labor movement. The ILO reported following its mission in the spring of 1986:

> This year, the mission was pleased to be able to make contact with the Executive Committee of the Federation of Workers, at its headquarters; it felt this meeting to be a sign that the situation is improving, especially as a list of demands to extend its activities, which are still limited, has been submitted to the competent Israeli authority. . . . There is no doubt that the fulfilment of these requests, especially those relating to the carrying out of trade union activities, would usher in an era propitious for the trade union movement in the territory of Gaza.[214]

Other activists, some of whom were Palestinians released in the prisoner exchange of May 1985, began making plans to revive the dormant unions in 1986, if necessary by defying the authorities' ban on union elections. At the end of 1986, six of the seven unions sent a formal request to the military authorities that they be permitted to hold elections, enclosing a petition signed by 130 of the unions' members.[215] The authorities responded in December, stating that no elections could be held unless the unionists provided them with the unions' budgets and with all the names, identity card numbers, addresses, workplaces, and names of the employers of the unions' members.[216] The unionists decided to ignore the authorities' request, seeing it as an unjustifiable interference in the unions' private affairs.[217]

On 21 February, the Carpenters and Building Workers' Union organized elections despite the military ban. The army was caught by surprise, and a lukewarm attempt was made to block the entrance to the federation building. Nevertheless, a number of union members, accompanied by the press, human-rights observers, and members of the Communist Rakah faction in the Histadrut, were able to push past the soldiers and enter the building, where they cast their votes. According to the local press:

> In the building, the elections then began. The committee in charge of the elections made a list of the names of the workers present. There were 71 workers, which according to union bylaws, did not constitute a legal quorum. The union has 326 dues-paying members who are eligible to vote. The bylaws provide for such a case by saying that under such conditions elections should be postponed for two hours. After that, they may be resumed and be legal with any number of workers present.[218]

After two hours, the elections were declared legal. Thus did the Carpenters and Building Workers' Union revive the union movement in the Gaza Strip.[219]

The military authorities responded with intimidation, using the threat of violence, and when this proved insufficient, actual violence. The Palestinian human rights organization Al-Haq reports that the army "threatened the newly elected executive board that they [would] close the whole federation if they [did] not cancel the results of the election, and also threatened to use physical violence against the union's leaders if they did not follow the authorities' orders."[220] One day following these threats, the son of one of the organizers was viciously beaten by soldiers and left for dead near the beach.

The unionists refused to back down. To the contrary, on 4 April, a second union, the Commercial and Public Services Workers' Union, organized elections. The army came better prepared this time to prevent the event from taking place. In the early morning hours, soldiers arrested several of the candidates for election and cordoned off the area around the Gaza federation building. The organizers had anticipated this, however, and had designated an alternative site: the compound of the International Committee of the Red Cross in Gaza City. Here the elections took place despite a heavy military presence in the immediate vicinity, which prevented a number of workers from entering the compound. In the end, 177 of the union's 391 registered members managed to cast their votes.[221]

After the two elections, changes were made in the makeup of the Gaza federation. Both unions sent two new representatives each to the federation's executive committee in an effort to tilt the balance of power in favor of the new activist and explicitly nationalist generation. This did not serve the military's interests, and the authorities responded with repression. Arrests and summonses of unionists were frequent during the following months. In letters to the head of the federation on 17 March and 26 May, the military warned that the two representatives from the Carpenters and Building Workers' Union were unacceptable because the elections in the union had been illegal. They urged that no further alterations be made in the federation council without their prior agreement.[222] They also informed the Commercial and Public Service Workers' Union that they did not recognize the new executive committee. In further communications, the military told eight members of the two new executive committees that they were barred from any union activity, and that they would face legal action if they were to violate this ban.

The two unions responded by sending a joint complaint to the ILO's Committee on Freedom of Association to protest the election ban and subsequent threats and repression.[223] The organizers also went public, condemning the army's actions to stymie labor organizing in the Gaza Strip in a press conference in Jerusalem on 16 June.[224] The ILO committee's ruling, in 1988, came down on the side of the Gaza unions.[225] This was a significant political victory, but by 1988 the development of the Gaza labor movement had been superseded by the intifada, and the two unions were therefore unable to capitalize on the ILO's recommendations to the Israeli government.

The revival of the Gaza labor movement in the spring of 1987 can in part be attributed to an injection of new ideas and energies in the wake of the 1985 prisoner exchange, and to a willingness, at least in the beginning stages, among activists from the different factions to work together. Several of the union organizers had spent long periods in prison, often sharing cells and therefore experiences. Once released, they automatically assumed leadership positions in their communities, and were able to challenge the authority of the notables and other traditional leaders, including in the labor movement. The Carpenters and Building Workers' Union, for example, was dominated by young Communist activists, while the Commercial and Public Services Workers' Union was controlled by organizers sympathetic to the political program of the PFLP. The veteran leadership of the Gaza federation, on the other hand, was either apolitical or tended toward a conservative pro-Fatah line. The elections in February and April 1987 posed a direct challenge to the continued control by these greying community elders.

In an attempt to head off a further erosion of Fatah's hegemony in the federation, the old leadership organized elections in two unions they controlled, the Textile Workers' Union and the Drivers' Union. These elections were held, without advance notice and in secret, in June. The two unions circumvented the procedures stipulated in the Egyptian labor law, and the military authorities closed their eyes to the elections, reckoning that if repression was incapable of blocking the revival of the Gaza union movement, internal divisions would soon upset the new balance of power in the federation's leadership and hobble further attempts at union development. Sure enough, serious differences arose between the pro-PFLP and the pro-Communist activists later in 1987, shattering the cooperation that had made possible the two watershed elections in February and April.

It is not clear what might have happened in the Gaza labor movement after 1987, because the uprising that broke out in December changed everything. At that point, Gaza unions were so weak that, unlike their West Bank counterparts, they played no role in the events. Although the activists' success in reviving the union movement must be seen in the context of the PLO's strategy of mobilizing the masses in the Occupied Territories generally, the special conditions that prevailed in Gaza, including the particularly severe military repression compared with the West Bank, militated against an earlier revival. Gaza unions were therefore wholly unprepared to deploy their infrastructure and leadership skills to help sustain the popular uprising in the Gaza Strip, which therefore assumed a character quite different from the West Bank intifada. Ipso facto, the negligible presence of the Gaza labor movement at the outset of the uprising also put in doubt any prominent role it might play in the next decade.

Chapter Five

THE WOMEN'S MOVEMENT

THE PUBLIC STRUGGLE of Palestinian women has been, throughout the twentieth century, a struggle aimed primarily at obtaining national rights. As such, the women's struggle was inextricably intertwined with the overall Palestinian national struggle, which has been dominated by men. Women were either co-opted into the structures of the national movement, or, when they did set up their own organizations, were called on to deploy these for the national cause. As a result, attempts to assert the rights of women as women, when they did occur, were relegated to the second plan or simply made subservient to the larger goals. When we speak, therefore, of a women's movement in Palestine, we are speaking primarily of the role of Palestinian women in the national movement, but including attempts to place women's issues on the national agenda.

The mobilization of women under the nationalist banner in the Occupied Territories after the mid-1970s runs parallel to the mobilization of workers. It, too, has been an integral part of the PLO's strategy to politicize the masses and involve them collectively in the struggle for national liberation. There are therefore significant similarities between the workers' and the women's movements, and the ways in which they developed:

1. Both movements have sought to reach out to all layers of the population, in towns, villages, and refugee camps.
2. Both have sought to recruit members by addressing the specific problems their constituencies face in their daily lives, but have placed nationalist concerns at the top of their agendas.
3. The recruitment of new members has led to a thorough democratization of existing and newly created structures, and this process has generated larger segments of well-trained cadres. Decentralization of the leadership has ensured a greater measure of immunity against the repression carried out by the occupying power.
4. Both movements have emphasized cooperation rather than confrontation with other sectors of society, who, it was argued, also suffered from the military occupation. This made class alliances possible.
5. Factionalism has been rife in both movements, reflecting schisms in the Palestinian national movement.
6. Both movements, by proposing and—to the extent possible—providing concrete solutions to people's daily problems, have increasingly succeeded in

undermining the institutional control exercised by the occupying power (in the form of the "Civil Administration" and local collaborators) and by Jordan (in the form of selective funding and the support of pro-Jordanian elements in local organizations, as well as of the traditional village elites). They began, in other words, to outadminister Israel and Jordan.

Despite these similarities, there are also some very important differences between the women's and the workers' movements:

1. Whereas the new workers' movement was able to use existing trade-union structures to propagate its cause, the women's movement only had the experience of (unorganized) women's activism to build on. Institutionally, women organizers had to start from scratch.

2. The main consequence of this historical fact has been that factionalism in the women's movement has been more subdued than in the trade unions, because the struggle over control between the Communists and the new nationalist-oriented organizers that characterized the labor movement did not occur in the women's movement in the absence of prior claims to hegemony by the Communists. Factionalism did raise its head in the women's movement, however: there are four committees rather than a single unified one. But the absence of bitter competition has made for a greater degree of cooperation and coordination, which has served the cohesiveness of the overall national movement.

3. The women's movement has suffered less from Israeli repression than the labor movement, probably because of the occupying power's patronizing conception of women and their role in society.

4. Most important, an unintended consequence of the induction of women into the national movement is a slow structural transformation of the status of women, a process set in motion in the mid-1970s that by no means has been completed today. Wage labor freed women from the confines of their homes, and participation in activities organized by the women's committees has started to free them from the restrictions imposed on them by their families. The traditional social values that consigned women to their homes and the supervision of their fathers, husbands, uncles, or brothers are being eroded, though very slowly. This has enabled women to take the initiative on some issues in their families and neighborhoods. Women are demanding to be granted equal rights, not after an independent state has been established, but before. In this, too, the women's movement differs from the labor movement. The growing participation of women in social and political work has also led to some access to the leadership level in local organizations, including trade unions.

The origins of the women's movement lie in the period before Israel's occupation of the West Bank and Gaza, but it is only during the occupation that Palestinian nationalism was articulated and channeled in such a way that women could be mobilized effectively. The work of women's committees in the 1980s has focused on pulling women out of their homes, raising their consciousness as women and as Palestinians, and drawing them into activities of an economic, social, and political character. The fruits of this labor can be seen in women's participation in the intifada. However, serious problems remain: too often, the issue of women's rights is made subordinate to the nationalist agenda, and then forgotten. And too often, tradition still prevails over new forms of interaction between men and women, so that today only a minority of activists can claim to have gained some of the rights that the movement as a whole has advocated for all women.

SERVING WOMEN: THE URBAN ELITE TRADITION IN THE WOMEN'S MOVEMENT

In the context of the Palestinian struggle for national survival in the face of escalating Jewish immigration in the 1920s, the women's movement was strongly nationalist in character. Predictably, its leadership derived from exactly the same class that produced the leadership for the national movement: the class of urban traders and rural landowners. During the period of the British Mandate, activist women were typically members of the wealthier and more prominent Palestinian families, like the Husseinis, the Nashashibis, the 'Abd-al-Hadis, the Budeiris, the Khalidis, and the 'Alamis. Such women were usually the wives or sisters of nationalist leaders.[1] According to Julie Peteet,

> upper-class urban women, usually kinswomen of prominent political personalities, organized charitable associations and women's organizations to assist in the national endeavor. Their goals and activities were oriented to achieving national independence and social development. Demands for improvements or reforms in women's positions were negligible, largely overshadowed by the pressing immediacy of national struggle. . . . Palestinian women were aware of the organic links binding their movement to the national movement and made little attempt to extract their own problems and prospects from those of the larger social body.[2]

Whereas in other Arab countries, such as Egypt and Tunisia, early women's organizations fought for such typically sociopolitical demands as the abolition of polygamy and summary divorce, and for the right to vote, in Palestine women demanded that the Balfour Declaration be revoked, that Jewish immigration to Palestine be restricted, and that Palestinian political prisoners receive better treatment.[3] The Arab Women's Union in

Jerusalem played an important role in organizing demonstrations against the establishment of Jewish settlements in the 1920s. The women who participated in these demonstrations were, according to Soraya Antonius, "heavily veiled and rode in closed cars. . . . [Their] emancipation . . . [came] as an accidental consequence of their determination to carry out some political action, such as a demonstration, which entailed a flouting of conventional mores."[4] The union provided the nucleus for further organized women's activities in Palestine, starting with the Arab Women's Congress in 1929.

Usually, though, the role of women during the Mandate period was limited to relief work in times of crisis, when male fighters needed women to provide them with food, clothing, and arms, and to take care of the wounded. Such a time was the period of revolt against British rule and Jewish immigration in 1936–39, as well as the 1947–48 war. In the immediate postwar period, women, according to Rita Giacaman,

> performed the crucial function of substituting for state services. They set up training centres for women nurses, establishing the profession as socially acceptable and respectable for women; they successfully operated first aid station[s] where even minor surgery was performed; they campaigned increasingly for donations ranging from canned foods to clothes to money; they organized soup kitchens and succeeded even in getting very bourgeois society women to participate in cooking; and they washed and mended the clothes they had collected and distributed them to those who needed them.[5]

During the period of Jordanian rule over the West Bank, and Egyptian rule over the Gaza Strip (1948–67), women's activities typically took place within the framework of already existing religious institutions, and were mostly charitable.[6] Women from the upper classes, referred to as the *shakhsiyat* ("personalities"), were instrumental in setting up charitable associations, including orphanages and centers for the elderly, which provided important services to the community not directly provided by the Jordanian and Egyptian governments. Few if any of these organizations were involved politically in national or women's issues. The Jordanian regime effectively prevented political organizing by means of harsh repression (banning of political parties, imprisonment of leaders, expulsions to the East Bank), and sought to control existing institutions by bureaucratic means (for example, through funding), thus defining the conservative character of most organizations.

After nationalist fervor swept the Palestinian community in the late 1950s and early 1960s, Arab governments set up the PLO to control, not organize, the Palestinian masses, in 1964. That same year, the Palestinian Women's Association (PWA) was founded in the West Bank, which sent delegates to the first PNC meeting, held in Jerusalem in May and June 1964. The next year, the General Union of Palestinian Women (GUPW) was set up as the women's branch of the PLO.

The PWA held its first conference in the West Bank in 1965. It began to branch out through the area, and the Jordanian authorities banned the organization in 1966, along with all other institutions affiliated with the PLO. The PWA nevertheless continued to operate "as a clandestine organisation under the cover of various charitable societies in the West Bank which organised literacy, sewing, first aid and nursing courses."[7] In that sense, the PWA can be seen as an ideological precursor of the modern women's movement in the West Bank. The onset of Israeli rule ended the struggle between the women's organizations and the Jordanian regime, and forced women to redefine their goals and adjust their methods of organizing to the new realities of military occupation.

The women's charitable organizations established during the period of Jordanian rule and after 1967 were located in urban areas and were highly centralized, dominated by women who, in the words of Rita Giacaman, saw their work as "a philanthropic expression of middle-class values."[8] If their activities were at all political, they were so indirectly. Even those who were more explicitly nationalist and promoted steadfastness (*sumoud*) under Israeli military oppression and land expropriation did not escape this overriding task: "Women were being trained in jobs that serve as backup for men's work: to be good housekeepers and mothers; and to have as many children as possible because this is their *wajib watani* (or national duty). The women's lives were not considered important."[9]

One of the most successful charitable societies in the West Bank, and one of the few with an explicit nationalist ideology, is the Society of In'ash Al-Usra in al-Bireh, which was founded in 1965 in response to pressing social needs in the Palestinian community during the Jordanian time, and changed as these needs changed with the onset of the Israeli occupation. One of the society's guiding principles since 1967 has been to train women, employ them in productive activities, and pay them for their work, especially in the production of traditional wares that do not compete with Israeli goods.[10] "We don't want our people to be beggars," the society's director, Samiha ("Um") Khalil, explained. "We want them to be trained and to find work."[11] The society is currently the largest charitable organization in the Occupied Territories.

The society's outlook on the role of women is typical of this generation of organizations. They provide opportunities for women to earn an income, but do little to educate and empower women politically. Rosemary Sayigh quotes Um Khalil: "When a girl begins to earn money she may begin to impose conditions on her family. We don't encourage such a spirit in our girls. To open the door too wide would cause a bad reaction." Sayigh concludes: "She is no feminist." In Um Khalil's view, the society's work aids the national cause: "This is the way to liberate our land."[12] Despite such limitations, however, organizations such as the Society of In'ash Al-Usra are important because they constituted the springboard for women's mobilization in the 1970s. According to Giacaman, "given the context in which [the older women's movement] evolved it was revolutionary. The women of the older movement fought to legitimize a social role for women, and therefore set the stage for the development of a more radical movement."[13]

ORGANIZING WOMEN: PALESTINIAN NATIONALISM AND THE NEW WOMEN'S MOVEMENT

The women's committees were established on the crest of the general efforts to organize the masses in the Occupied Territories, and at the same time in reaction to the perceived limitations of existing organizational frameworks. At the end of the 1970s, a generation of women who had been in their teens at the beginning of the decade was now coming of age, entering universities or the labor force, and attempting to make their voices heard in the established organizations: student committees, voluntary work committees, trade unions, and charitable societies. In their effort to articulate their needs and aspirations, they encountered a number of obstacles in all of these organizations: their exclusion from participation as women, especially at the leadership level (except in the charitable organizations), and exclusion from discussion of the issues they raised. Yet they knew from their own experience, for example in the voluntary work and student groups, that they had an important role to play.

The charitable societies, despite their role in preserving the Palestinian heritage and organizing literacy and educational programs and vocational courses, were, according to Giacaman, "unable to extract themselves from the charitable perspective and their efforts, in spite of attempts to fill the gap, remained a palliative treatment to a recurring disease."[14] They provided care for a sector of the population, especially women, but they did not provide these women with the tools that might enable them to involve themselves actively in the operations of Palestinian society and effect social change. As for the trade unions, they might have offered this opportunity to women workers. However, social restrictions that kept women from joining organizations that were seen as men's institutions and a perceived lack of a receptive interest on the part of the unions' male leadership in the problems encountered by women in the workplace proved generally prohibitive to the recruitment of women in trade unions.[15]

A new generation of activists, prompted by pressing social needs and encouraged by the political leadership, therefore looked for frameworks in the 1970s that would accomodate their interests. When they found none, they set up their own.

Emergence of the Women's Movement in the Late 1970s: Creation, Factionalism, Expansion

In 1978, activists in Ramallah/al-Bireh, some of them students at Bir Zeit University, formed the Women's Work Committee (WWC). The founders were women from predominantly petit-bourgeois families involved in commerce or in the professions.[16] Yet they broke from the past by deciding to address the problems of working women, of village women informally employed in agriculture, of students, and of housewives. Two surveys, carried out in the Ramallah area, expressed the new focus and formed the basis for the WWC's work: one was a survey conducted among working women employed in workshops in Ramallah and al-Bireh; the other targeted housewives.[17] The purpose of the surveys was to determine the conditions under which West Bank women lived, and to develop strategies to recruit these women into the trade-union movement, which was also just being revived, and the WWC.

The fledgling organization did in fact succeed in attracting a following, and in encouraging others to join the union movement. The Textile Workers' Union in Ramallah in particular experienced an influx of women in this period as a result of the WWC's efforts. In other towns, too, branches of the WWC were established. During its first years, the organization reached out to women in villages and camps while remaining firmly ensconced in the towns. Only later, when a solid organizational nucleus had been created, did similar committees arise in villages and refugee camps, and they affiliated themselves with the WWC in Ramallah.

The WWC and the committees that soon followed it made it very clear from the beginning that their work would be different from that of the charitable societies. One activist from the Hebron area said: "We do not see ourselves as an alternative to any other union or committee. We founded this committee to support other organizations. The necessity to set up the committee stemmed from the lack of activities of the other committees and organizations. This lack of activities is due to the traditionally minded people who are in charge of such activities. They are not giving the younger generations the opportunity to fully utilize their energies."[18]

A Nablus activist who had been a teenager in the 1970s described her trajectory from charitable women's work to militancy as follows:

In 1976 I began working with the women's charitable societies. They are bourgeois organizations. In their meetings they talk a lot about clothes and that sort of thing. So I soon realized that this was not what I was aiming for. I saw the need for direct contact with housewives and working women. In 1980, when I was still in high school, I heard that some women were changing things, especially in the unions. So I went to the union [the Textile Workers' Union in Nablus] to see if they needed help. In the four years that I was a student at Al-Najah University, I continued to volunteer my services to them.[19]

Unlike the charitable societies, whose leaders are usually members of prominent Palestinian trading or landowning families, the new women's committees derive their cadres and membership from across the spectrum of Palestinian society. Although university-educated women figure prominently in the national leadership and in some of the urban committees, many blue-collar workers and village women play important roles in the movement, especially on a local level. Rosemary Sayigh noted, following a visit to the Occupied Territories in 1980, that "unlike the charitable associations whose structure reproduces class boundaries (the middle class directs for a needy clientele), [WWC] members include professional, clerical and factory workers." Sayigh quotes a WWC activist as saying: "We formed the Committee because the older societies did not encourage working women. They only give money and services, don't have development projects, don't try to change consciousness. We go to women, try to involve them in social and political activities. At first the older societies resented us as newcomers. This has been a big problem. But now some of them help us."[20] As if to underline the activist's point, the director of In'ash Al-Usra, Samiha Khalil, stated tersely when asked about her organization's view of the women's committees, "We have no relations with the women's committees."[21] Yet most of the committees, which are not formally registered with the military authorities, operate under the aegis of a local charitable society to avoid the problem of registration. By not being registered, the committees cannot be monitored as easily by the Israeli military authorities (the Department of Social Affairs of Israel's Civil Administration). This has given them space to maneuver. Additionally, registered organizations were supervised for twenty-one years (until July 1988) by the Jordanian Ministry of Occupied Territories Affairs, which attempted to manipulate Palestinian institutions through its control over funds. The new women's committees succeeded in eluding Jordanian control as well.

On its founding, the WWC adopted a nationalist line without, however, affiliating itself with any particular faction. It was clear, though, that most of its founding members were inspired by the political program of the

DFLP. Given the primacy of nationalism in the Occupied Territories, worsening tensions in the Palestinian national movement inside the Occupied Territories and in the PLO outside produced a split in the women's movement in the early 1980s, as it did in the labor movement. Schisms in the PLO increased factional competition on all levels of organization in the Palestinian community. The readiness to cooperate in unified structures evaporated, so that if a particular faction was unable to control a local organization, it would leave that organization and create a new one parallel to it.

Thus, WWC members who disagreed with the pro-DFLP orientation split off in 1981 to set up new women's committees according to their own political beliefs. On International Women's Day 1981 (8 March), pro-Communist women in Jerusalem and Ramallah founded the Union of Palestinian Working Women's Committees (UPWWC) with branches in all the major towns in the West Bank, and later in a number of villages. That same year, activists in the Bethlehem area who identified with the program of the PFLP established the Union of Palestinian Women's Committees (UPWC). The next year, pro-Fatah women founded the Women's Committee for Social Work (WCSW). The WWC meanwhile changed its name to the Union of Women's Work Committees, which was renamed in 1989, the Federation of Palestinian Women's Action Committees (FPWAC).

The four committees have shared a program on the question of organizing and mobilizing women, although the WCSW has tended to be less militant than the others, often copying the service-oriented activities of the charitable societies. On tactical positions within the national movement, however, differences are considerable. According to a UPWC organizer, "our committee's activities are pretty much the same as those of the other committees. We are different in our politics, in how we recruit women, on the basis of what program. Political differences center on the national question, on the main goals of the Palestinian movement."[22] Hamida Kazi has noted that while "women in all these committees are active in the unionization of working women, generating social and political consciousness, supporting prisoners' families, etc., the divisions which led to the establishment of the four different committees seem to reflect the factionalist trend in the larger movement. The membership of these committees reflects the ideological views of the factions in the larger movement itself."[23]

The women's committees, although divided along political lines, have not experienced the type of rivalry and sometimes outright conflict that has marked the trade unions in the West Bank. The reason for this is probably the specific history of the labor movement, where unions openly espousing nationalist aims were set up in reaction to the perceived inactivity, especially on a nationalist level, of the existing union bloc, which, however, continued to control the general federation, thereby thwarting the newer unions' immediate aspirations. The history of the women's committees differs considerably. In the words of one of the leaders of the WCSW: "The WWC was the first women's committee in the Occupied Territories. Most active women became members of the WWC, which in the beginning did not have a clear political orientation. Then people began identifying with factions, which led to a split, and women began to set up their own committees."[24] WWC activists claim that they did not see this development as a threat to their own existence, even though they deplored the split. Said one of the WWC's founders:

> There was no real split. Those who started with the WWC are still with us. Those in the other committees would have continued with us if they had really believed in building a united women's movement. In the beginning we were very careful to work with all societies and clubs and refugee-camp directors in order to clarify the WWC's goals. But there are always people who want to work only for their own party. In [the Ramallah area village of] Beitin we worked with the local club. We had sixty solid members. We cooperated with the club in opening a kindergarten. We had worked out all the details, but then one of the women of the club decided that she did not want a link with the district committee [in Ramallah]. So then we gave everything to the club, except our name, which they had also wanted. Then they set up their own women's committee alongside the club.[25]

A UPWC activist expressed a sentiment shared by the other committees when she remarked that "it is a good thing to have more than one committee: it creates honest competition and offers women who are trying to leave the prison of their home more options."[26] Factionalism and competition among the four committees almost certainly spurred recruitment, as it did in the labor movement. Yet competition can become a curse when it is transformed into a struggle for representation in the national movement. Such fears have been expressed by Rita Giacaman, who has said that the "problems of women have been reduced to serve the interests of thoroughly secondary, and possibly very petty, struggles between political factions, at the expense of the women," struggles that stem from "certain groups' attempts to achieve hegemony over political activities, including developmental and popular institutions and organizations, in the area."[27]

It is not clear that relations among the four committees ever deteriorated to that extent. In 1984, the four committees set up a framework for informal coordination, especially on activities that responded to Israeli repression affecting Palestinian women regardless of affiliation, and that therefore did not require the committees to take separate political stands.

Hunger strikes carried out by political prisoners, for example, have been an occasion par excellence for women's committees to organize joint sit-in demonstrations of mothers and wives of detainees at local Red Cross offices. Such coordinated sit-ins took place frequently before the intifada, for example in June 1986 when the four committees staged a sit-in at the headquarters of the Red Cross in Jerusalem. The committees issued a joint statement denouncing a noted deterioration in prison conditions and linking this, as reported in the local press, "to the escalating campaign against the Palestinians in Lebanon" and to the actions by religious groups in Gaza (the Muslim Brotherhood) against the national movement. The only way to overcome this continuing assault on Palestinians in the Occupied Territories and in the diaspora was in the committees' view by restoring "the unity of the PLO on a basis hostile to imperialism and Zionism and responding positively to the Algerian invitation to overcome the splits in the Palestinian ranks on the basis of the Aden-Algiers accord."[28] Later, following the reconciliation of PLO factions at the eighteenth PNC meeting in Algiers in April 1987, ties were strenthened further.

Relations between the committees and other Palestinian organizations such as charitable societies and trade unions have generally been cordial, not least because committee members maintain close links with such organizations, either as members or as employees, and can therefore exert some influence on such organizations' agendas. The historical role of these organizations should not be underestimated. Regardless of how they saw their role in Palestinian society, they groomed the activists of today. The women's committees clearly did not arise in a vacuum. More often than not they built on existing but unorganized (or at least uncoordinated) attempts by activists within established organizations to mobilize women around particular issues of local concern. For example, the UPWWC branch in Nablus grew out of a core of Nablus women who had already been active as a women's committee inside the Textile Workers' Union since 1977.[29] The Nablus branch of the WCSW consisted of women who had been active as a group, together with other women, in Nablus since 1976.[30] Most of the members of the UPWC branch in Hebron are also members of one of the following organizations: the Hebron Women's Charitable Society, the Hebron Young Women's Club, or the Hebron branch of the Red Crescent Society.[31] When the city-based committees grew and started to turn their energies toward the villages and camps, they approached women, usually of similar political persuasion, who had already been active on a local level, either as individuals or as members of existing organizations, including youth clubs.

Yet strains have occurred in relations between the four committees, on the one hand, and the charitable societies, on the other. In a question-and-answer overview of the UPWC and its work, UPWC leaders said, when asked how they viewed the relationship between their committee and other women's groups:

> We regret to say that this relationship is not positive, with variations here and there. Some societies have not offered us support, even though we have continuously asserted that our committees are not alternatives to [existing] institutions or societies, but complement them. Our experience in Ramallah was different, where we encountered some cooperation in some societies, particularly In'ash al-'Usra which has offered us moral, and sometimes material, support. We have had a similar experience in [the town of] Beit Sahour [near Bethlehem].[32]

In 1987 the women's committees had grown to a membership of thousands of women throughout the West Bank and, in the case of the three leftist committees (UPWC, FPWAC, and UPWWC), the Gaza Strip as well. In Gaza, committees have been most active in the refugee camps, such as Jabalya and Shate'. UPWC activists, who began to display an interest in organizing Gaza women in 1983, said:

> [Recently] we paid a visit to the Gaza Strip and contacted a number of girls who showed an interest in women's activities and who were ready [to organize women]. We agreed on opening a UPWC branch in Jabalya Camp. Two points are noteworthy, however. First, social conditions in the Strip are different from those in the West Bank, and this is reflected in the speed in which committees can be started there, and in the nature of their activities. Secondly, we feel that the responsibility for setting up a women's committee in the Strip falls onto women in Gaza, besides women in the movement in general.[33]

By 1987, the women's movement in Gaza, which is allied with the four West Bank committees, has grown considerably and, although the committees are faced with harsher repression than their colleagues in the West Bank, they have been just as active. The FPWAC, which began organizing in the Gaza Strip in 1983, reported in 1986 that it had seven hundred members and was aiming for a thousand by the end of that year. In February 1986, the Gaza branch of the FPWAC held its first regional conference at its center in Shate' Camp.[34]

From the mid-1980s on, the women's committees played an important role in putting pressure on the leadership of the various factions in the national movement to effect national reconciliation after half a decade of splits and factional struggles. The committees, as well as other Palestinian popular organizations, were instrumental in facilitating the convening of the eighteenth PNC meeting in Algiers in April 1987 by coordinating their activities even though their national leadership remained divided. The four committees for the first time in their history organized a joint event,

in the Al-Hakawati Theater in East Jerusalem on 4 March 1987, to celebrate International Women's Day. It is worth quoting at length from the
report of the celebration in the weekly *Al-Fajr* to get a feeling for the
delicate balance that was maintained throughout this event, which was
attended by 350 members of the four committees who later each held
their own separate celebrations, reportedly with a lot more enthusiasm:

> The four speakers [each representing one committee] had both major points
> in common and major points of disagreement. They were all strongly critical
> of class, social and political, and personal oppression Palestinian women face.
> All four also condemned the war against the camps in Lebanon. The speaker
> from the WCSW specifically attacked [Syrian president] Hafez al-Assad for
> his role; the other women more generally accused the Arab reactionary
> forces.
>
> Speakers all spoke in favor of unity among Palestinians. Those from the
> [UPWC] and [UPWWC] proposed the establishment of unity on an anti-
> reactionary and anti-imperialist basis. The woman from the WCSW spoke of
> creating unity by reintegrating other groups within the PLO. The person of
> the [FPWAC] simply spoke of unity. All four groups were opposed to Jordan
> and Israel sharing power in the occupied territories; to the Jordanian devel-
> opment plan; and to the appointment of mayors and municipal councils in
> cities in the occupied territories. Possible issues of discord, such as the 1985
> Amman Accord between the PLO and Jordan, were not raised.
>
> The idea of holding a joint meeting of the women's groups should be seen
> as an integral step in efforts to create unity among Palestinians in the occu-
> pied territories and abroad. Attendance at the meeting was small in compari-
> son with meetings of each committee, which sometimes attracted 500 partic-
> ipants. Supporters of each committee sat separately and applauded only their
> own speaker.[35]

The call for unity and the mere fact that this event took place at all constituted a giant step forward from Women's Day celebrations in 1985, when
a UPWC statement calling for a wide national front in the PLO was
"loudly vetoed from the floor" during the celebration organized by the
FPWAC.[36]

In an interview in 1985, one of the leaders of the FPWAC said that "we
are the people who can decide about unity [in the national movement]. It
cannot be done at the higher levels of the PLO, but only in the mass
movement."[37] The moves toward reconciliation at the eighteenth PNC
meeting following concerted pressures by popular organizations, including women's committees, in the Occupied Territories, bear out the valid-
ity of the activist's words.

The military authorities have at times tried to block the growth of the
women's movement, but the committees have suffered relatively little

compared, for example, with the trade unions. One reason for this, according to FPWAC activist Amal Wahdan, who has herself been under town arrest on more than one occasion, is that the authorities "already believe they have paralyzed the national front, so they do not have to go after the women. At least, that is what they told me when they came to arrest [my husband] Muhammad [al-Labadi, who was put in administrative detention in October 1985]."[38] Another reason may be that the women's movement is too large and amorphous to be easily repressed. Rita Giacaman has argued that

> in the past, with the traditional charitable society structures, if something happened and the Israeli military was upset, they could close down the center and the work would cease; or the Israelis would put one of the leaders under town or house arrest and activities would almost break up. But with the women's committees, when several centers were closed down, the work went unharmed because it's a popular grass-roots organization, a movement that affects all women, that involves all women doing things for themselves. This kind of movement doesn't depend structurally on the presence of one or two or even ten people. And you can't put sixty to seventy thousand peasant women in jail.[39]

As in the case of the trade unions, repression of the women's committees is graded, starting with manipulation of licenses and permits, and by way of harassment and intimidation ending up with such administrative punishments as restrictions on movement, and then administrative detention. According to Giacaman, the authorities have been particularly effective in stemming the flow of funds from outside: "The issue of finances, donations and budgets has . . . become, particularly the last few years, a major controlling force that the military government exercises against women's and men's institutions alike."[40] The authorities try to control the budgets through existing Jordanian laws governing charitable societies and trade unions, and have put limits on the amount of money that can be brought into the country by any single person. During the uprising in February 1988 this amount was reduced from five thousand dollars to one thousand dollars per person. In addition, Israeli military orders prohibit a person from accepting money from "banned organizations," which of course include the PLO.

The authorities have interfered with the committees' activities through raids on exhibits, confiscation of materials, and closure of offices. For example, the military disturbed the celebration by the Nablus branch of the UPWWC of International Women's Day on 8 March 1983, which was held in the building of the GFTU-Ghanem, forcing the women to leave. They continued their celebration in a different location.[41] The WCSW's exhibit of national products, folklore, and handicrafts, held in Tulkarem in June

1983, was raided by the army, who confiscated materials and arrested three of the committee's members. [42]

Sometimes less visible pressures are put on women organizers. A UPWWC activist in Nablus reports that one of her branch's members was called in by the authorities in 1985 and told to provide them with information on a weekly basis or risk losing her job as a sewing teacher. She reportedly lost her job. [43] A Gaza organizer claims that the authorities work through Palestinian collaborators, who talk to heads of families to pressure them to ensure that their female family members cease any public activities in the community. [44] Many committees report that their members are regularly called in for questioning at the local military headquarters.

A number of leaders of the women's committees face travel restrictions or are placed under town arrest. For example, the chairperson of the FPWAC, Zahira Kamal, was under town arrest in Jerusalem intermittently between 1980 and 1988—for almost eight years—without being accused of any specific offense and without being able to defend herself in a court of law. [45] Nine (or according to some reports, ten) women activists from the various women's committees, including the head of In'ash Al-Usra Samiha Khalil, were barred from leaving the Occupied Territories in July 1985, which prevented them from attending the International Women's Conference in Nairobi that month. [46] One of those who was unable to obtain a travel document (or laissez-passer) was Amal Wahdan, who said that following the refusal she asked Nitza Libai, advisor on the status of women to then–prime minister Shimon Peres, to intervene. Libai contacted the defense minister, Yitzhak Rabin, who answered that Wahdan was not allowed to travel because this would "harm the security of the state." [47]

The committees have sought to protect themselves from Israeli repression by building up an international network of support, including in Israel. To this end they have issued publications in English and have given lectures abroad and participated in international conferences on the position and rights of women. An event of particular importance to the committees was the U.N.-sponsored International Women's Conference in Nairobi in 1985, which ended the International Decade for Women. During the previous conference, in Copenhagen in 1980, U.N. member states submitted a resolution, opposed by the United States, Canada, and Israel, recognizing the PLO as the representative of all Palestinians and calling for the support of Palestinian women. [48] In 1985, the Israeli delegation sought to counteract the damage done to Israel's image in 1980, but again Palestinian women made a strong showing, despite the fact that a number of women from the Occupied Territories had been barred from traveling abroad by the military authorities. Participants discussed the results after-

1. Fish vendors in the Shate' refugee camp in Gaza, June 1990. Photo: Rick Reinhard.

2. Woman churning butter in the village of Yatta (Hebron), 1986. Her family was living in a cave for a year after the army demolished their home. Photo: Joost R. Hiltermann.

3. Metalworkers in Hebron. Photo: John Tordai.

4. Worker at textile factory in Bethlehem, 1989. Photo: Fred Solowey.

5. Workers in the weaving industry, 1989. Photo: Fred Solowey.

6. Women weaving in the village of Dura (Hebron), 1986. Photo: Joost R. Hilter-mann.

7. Member of the Gaza truck drivers' union shows his union card, 1989. Photo: Fred Solowey.

8. Trade unionist in his Nablus office,
1985. Photo: Joost R. Hiltermann.

9. Trade unionists in their Hebron office,
1985. Photo: Joost R. Hiltermann.

10. Unionized worker at the Jordan
Vegetable Oil Company, Nablus, 1989.
Photo: Fred Solowey.

11. Palestinian workers in front of West
Jerusalem post office, 1985. Photo: Joost
R. Hiltermann.

12. Nablus workers take a break on the Jewish settlement of Ariel, 1985. Photo: Joost R. Hiltermann.

13. Day laborers in dispute in the Musrara "slave market." Photo: John Tordai.

14. Day laborers in the "slave market" in Gaza, 1988. Photo: Rick Reinhard.

15. Woman from Ya'bad who works seasonally in Israel, 1985. Photo: Joost R. Hiltermann.

16. Women's production cooperative in the village of Sa'ir (Hebron), June 1990. Photo: Rick Reinhard.

17. Village women protest land confiscation. Photo: John Tordai.

18. Women's committee child-care center in Beit Hanina (Jerusalem), 1988. Photo: Rick Reinhard.

19. Schoolgirl harangued by border police, East Jerusalem. Photo: John Tordai.

20. Deportation of trade unionist 'Ali Abu-Hilal, High Court, Jerusalem, 30 January 1986. Photo: Joost R. Hiltermann.

ward, stating that similarities drawn between the predicament of Palestinian women and that of women in, for example, South Africa, strengthened the Palestinian case. Attorney Mona Rishmawi said:

> The Israelis were always on the defensive, claiming that Zionism is not equal to racism, that Zionism is a liberation movement. In the NGO Forum they failed because their arguments were not valid, mainly because many similarities were drawn between women from South Africa and women from Palestine. South African women really helped us a lot by drawing out the similarities. Every time Israelis spoke about Zionism as a liberation movement, South African women would repudiate it, saying how similar it was to apartheid.

Participant Samar Miri of the UPWWC reported that South African women continued to emphasize the Israeli government's support for apartheid through arms sales and the sending of experts.[49]

The most significant result of the Nairobi conference, however, was that the Palestinian participants were able to make contact with members of other women's organizations. An international network of support for Palestinian women might be crucial in the event of an Israeli crackdown on the committees in the Occupied Territories.

Membership, Recruitment, Structure

The outstanding accomplishment of the women's committees during their first decade has been the recruitment of women from all layers of the population, and their involvement in the organization and leadership of their communities. It is this that sets the modern women's movement apart from previous women's organizing in Palestine.

In 1986, the FPWAC claimed a membership of 5,000, divided into 107 centers.[50] A UPWWC spokesperson said at the end of 1985 that her federation had 5,000 members, divided into 54 branches.[51] The WCSW said it had between 3,000 and 4,000 members in 1985.[52] The UPWC claimed in 1985 that it had a membership of 1,450 divided in 40 centers.[53]

These official membership figures appear inflated, especially compared with figures given for individual branches during private interviews: they simply do not add up to the official totals. There appears to be a tendency to include nonmembers in membership figures, if only because social restrictions make it impossible for many women to become formal members of the committees or trade unions. They are followers who can be relied on to participate in activities organized by the committees, especially at times of local or national crisis, as the intifada has shown.

Membership tends to be concentrated in the larger towns such as Jerusalem, Nablus, Ramallah/al-Bireh, and Hebron. The following figures merely give an indication of the pattern. The Nablus branch of the FPWAC said in 1985 that it had over 400 members in the entire Nablus area: 250 in the city itself, and between 150 and 200 in the camps and villages.[54] The Hebron branch of the same federation gave a figure of "approximately 1,000" for the area, divided into five centers in Hebron and twenty-one units in the villages and camps.[55] The FPWAC in the Gaza Strip, which started up in 1983, counted around 600 members at the beginning of 1986: 300 in Abasan and the eastern villages, 100 in Shate' Camp, 100 in the Mughazi and Nuseirat refugee camps, and another 100 in the other camps.[56] The UPWWC branch in Nablus in 1985 had 250 dues-paying members, while the Hebron branch had 300.[57] The UPWC in Hebron had 120 members in 1985.[58] The WCSW claimed to have between 120 and 150 members in its Nablus branch at the end of 1985.[59]

Any woman can join one of the committees, but she must fulfill a number of conditions, according to the bylaws. The WCSW, for example, stipulates that the prospective member must be Palestinian; must agree to the WCSW's program and cannot be a member of another committee whose program is at variance with the WCSW's; and must be "committed to the just national cause."[60] The WCSW lists three categories of membership: (1) full members, who have the rights and duties of all members (but can be elected to administrative posts only if they are eighteen years or older); (2) youth members—girls who are not yet fifteen and who have all the rights and duties of full members except the right to vote; and (3) supporting members—any women who offer moral or material support without formally enlisting, who have the right to participate in the committee's meetings and activities.[61]

Membership in the committees is generally open to women regardless of their political commitment within the national movement (if they have at all committed themselves, which is usually, especially on a village level, not the case). The only conditions placed on membership tend to be adherence to the committee's bylaws and active participation in the committee's activities, insofar as possible. An FPWAC organizer said: "We do not ask people for their politics. Factions are a reality in the PLO [outside the Occupied Territories] and in the Occupied Territories. But our committee's approach to overcoming factionalism is different [from that of other committees]. We believe in working toward unity [of the women's movement]."[62] And an activist in the WCSW said: "We are trying to make political commitment not affect our activities. Some members actually have changed their political alliance, for example because of marriage [to a man belonging to a different faction], but these members are not expelled, and they can continue to join all our social activities."[63] Implicit in this statement is that such members have little chance of ever being elected to leadership positions in the committee, since the leadership's commitment to a particular current in the national movement is, at least on the strategic level, unshakable.

The committees' recruitment strategies reveal the parameters of women's organizing in the Occupied Territories. Rita Giacaman, who observed the emergence and development of the committees from close up, argues:

> In their beginning phase in the latter part of the 70's, the women's committees were perceived by their organizers as the means through which they could achieve the goal of mobilizing this largely untouched section of the Palestinian population towards the struggle for national rights and the right of self-determination and the construction of an independent Palestinian state. The aim necessitated the creation of a mass women's movement all over the occupied territories. Experience in the field, however, was quite revealing. The organizers were shocked by the realization that, with the existing conditions of women's lives, particularly in the villages and among the poor urban dwellers, it was impossible for them to effectively mobilize women in the national struggle. Illiteracy, overwork, poverty, economic dependence, the limited interests of women that result from all this and the general low status were crucial stumbling blocks. And it is precisely this realization of the Palestinian women's condition that precipitated the awareness for the need of women to organize around their own problems, and for the need to adopt specific programs aimed at the improvement of women's lot. Accordingly, the women's committees proceeded to adopt programs of literacy, activities aimed at solving some of the women's problems (such as setting up nursery schools which allowed women to leave their "prisons" and attend literacy and vocational training classes), general services (such as health) to alleviate the burdens of everyday life, and productive projects aimed at providing women with some means of earning an independent income.[64]

Giacaman claims that several factors contributed to a changed societal perception of the role of women, enhancing their recruitability. These factors are the increasing participation of women in the labor force and the increase in the level of women's education, especially in light of the accessibility of university education in the West Bank itself from the mid-1970s on, including to village women. The result was, according to Giacaman, a changed perception of women's "ability to participate in all aspects of Palestinian life."[65] In the 1980s, therefore, the membership consists not only of educated, middle-class urban women, but increasingly of working women and housewives living in villages and camps as well.

Sixty-five percent of the UPWWC's membership in 1983 consisted of either wage or salaried workers; the remainder were either students or housewives, some of whom were engaged in part-time agriculture.[66] Because of its Communist inclinations, the UPWWC has focused on blue- and white-collar women, the majority of whom are to be found in the towns, and has not spent commensurate efforts in the villages, where many women are informally employed in agriculture. Most of the UPWWC's members are young, unmarried women. Frequently, members leave the committee when they get married, although "this depends on the husband."[67]

The membership of the UPWC, on the other hand, consists predominantly of students and professional and office workers, betraying the committee's petit-bourgeois roots.[68] Much UPWC support stems from an educated stratum of retailers and traders. Yet the UPWC has stressed the importance of organizing women workers and women from the poor sectors of society:

> It is necessary for [all] the women's frameworks [committees] to move toward recruiting women from the sector of working women, and it is extremely important for the federation to include women who are themselves poor or come from poor working families. The reason for this is that these women are most in need of being educated, enlightened and pushed toward participating in social work with a definite purpose: to play a role in liberating women politically, economically and socially.[69]

The UPWC also claims that its organizers regularly visit factories to recruit blue-collar workers. This does not seem to have significantly affected the makeup of its membership. The fact that the group's trade-unionist counterpart, the PUAF, is relatively small itself may in part account for the absence of serious unionist activities in the UPWC.

The FPWAC branch in the village of Abasan in the Gaza Strip has claimed that its membership consisted of 25 percent working women, 25 percent students, and 50 percent housewives, who are officially unemployed but may be involved actively in agricultural work.[70] Abasan is not an exception in the FPWAC, which has laid the emphasis on recruiting housewives. In 1985, the FPWAC stated that "housewives in villages and camps have no framework for organizing except for the FPWAC. It is therefore necessary to get their support, and to organize them in order to activate this large sector of women and attract it to the arena of social and national activity."[71] The FPWAC has attempted to obtain a mix of women, however: "The ideal committees are those which include a majority of housewives, some employees, and working women, and they must also include a good number of women from the age group 30–50, and what we could call 'ladies,' [those women] who usually have influence and social status in the area."[72]

The FPWAC's recruitment strategy is to get women who look like potential members acquainted with the committee's program, and to encourage them to set up their own units in their villages or camps, with the more active women spurring on the more hesitant ones, who are gradually

involved in the group's activities. The point, according to FPWAC officials, is to give potential organizers a measure of local responsibility before inducting them into regional and national frameworks. In the words
of one organizer: "Sometimes women come to us, and then we give them
all the information about how to organize themselves. Through guidance
we encourage them to attend district committee meetings. Sometimes we
help them at the beginning by sending a woman to monitor. We advise
them to elect a preparatory leadership. After that there will be real elections, once they have a membership."[73]

During a visit to al-Far'a refugee camp in December 1985, I was taken
by an FPWAC activist to the local camp branch of the Nablus FPWAC,
the only women's committee in that camp at that time. In the back room
of a house in the middle of the camp, some fifteen women were working
on designs for clothes, cutting up newspapers to practice before they applied their skills to cloth. The young women—their average age perhaps
seventeen or eighteen—had not finished high school, nor were they likely
to: books, notebooks, pencils, and school uniforms are very expensive,
and boys get priority treatment in a family. Many girls have therefore
joined the labor force at an early age. A great number work in Nablus,
some twenty kilometers away, in sewing workshops, as secretaries in offices, or as teachers. Others travel daily across the Green Line to find
work in Israeli factories or agriculture. Their earnings are minimal: not
much more than one or one and one-half Jordanian dinars per day (approximately three to four dollars at that time), which is hardly enough to buy
bread for the whole family; it is simply a contribution to the family income. The FPWAC activist explained that the women in this committee
gained their political consciousness by leaving their homes for short periods of time (the sewing class meets twice weekly for a few hours), by
working together and by talking together about the situation they are in.

The other committees have similar recruitment strategies. Aiming at
the sector of women that because of specific problems or a specific consciousness is prone to be inducted in the women's movement, they reach
out through personal visits and by providing concrete services in the various localities themselves, thereby slowly familiarizing potential members
with the work of the committee, assuaging the fears of (usually male or
older) relatives of organizations such as the committees that take public
political positions, and gradually implicating women in both the women's
and the national struggle. The UPWWC, for example, which maintains
close relations with the nonpolitical Union of Palestine Medical Relief
Committees (UPMRC), will draw the UPMRC's attention to the needs of
women in a particular location, assist the UPMRC in its work there, and
thereby enhance its own standing in the eyes of the women it has thus
served.[74] This is the crucial first step on the way toward recruiting at least

some of these women, over the objections of their menfolk, who may be of a different ideological persuasion or who resist the efforts by women to gain a measure of autonomy from the male-dominated domestic sphere.

The committees' structure has facilitated the recruitment of a mass membership. This was not the case with the charitable organizations. Rita Giacaman has pointed out that

> the old organizations operate on a centralized model, with the society head-quarters almost always in cities and towns, where activities are controlled by an elected executive body that is usually largely composed of bourgeois town and city women. Activities and programs are based on the perceptions of the controlling body of the needs of the recipient population, whether rural or urban. In other words, the organizational and structural framework of the old movement does not really allow for the representation of the needs and aspirations of women from all sectors of society, thus reducing most of those involved into the role of beneficiaries.[75]

The structure of the modern committees, especially the three that identify with a Marxist-Leninist ideology (the UPWWC, the FPWAC, and the UPWC), has the trappings of a decentralized system with the higher committees retaining overall control of policy. The power of the base units ensures representation from the bottom up, as well as lively discussion of all matters affecting women and the committee across membership ranks. The WCSW differs in this respect. Identifying with the mainstream current in the Palestinian national movement, the WCSW has never aspired to organize the masses but rather to gain the masses' support through charisma and patronage. With the emergence of the new women's movement in the late 1970s and 1980s, which was spurred by the leftist factions, the mainstream did not wish to fall behind, and it stepped up its organizing activities. The work of the WCSW has remained limited to Jerusalem, Ramallah/al-Bireh, and Nablus, with a few active pockets in refugee camps like Balata and Jalazon. Although the WCSW, like the other committees, does have base units in smaller areas, they are more clearly appendages of the central leadership. In the words of a top WCSW organizer:

> Each of the four areas has an executive committee that controls activities in that area. Members of these four committees form the federation council, which on a yearly basis elects a five-member executive committee. However, elections have not yet taken place because the organization is still young. There are still problems in organizing the north and the south, and the Gaza section is still very small. Only in the Ramallah area [which includes East Jerusalem] things are pretty much settled. So the five members of the execu-

tive committee have been selected. From the beginning the hierarchy was from the top down. But now we are transforming it from the bottom up according to the bylaws that were adopted in 1983. We are now working on creating responsible individuals in the organization. As for now, for each new [base] committee, the central committee imposes an executive committee for six months. After that candidates will appear who can be elected.[76]

The WCSW, unlike the UPWWC and the FPWAC, which have policy-making federation councils of over a hundred people, does not have a formal general federation of affiliated committees, or branches, but an informal, and informally operating, federation comprising a small number of appointed active members.[77]

The UPWC does have a federation council, which is the highest legislative authority in the committee, but because of the UPWC's limited size in the Occupied Territories, representation from the bottom to the top is still minimal. The UPWC has a basic structure of a federation council with an executive committee of between nine and fifteen members, regional committees represented in the federation council, and subcommittees in the neighborhoods, camps, and villages.[78] The federation council, which meets yearly in July, is the highest legislative body in the UPWC. Each year it elects a new executive committee whose budget it must ratify.[79] The UPWC has been most active in the Bethlehem area, including the Deheisha, Aida, and 'Azza refugee camps, Jerusalem, Ramallah/al-Bireh, and Hebron.

The UPWWC has been set up along similar lines. There are branch committees in camps, villages, and town neighborhoods. Each branch sends one of its members to the area committee, which is based in the nearest town. Each cluster of fifty members sends one representative to the general council. Elections to the general council take place on a yearly basis, but are planned individually by each branch. New committees that are not yet ready to hold elections may send observers to the general council. The council elects an executive committee from among its members.[80]

The FPWAC has the most elaborate structure of the four committees. Its smallest unit is the base committee, which consists of between fifteen and thirty members, and is headed by an administrative committee of seven to nine members, including a general secretary, her deputy, and a treasurer. As soon as the unit expands beyond thirty members, a new unit is created along similar lines, and the two committees together form a branch with its own administrative committee. This structure on the grass-roots level allows for a large measure of participation by all members and smooth access to higher levels of leadership.[81]

Base units and branch committees send one representative each to their district committee, and district committees send three members each to the higher committee. From this is drawn the seventeen-member national executive committee. The executive committee is broken up into various other committees controlling all aspects of the FPWAC's work: the Internal Affairs Committee, the Financial Committee, the Kindergarten and Nursery School Committee, the Public Relations Committee, the Education Committee, the Workers Committee, the Prisoners Committee, the Youth Committee, the Training Courses Committee, the Coordination Committee, and the Social Committee, which is subdivided into the Committee for Centers to Abolish Illiteracy, the Health Committee, the Consumer Market Committee, and the Defense of the Camps and the Land Committee. The highest legislative body in the FPWAC is the general assembly, which consists of representatives from all the base units and branches. It meets annually to review the FPWAC's activities, to discuss the general situation in the Occupied Territories, to amend the FPWAC's program and bylaws, and to give direction to the federation's future program.[82]

The four women's committees are financed mainly by contributions from their own members, who pay an admissions fee and an annual membership fee (usually one dinar, approximately three dollars), by donations, and by revenues from periodical sales. The committees have also attracted the attention of foreign donor organizations such as Oxfam and War on Want in England, and NOVIB in the Netherlands, which have funded individual projects.

The Work of the Committees

Although they are divided along factional lines in the national movement, in practical terms the four committees agree on the need to free women from their household chores and involve them in social and economic activities outside their homes and the family sphere. The committee activists noticed early on that working women could be organized by the committees and by trade unions more easily than women who are at home. The committees have therefore had a clear interest in encouraging the process of proletarianization. To this end they have strived both to enhance women's consciousness of their position as women, particularly as Palestinian women, and to provide certain facilities to smoothe the transition from home to wage labor or to make the dual tasks of wage labor and continuing household responsibilities, including child raising, possible. In the words of one commentator: "Encouraging women to break away from a dependent life is possible only by providing alternatives; thus the women's committees try to complement one activity by another: child care frees women to leave the home to attend self-improvement classes; sewing classes can give women a basic skill for outside jobs; and health information helps self-reliance."[83]

Through these activities, the women's committees have accomplished two important tasks. They have, in cooperation with the trade unions and other popular organizations, built an increasingly effective institutional counterweight to the military occupation; and, by raising women's consciousness, they have kicked off the long process toward bringing about changes in the position of women in Palestinian society.

The committees have made great strides, especially in the area of providing child care. Today child-care centers and kindergartens can be found in most towns and refugee camps, and in a number of villages as well. They allow women with children to leave the immediate vicinity of their homes to join the labor force or, during the intifada, to be active politically. The focus of such centers, according to one FPWAC organizer, is "not the child but the mother. If the committee takes care of the kid, the mother has time for the committee."[84] Another leading FPWAC activist explained that in the absence of a national authority, kindergartens fulfill those needs of children that would otherwise be fulfilled by national institutions, including preparing them for elementary school. In 1985, the FPWAC already had twenty-two day-care centers with one thousand children. "If we have one thousand children," the organizer said, "we must also have one thousand members"—the children's mothers.[85] The FPWAC has criticized the provisions concerning maternity leave in the Jordanian labor law for not protecting women, and has encouraged individual committees to fill the gap: "We lack sufficient childcare centers that would help in taking part of the burden off working women. We hope to be able to build a sufficient number of childcare centers [to reach a situation] like in the socialist countries, most particularly in the Soviet Union."[86]

The UPWWC has been equally successful in establishing day-care centers. A UPWWC program pamphlet states: "The severe shortage of preschool facilities in the Occupied Territories restricts women's ability to work outside the home. Twelve kindergartens have been set up by the [UPWWC] run by trained kindergarten staff and supervised by parent-teacher councils."[87] The WCSW claimed to have twelve kindergartens in 1985.[88] The UPWC claimed to have fourteen kindergartens with 535 children in 1985.[89]

Having loosened the ties linking women to their families, especially their children, the committees aim to prepare women for the labor force to ease, or spread, the economic burden on the family, and to amplify the

role of women in the economic sphere and, by implication, other sectors
of daily life as well. To that purpose they have organized training courses
in such traditional economic activities as dressmaking and food preparation and preservation, and have assisted women in finding employment or, for those who work at home or at the committee, in marketing
their products. One of the main aims of the FPWAC is, according to its
program,

> to improve women's professional skills and to increase their opportunities
> enabling them to become active and productive members in their commu-
> nity by:
>
> (a) establishing vocational training centers which will help women in devel-
> oping their professional experience and gaining new experience in order to
> improve their economic situation as well as the conditions to carry out their
> work, and which will contribute to increasing their opportunities to find
> work;
>
> (b) encouraging the setting up of new production cooperatives to support
> women's contribution in satisfying the economic needs of their families; and
> encouraging [the production of] domestic goods, to be marketed via exhibi-
> tions and bazaars;
>
> (c) establishing marketing cooperatives so as to reduce the burden of the
> economic crisis and to fight the high cost of living which has been placed on
> the shoulders of our Palestinian working families, by marketing national
> products at production cost and by setting up permanent consumer coopera-
> tives for housewives.[90]

Typically, activists in a locality will open their houses to training
courses on a once- or twice-weekly basis, or rent rooms in their neighborhood. If a committee has its own facilities, it may try to combine child care
with training courses. The UPWC reports that it offers courses in knitting,
sewing, embroidery, and pottery making "to help women be productive
and to preserve our heritage and Palestinian identity." The UPWC had
fourteen sewing courses with 160 trainees and twelve knitting courses
with 120 trainees in 1984.[91] The FPWAC position, according to an activist,
is that "there is a need for every family member to work because of the bad
economic situation under occupation. After their work, women may per-
form productive activities for the committee. They themselves are responsible for marketing the products, for example school uniforms."[92] The
committee will also assist in this, selling the women's products at its bazaar in exchange for part of the profit.[93]

Many of those who have graduated from an FPWAC training course try
to find work in the sewing industry in the Occupied Territories (often
providing finished products to Israeli companies on a subcontracting

basis) or even in Israel itself. In some cases, women who have finished a sewing training course are provided with a machine and a regular supply of raw materials so they can do piecework at home. The finished products are then bought by the committee and sold at its periodic bazaars.[94] The UPWWC follows the same strategy.[95]

The women's bazaars, in addition to generating an income for the committees and their members, play a role in promoting Palestinian products. In the words of a UPWWC activist: "We exhibit national products to discourage people from buying Israeli products, by showing them that there is a national alternative. When they see the products, they will know that they exist, and our endorsement of these products will encourage them to buy them even if they are of lower quality than the Israeli ones. This is how we seek to support national industries."[96] This effort was escalated, with considerable success, during the intifada.

The committees' income- and employment-generating projects have focused on traditional Palestinian products, such as embroidery, which do not compete with Israeli products. Before the uprising, such projects were still rare because of lack of seed capital, social obstacles to women setting up their own cooperatives, and the economic problem of marketing traditional products, such as embroidery. The FPWAC and other committees have made it a primary goal to set up income-generating cooperatives, and they have tried to steer away from producing embroidery, which as a luxury good is relatively difficult to market. In Abasan, a village in the Gaza Strip, six women set up a cooperative bakery in 1986 producing biscuits and cookies. The FPWAC has two shares in the bakery as well. A 1986 FPWAC newsletter explained:

> For some time, the committees have been discussing the problems of productive activity: it was decided that the production of basic goods which are needed on a regular basis by all communities would provide a more reliable source of income than expensive embroidery, which focuses on fickle or elite markets in urban areas or overseas. Since food had always been women's province, it seemed logical to start with food processing. . . .
>
> At the beginning, the six workers gave their labour free so that the project could get established, but they soon hope to sell shares to other members, which should eventually enable them to pay shareholders dividends from the profits and to pay themselves for labour. They also hope that the profits from the cooperative will make the Abassan Women's Work Committee more self-reliant so that they can expand their services to the community.
>
> The enterprising women in Abassan are not only creating employment for rural women and helping the [FPWAC]; they are also challenging the accepted role of women as dependents of men and providing an inspiring example for others to follow.[97]

The Abasan project remained one of the exceptions before the uprising, however, and its small size precluded any significant changes in the status of women in Abasan or beyond. However, it marked an important first step in the process of consciousness-raising and mobilization.

Another focus of the women's committees has been the eradication of illiteracy, again with the aim of raising women's awareness of their position in society by providing them with the basic tools and venues to articulate the problems they face on a daily basis in the domestic sphere. Illiteracy is a serious problem in the Occupied Territories, especially among village women. The UPWWC has reported that the "level of illiteracy among women in rural areas in the occupied territories is estimated to be about 60 percent, although in some places it has been shown to be as high as 74 percent, substantially higher than that for men." The UPWWC continued: "In response to this the UPWWC has opened five literacy centres in villages in the Jerusalem and Ramallah area and in Nablus."[98]

The other committees also report being active in organizing literacy courses in the villages and camps, and drawing women, mostly the older ones, into the activities of the committees. These courses, in the tradition of Paulo Freire, are not devoid of politics but rather aim to teach women not simply to read but to educate them about their rights as women. Typical reading materials include committee documents, orders and notices issued by the military authorities, and readings in Palestinian history. According to two German researchers, literacy teachers "try to teach subjects of social-political content and to give practical help to [women] in their situation as oppressed women. The female teachers read the land confiscation notices of the military authorities together with the women. They show them how to fill out forms or practice reading medical prescriptions."[99]

Health education is of similar importance. All committees offer medical care to members at reduced cost through arrangements with local clinics, doctors, and pharmacists. Some committees cooperate closely with grass-roots medical groups involved in providing low-cost health care in villages and camps, such as the Union of Palestine Medical Relief Committees (UPMRC), and with institutions that provide information on health-related matters (for example, concerning nutrition and breast-feeding), such as the Bir Zeit Community Health Center. The UPWWC, for example, works with the UPMRC, "arranging medical relief visits to rural communities which lack health services, and to women working in factories."[100] There is a division of labor: the UPMRC provides the expertise and the UPWWC provides the clientele.[101]

On the local level, the committees organize first-aid courses, training women in basic medical skills. They distribute health and nutrition information, having rewritten the material published by local health institutions so it can easily be understood by women who have no previous experience in health matters. A FPWAC activist said that the health committee of the FPWAC

> follows up on the health situation of women in camps and villages, coordinating activities with the Union of Health Care Committees [UHCC], which consists of doctors, pharmacists, and other health professionals. The committee promotes preventative health care through dental and medical check-ups, and offers health education through films, lectures, and panel discussions. The committee also pays attention to public health issues such as hygiene and sanitation. It offers instruction on matters such as maternity and delivery, on epidemics, and on how to apply health principles in daily life.[102]

The FPWAC reported in 1984 that it had opened clinics in Ramallah, Nablus, and Tulkarem. A first health bulletin was put out by the committee, discussing "health issues such as pregnancy (toxemia and uterine bleeding), first aid, breast-feeding, and burns." A later bulletin, sponsored by the French organization Terre des Hommes and aimed at those who have only basic reading skills, "featured articles using simple language and illustrations on pregnancy, cuts, prevention of disease, dental and gum disease, and [obesity]."[103]

Organizing Working Women

One of the main tasks of the women's committees in the Occupied Territories has been to organize working women in towns, villages, and camps. In this effort they have been forced to define their relationship with the trade unions, whose primary role has been to recruit any and all workers, including women, but whose performance in protecting the rights of women has been less than exemplary. The relationship between the women's movement and the trade-union movement reflects the main contradiction that permeates the ideological foundations of the popular movement in the Occupied Territories: that of the pursuit of national versus social rights. This contradiction is exacerbated by the countervailing pressures of the nationalist-inspired strategic and tactical directives issued by the Palestinian leadership, both inside the Occupied Territories and abroad, on the one hand, and of the genuine aspiration on the part of certain interest groups and their individual members (such as women) to realize universally recognized rights in the particular situation of Palestinian society, on the other. The reactivation of the union movement and the emergence of the women's movement therefore were, although concurrent, not harmonious processes. Many working women activists found in their organizing efforts in the late 1970s that the leadership of the unions to which they hoped to be admitted was controlled by men who so far displayed little understanding, or even willingness to try to understand, the particular problems women face at home and at work. An event at the PWB-controlled Textile Workers' Union in Nablus may serve to illustrate this point.

During a discussion about the activities of the union in the union's office in Nablus, in the presence of several members, including women, in January 1986, the union's general secretary remarked on the difference in wages earned by men and women in Nablus sweatshops. He attributed the women's lower wages to their lower productivity, which in turn he attributed to their lack of work experience compared with men. At that point in his explanation the unionist was interrupted by one of the women present in the room, Samar Hawash, a member of the union's administrative committee, who exclaimed: "Now you see why we have set up women's committees!" She later explained that she was also a member of the administrative committee of the Nablus branch of the UPWWC. She and the other original members of the UPWWC in Nablus set out as card-carrying members of the Nablus Textile Workers' Union in 1977. After 1981, however, when the UPWWC was established at a national level and the women's dissatisfaction with their position in the union grew, they split off from the union to create an independent unit. The committee offered advice to women who faced problems at work, but sent them to the union if what they needed was trade-union support. At the same time, many of the committee members remained active in the union. In fact, Samar Hawash became the first woman to be elected, through her position in the Textile Workers' Union, to the executive committee of the GFTU-PWB, in April 1987.[104] Several other women's committees, such as the UPWWC branch in Hebron, started in the offices of a local PWB union, in this case also the local Textile Workers' Union, until criticism from male workers and denunciations in the mosque drove them out.[105] The UPWWC branch in Tulkarem also started off in a local PWB office.

The women activists' ambivalent attitude toward the male-governed unions is a major theme in the development of the Palestinian women's movement in the West Bank. On the one hand, unions are recognized as ready-made structures geared toward defending workers' interests, but on the other hand women activists complain that the unions so far have not proven themselves to be appropriate vehicles for working women to defend their particular interests. At the same time, the problem of the relationship between working women and trade unions must be addressed because growing numbers of women are entering the work force.

There has not been a unified strategy used by women activists in dealing with their role in unions. Whereas the UPWWC branch in Nablus, for example, set up a committee of women drawn from the Textile Workers' Union who continued to cooperate with the union, activist members of the FPWAC in Ramallah, by contrast, launched a drive to induct working women from the area into the local trade unions. Especially in the case of the FPWAC and the WUB, a convergence between unionist and women's goals took place. According to 'Amneh Rimawi, a WUB unionist and the first woman in the West Bank to be elected deputy general secretary of a labor federation, the GFTU-WUB, one of the first things the FPWAC did after its establishment in 1978 was "to call for the economic liberation of women, which then would lead to other women's rights. The FPWAC program encouraged women to come out of their homes to take part in the productive process and gain social awareness."[106] Once employed, they could be recruited into unions.

Women in Trade Unions

According to Amal Wahdan, another WUB woman activist and one of the founders of the FPWAC, the women's role in the unions grew after 1978, following the creation of the FPWAC: "This was not because of the unions' reaching out to working women, but the other way around." The FPWAC carried out a survey among a sample of working women in the Ramallah area primarily employed in textile factories and agriculture in Israel.[107] One of the purposes of the survey was to find out why women had not joined trade unions, and to encourage them to do so. About 150 women were recruited by FPWAC activists into the PWB-controlled Construction and General Institutions Workers' Union (CGIWU) in Ramallah/al-Bireh during a period of one month that year. "We set up a working women's committee inside the Construction Union in Ramallah. In other words, we imposed it on them, and they accepted it because they had no access to working women. The Construction Union had nothing for women in their union, however, and it still does not have a grass-roots basis of women. The WUB then set up its own Construction Union [in 1983], and women were part of it."[108] 'Amneh Rimawi was elected a member of the executive committee of the WUB-controlled CGIWU in 1979. By 1985 the council of the CGIWU had six hundred members, one-third of whom were (predominantly unmarried) women: factory and office workers from Ramallah and the surrounding villages and refugee camps. "Perhaps twenty-five of the women are active in union life," Rimawi commented. "The others are active in the place of work; that is how they became members to begin with."[109]

Other unions followed in the CGIWU's path. A new union was set up in Ramallah on the initiative of FPWAC-affiliated activists to serve women working in the local sweatshops: the Textile Workers' Union, in 1981. Its general secretary in 1985 was a woman, Karima Dib. From this union sprang the WUB-controlled Federation of Textile Workers' Unions in the

West Bank. Among the thirty-five members of its executive committee in 1985, four were women.[110] In addition, the FPWAC was instrumental in establishing the WUB-controlled Textile Workers' Union in Tulkarem. Members of the FPWAC are also active in the Health Services Workers' Union in Nablus and in the Health Services Workers' Union in Hebron.[111] At the WUB's first general conference in Jerusalem in July 1985, twenty percent of those present reportedly were women.[112]

The WUB unions with high rates of women's participation exist quite separately from the FPWAC, which launched the drive to recruit women into the unions, and their activities in principle do not overlap. Still, there is a great deal of cooperation between the women active in the WUB unions and those active in the FPWAC, and many working women who are members of the FPWAC are also members of the WUB. The FPWAC's official policy toward working women is that they "must be organized in the Workers Unity Bloc and become members in its individual unions [WUB-controlled unions]. In addition, they must organize within the framework of the FPWAC and take part in its activities and social programs, especially those which concern them directly."[113]

One of the aims of the UPWWC has been, despite its bad experience with individual unions,

> to talk to the workers at their homes and at work and to try to recruit them into the union movement represented by the General Federation of Trade Unions in the West Bank and Gaza Strip [the GFTU-PWB] and the Progressive Workers' Bloc. The UPWWC has participated in this field by forming unions for sewing industry workers in Ramallah, al-Bireh, Bethlehem, and Beit Sahour. This effort was crowned by the formation of the Federation of Workers in the Clothes and Sewing Industry [in the West Bank] as a higher form of unionist organization, accomplished through the joint efforts of the UPWWC and the PWB. In Jerusalem a union for nurses was established, and in Bethlehem a union for workers in health professions.[114]

The effort to have women join unions was beset with problems. Unionist Rimawi claimed in December 1985 that between 10 and 15 percent of unionized workers in the West Bank were women, blaming the low number on the following factors:

1. The number of working women is limited. The female work force grew only during the last ten years. The working women's role has been almost exclusively in education, nursing, and office tasks, not in the production process.
2. Social customs restrict women from mixing with men in unions.
3. Factory and workshop owners isolate working women from the unions by providing them with transportation from their homes to work and back.

4. The unions have not really yet opened their doors to women's participation. This is now changing, but very slowly.[115]

The case of the village of Abu Dis, on the outskirts of Jerusalem, is illustrative. The village counts a number of workshops employing women who service Jerusalem's tourist industry (for example, producing yarmulkes for religious Jews). The village also has an active union, the WUB-controlled Construction and General Institutions Workers' Union. Yet the union's efforts to recruit the women from the workshops have largely been frustrated. In the words of Amal Wahdan, who was active in Abu Dis in the early 1980s: "We had a committee of working women [inside the union], but because of traditional social obstacles as well as the political situation, many women could not come to us. Still they would come to union celebrations to which the whole village was invited. These days women are allowed to go and work in factories because of economic needs, but they are not allowed to visit unions. They [and their families] don't know enough about the unions."[116]

Another representative case is that of the Tako and Silvana factories in Ramallah. According to unionist Wahdan, who used to work at the Tako tissue-paper factory, men and women workers are kept separate and do different types of work. Women are collected at a pickup point in Ramallah by a company bus in the morning, and returned there in the afternoon. If organizing the women at work proved difficult, attracting them to the union office was impossible. "To attract the Tako women, we invited them to our women's committee's office, not to the union," Wahdan said. This way a de facto division of labor emerged, with the union serving male workers, and the women's committee serving female workers.[117]

At Silvana, a sweets company in Ramallah, other problems occurred. A company bus picks its female workers up from their homes every day, and returns them there in the evening; many come from Jalazon refugee camp outside Ramallah. These women have no way of going into Ramallah to visit a women's committee, let alone a union. So activists had no choice but to try to organize women in the workplace at Silvana. In Rimawi's words, "women established a workers' committee inside the factory. The seven activists who started it were fired, but the other women continued fighting on this issue until the owner was forced to accept the idea." Yet the women employed at Silvana are still not organized in a union.[118]

One problem that women organizers face is the fact that many women remain employed only until they get married or at the most until they have their first child. They are subject to pressures both from their husbands, who want them to quit their jobs and stay at home to care for the child, and from their employers, who are known to have laid off women because they gave birth. Due to the high turnover of women in wage labor, unions face the same turnover. Women who leave work automatically lose their union membership unless they are actively looking for another job.[119] The women's committees in this sense also constitute a real alternative to the unions for women, since such restrictions on membership do not exist.

One sector of working women that has proven difficult to organize are the women in the cottage industries, producing clothes for Israeli companies via Palestinian subcontractors.[120] These women are often village or camp women; in other words, they live in places the town-based trade unions do not easily reach. Again, it is the women's committees who have tried to fill the gap.

The women's objectives in the union movement are limited. This is in part due to the relative newness of their involvement in union work, and in part to the overriding needs of the national movement. As regards the latter, 'Amneh Rimawi remarked: "There is a strong link between national and social liberation. The WUB has made this very clear. How can men give [sic] women their rights as long as they are both living under occupation?"[121] The WUB women's first slogan was to fight for "equality in wages for men and women who are doing the same job in the same location, in order to improve the position of women in society."[122] Other agenda items include: (1) to fight for work contracts for women workers, since few exist (even for men); (2) to demand annual vacations for workers; (3) to demand maternity leave, and to encourage employers to hire married women (since most employers, except for institutions like Bir Zeit University, and the UNRWA, resist hiring married women); and (4) to fight for paid sick or injury leave, and for paid vacations.[123] One of the unions that has a large female constituency, the WUB-controlled Textile Workers' Union in Ramallah, has addressed a number of specific problems. It has sought to negotiate collective contracts with employers, because, in the words of unionist Karima Dib, "bosses are sometimes ready to make concessions regarding salaries and work breaks, but they are never prepared to put them down in contracts."[124] The union has also fought for minimum salaries for women in the sewing industry, for fixed hours and working days, for paid holidays, for maternity leave, and, most importantly, to be granted the right to unionize, since employers have been in the habit of blacklisting and firing union organizers.[125]

The unions with high percentages of women as members do not differ from other unions in their position vis-à-vis Palestinian employers. Strikes are not shunned, although they are clearly seen as a last resort. Moreover, it is clear that unions will avoid confrontations with employers for nationalist reasons. There are several examples of successful actions by women to secure their rights as workers in particular situations, as well as failures, illustrating the continuity of the women's struggle in the West Bank. In

1979, for example, male and female workers employed at the Star chemical factory in Ramallah attempted to set up a union for workers in the chemical and pharmaceutical industries. The owner became aware of the attempt and fired two of the activists, one of whom was 'Amneh Rimawi. When others were fired, the organizing effort collapsed.[126]

In 1983, the Ramallah Textile Workers' Union supported a strike by women workers at the Dajani factory in Ramallah. The workers succeeded in gaining a 50 percent raise in their average salaries, and an even larger raise in their starting salaries.[127] In 1984, the owner of the Silwadi tailoring workshop in Ramallah sold his enterprise to someone else. The women employed at Silwadi were laid off, although they had wished to continue their jobs. The Textile Workers' Union then intervened, forcing the previous owner to pay the women compensation. They were rehired by the new owner, who made an oral agreement with the women about working hours, monthly wages, overtime, minimum wage, and bonuses for productivity, but he could not be convinced to sign a written agreement on these matters.[128] In 1985, the Textile Workers' Union in Ramallah intervened on behalf of women employed in the Al-Ra'ed textile workshop in Ramallah, who complained that the owner was always late in paying wages. The action was successful.[129]

Unions face additional problems in their attempt to organize women from the West Bank employed across the Green Line in Israel. Palestinian unions have no jurisdiction in Israel, and have therefore less to offer to these women than to those employed in the Occupied Territories. In addition, the exploitation women face in Israel, where many work seasonally in agriculture, is greater than what they are subjected to in the West Bank and Gaza because of the ambiguity of their legal status in Israel, especially if they are employed without a permit—as most of them are—and the consequent ease with which their rights can be violated by employers who have little reason to fear legal action. West Bank unions are not allowed formally to organize West Bank Palestinians in the Israeli workplace, nor are they by Jordanian law permitted to organize workers employed in agriculture. But, said 'Amneh Rimawi, "we ignore this Jordanian law and try to organize these women and men anyhow."[130] Yet few women employed in Israel have joined unions—and in fact none has joined Rimawi's union, the Construction and General Institutions Workers' Union in Ramallah/al-Bireh. In the words of Amal Wahdan: "There are women from Abu Dis working in Israel, but they are usually older women. Some work as cleaners in places like Hadassah Hospital [in West Jerusalem]. So far the union [the Construction and General Institutions Workers' Union in Abu Dis] has not been able to do anything for these women. They themselves don't want it, nor do they think that the union can help them. Also they are afraid of losing their jobs."[131]

Unionist Rimawi said the main reason for the paucity of women employed across the Green Line in West Bank unions was that their families are ashamed of having to send them to work there, and would not want this to be widely known. In Jalazon refugee camp, for example, several thirteen- and fourteen-year-old girls work seasonally in Israeli agriculture, but their families were too ashamed to admit this when the FPWAC did its survey.[132]

Women unionists have suffered the same repression as other unionists in the Occupied Territories insofar as Israeli actions concerned the unions, not individuals. The only punishments individual women unionists are subjected to with any frequency are travel restrictions and town arrest. 'Amneh Rimawi and Amal Wahdan of the WUB, for example, were both under town arrest in al-Bireh in 1986 and 1987.

The limitations on women activists and the opportunities they are able to create for themselves, are starkly outlined in the personal history of 'Amneh Rimawi. Having played a major role in the FPWAC's drive to encourage women to join unions, she has risen to the top of the WUB-controlled Construction and General Institutions Workers' Union in Ramallah/al-Bireh. She was elected a member of the union's executive committee in 1979, the first woman to be elected to this level in the union hierarchy in the West Bank. In 1981, Rimawi's father was openly canvassing support for her candidacy in WUB elections in the West Bank, much to the surprise of other union members who "found this strange, but it just shows how far we [women] have come." In January 1986, Rimawi was elected deputy general secretary of the GFTU-WUB. Again, she was the first woman to reach that rank in the West Bank labor movement. During the late 1970s and early 1980s she was fired three times by successive employers for her union activities in the workplace. In July 1986, the Israeli military authorities issued a six-month town arrest order against her, restricting her to al-Bireh. The order was renewed for six months in January 1987, and again in July 1987. She had no legal recourse, and became unemployed.[133]

The Committees' Unionist Work

Committees have continued to do union work as long as their activities do not overlap with those of the regular trade unions. They have tended to intervene there where the unions are not seen to be doing their work or where they cannot reach, especially concerning problems faced specifically by working women.

The UPWC, for example, has stated that the committee does "not consider [itself] as an alternative to unionist organizations, because it is the trade unions which express the economic demands of workers."[134] But even though the UPWC routinely encourages working women to join trade unions, at the same time it has sought to represent women workers in factories in the Occupied Territories and to negotiate working terms with employers, such as paid holidays on national anniversaries, presumably in those localities where no unions are active, or where no unions sympathetic to the UPWC's aims (PUAF-controlled unions) are active.[135] Coordination between committees and trade unions on issues concerning the rights of women has been considerable whenever committees and unions have identified with the same program in the national movement.

Because of the restrictions on women to join trade unions, which are considered places for men only, the FPWAC created a special place within its structure to teach working women about their rights, and to encourage them to join unions at a later stage. In the words of FPWAC-WUB activist Amal Wahdan: "In every village or camp where there is a branch of the Federation, a subcommittee of about 10 working women meets regularly to organize around the specific situation of women in wage labor. They discuss specific problems and offer practical assistance like negotiating with factory owners, for example."[136] The need for the FPWAC's unionist role is greatest in the villages where branches of city-based trade unions are often lacking. Because of the distance involved, working village women often do not have the opportunity to join trade unions even if they are not otherwise restricted. The FPWAC has attempted to fill the gap by providing basic unionist services where necessary.[137]

The FPWAC has stated that it wants to create a full-scale unionist program within the federation, focusing on the following:

(a) fixing working hours to eight hours each day;

(b) struggling to increase wages under the slogan "equal wages for equal work!";

(c) building nurseries and child-care centers in cooperation with the union movement to guarantee good care for the children while their mothers are at work;

(d) guaranteeing the right to sick leave and maternity leave for working women.[138]

Women's committees play an important role in providing working women with information about their rights. The FPWAC has found that not only are there major gaps in the Jordanian labor law, but that West Bank employers do not even apply the law as it stands, for example by not granting women maternity leave. The result is, according to the FPWAC, that "working women are either forced to quit their job and lose it, or to take a maternity leave without pay. Some institutions even go so far as to not employ married women or to expel women as soon as they get married." The FPWAC recommended not only negotiating with employers on this issue, but also that the FPWAC step up its efforts to establish more child-care centers to avoid the problem of protracted absences due to childbirth and child rearing.[139]

Regarding working women and the national question, the FPWAC's position has been that

> the working woman is part of the Palestinian working class, and therefore she should struggle from the same position as her male colleagues against class discrimination and national oppression. Therefore the unionist program of the working women coincides with the aims of the general program of struggle of the unionist movement and the working class, i.e., to remove the occupation and achieve the aims of our people: the right of return, the right of self-determination, and the right to establish our national independent state on Palestinian soil.[140]

In Gaza, the FPWAC has been active on behalf of working women in the absence of a vibrant union movement. In the words of one organizer: "The unions do not really function. If you want to spread information, you have to do it via the committee. . . . Women do not know they have the right to holidays, to maternity leave, etc."[141] The FPWAC in Gaza has a workers' committee that organizes activities for workers, such as lectures and discussions on specific problems faced by women workers. In 1986, the committee reported that it had visited thirteen factories in the Gaza Strip to distribute cards to workers on the occasion of International Women's Day, 8 March, and that three employers had complied with their demand that 8 March be a paid holiday.[142]

The UPWWC, aside from attempting to recruit women into the unions, has sought

> to press for workers' rights and to resist workers' exploitation through:
>
> fighting wage inequality in the workplace;
>
> defending the right of women to paid maternity leave;
>
> demanding recognition of unions;
>
> encouraging women to organise and press for women's representation at union level;
>
> demanding recognition of the 1st of May and International Women's Day, March 8th, as paid holidays;
>
> publicising workers' issues in the local and international press.[143]

In 1986, the committee reported that it had achieved a number of results in its efforts to protect the rights of working women. The UPWWC had negotiated collective contracts for knitting workers in Nablus in 1982, at the Mourad sewing workshop in Ramallah in 1984, and at the Al-Ra'i knitting workshop in Beit Sahour in 1985; it had established a number of workers' committees in factories and workshops in Nablus, Bethlehem, and Jericho; it had organized training courses in dressmaking and handicrafts (fifteen courses in eleven towns, villages, and camps in the Occupied Territories between 1982 and 1985); it had organized a unionist training course for UPWWC cadres in cooperation with the PWB; it had organized a number of lectures and discussions on the conditions of Palestinian working women; it had participated in the annual 1 May celebrations by putting up exhibits at the various local committees' offices; it had succeeded in having International Women's Day, 8 March, declared a paid holiday in 136 workshops and institutions in the Occupied Territories; it had supported a strike of knitting workers at the Robotnix company in the Israeli settlement of Khan al-Ahmar near Jerusalem in 1983; and it had organized a competition for literary and artistic creativity among women workers in 1985.[144] A PWB unionist of the UPWWC in Nablus said: "The role of the committee is to encourage women and to tell them that they are not only working for money, but also for themselves."[145]

NATIONALISM OR FEMINISM: THE PROGRAM OF THE WOMEN'S MOVEMENT BEFORE THE INTIFADA

What accounts for the rapid growth of the women's movement in the 1980s? Why and how were women attracted to the committees? In Palestinian society, affiliation with groups that are often perceived to be "Communist" is frowned on, especially in the case of women. Appeals to people's nationalist sentiments have tended to break down many barriers, however. The committees' nationalist penchant has therefore worked in their favor, as long as they played down their ideological, primarily leftist, leanings. In addition, the committees' concrete work has in many cases earned them respect in the communities where they are active.

Three of the four committees, the UPWWC, the FPWAC, and the UPWC, claim adherence to Marxist-Leninist ideology, and have leaned, at least until 1990, toward the Soviet Union politically. The two stances, ideological and political, are not necessarily related. The greater sensitivity displayed by the Soviet Union toward the Palestinian struggle for national liberation has given it a larger measure of genuine support among Palestinians than the United States. The WCSW, on the other hand, has no strong ideological leanings, and is politically flexible, mirroring the stand of Fatah in the national movement.

The Marxist-Leninist convictions of the three larger committees appear to be confined to leadership levels. At the base, ideological beliefs may be echoed, but there is little in-depth analysis of structural problems affecting Palestinian society and the role of women in it. Foremost in everyone's minds is the military occupation and how to oppose it effectively. The four committees told women from other parts of the world in Nairobi in 1985:

> In view of the racist policies of the Jewish State, and in the absence of a Palestinian National State, the role of the Palestinian woman has proved decisive in development as the basis for steadfastness in the face of liquidation of the cause of our people, and for continuing the struggle to end occupation and to exercise the right to self-determination and the establishment of an independent Palestinian State under the leadership of the PLO, the sole legitimate representative of the Palestinian people.[146]

Political discussions also tended to be confined to leadership levels, at least until the intifada. In the words of Rita Giacaman, "the available evidence indicates that at least the organizers of these movements perceive their activities as political and national, in addition to being a woman's movement aimed at the improvement of the economic, social and cultural status of women."[147] Though discussions of a national character do take place at a mass level, the efforts of women who join base units in the villages, camps, and neighborhoods are clearly directed, as a matter of accepted and unquestioned priority, toward concretely improving their living and working conditions.

The real differences among the four committees lie less in their ideological persuasions or their individual approaches to women's problems as in the particular positions they take in national politics. A UPWC activist said: "Our activities are pretty much the same as those of the other committees. We are different in our politics, in how we recruit women, on the basis of what program." That is, on the basis of what *political* program: "Political differences center on the national question, on the main goal of the Palestinian movement."[148]

Yet during the past few years, another real difference between the committees has emerged, which is indirectly linked just as much to the national question as are the committees' explicit political positions. In the words of a FPWAC organizer: "Our approach is different from that of the others. . . . Our concern is the women who have previously not been organized, such as housewives and peasant women. Perhaps this is the secret of our success. The others focus on the well-educated women."[149] The FPWAC defines itself as a framework of democratic women that includes in its ranks

> women from all national classes, and which works to unite the struggle of all women in the defense of all national rights: the right of return, the right to self-determination, and the right to establish an independent national state, and which also works in the interest of women's causes, the improvement of women's social, economic, and cultural situation, and the defense of women's

right to work, be educated, acquire experience, develop their personality, and involve themselves in the development of society.[150]

The FPWAC showed its nationalist colors in the federation's fourth conference in March 1986, when delegates adopted resolutions calling for the abolition of the "11 February Agreement" of 1985 between Jordan and the PLO, condemning King Hussein's attempts to create an alternative leadership to the PLO, rejecting U.N. Resolutions 242 and 338, which deal with the Palestinian case as a problem of refugees, and condemning Israel's Iron Fist policy in the Occupied Territories.[151] Other statements by FPWAC representatives, covering a range of issues, such as the U.S. attack on Libya in 1986, abound.[152]

On the relationship between the national struggle and the rights of women as women, the FPWAC has said that the "liberation of the Palestinian woman is bound up with the general struggle for political independence and the achievement of the legitimate rights of the Palestinian people. . . . This is a necessary condition for later transition to a radical solution of the problem of women through stages of struggle to reach a society in which equality between men and women will be achieved."[153] To what extent the two struggles are linked—how much weight will be given to either one of the two struggles at the expense of the other—depends on to whom you talk in the FPWAC. Moreover, the FPWAC's official view has evolved over the years. Gradually, more weight is being assigned to the struggle for women's rights, at least in official discourse. Amal Wahdan, an activist in the WUB and one of the founders of the FPWAC, has said: "The struggle for our rights as workers and as women should start now or we'll end up with another bourgeois state and another kind of regime that will oppress women and the working class. It all has to go side by side."[154] Sama Liftawi, an FPWAC activist who represented her federation at the women's conference in Nairobi in 1985, said: "If a woman is going to participate only in the national struggle, she'll have to start at square one after liberation."[155] Similarly, according to a 1985 FPWAC newsletter, "the restoration of national rights will only be achieved by a strong self-reliant people, and for this the liberation of women is a pre-condition."[156]

Given its aim to recruit as many women as possible around a nationalist program with a view to effecting concrete changes in women's conditions, the FPWAC has reached out primarily to housewives to bring them out of their homes so that they can "take part in the productive process and gain social awareness": "At the same time as the FPWAC moves toward organizing in its ranks all women regardless of their social or professional position, it takes particular interest in organizing housewives and village women first, and then employees, teachers, workers, and artisans in general."[157] To this end, the FPWAC has set out to create, or to encourage the creation of, vocational training centers for women, cooperatively based productive projects, cooperative shops selling national products, literacy centers, and day-care centers and kindergartens.[158] They are all aimed at freeing women from the constraints that have traditionally been imposed on them and involving them directly in the processes of society in order to improve their conditions of life and work—and, ipso facto, to recruit these women to the national cause.

The UPWWC differs from the FPWAC in two important respects: in its political stances within the Palestinian national movement, and in its particular focus on recruiting working women. The UPWWC defines itself as "a democratic women's organization" that strives "for the national, economic, and social liberation of Palestinian women."[159] In 1987, the UPWWC went on record to "assert the right of all peoples to self-determination, and call for the establishment of an independent Palestinian state in the West Bank and Gaza Strip under the leadership of the PLO, and the right of return for all Palestinian refugees."[160] At the same time, the UPWWC said, "In our struggle in the Occupied Territories the Union of Palestinian Working Women Committees considers the liberation of women to be an integral part of the movement toward national liberation. In our belief women's organizations are an agent for progressive change in the Occupied Territories."[161]

The UPWWC has been as ambivalent as the FPWAC on the issue of the struggle for women's rights. A UPWWC representative, Samar Miri, told the Nairobi conference:

> Women need to use more energy and strength to fight for their rights. It is the task of women's organisations now to make more united actions, and to participate effectively in all fields, especially politically. We must speak to more women, to raise their awareness so that we are able to participate effectively in the liberation movement. . . . We will not progress or improve our situation until the occupation is ended. Because nothing is developing, everything is going backwards.[162]

With such a view of the overwhelming influence of the occupation on all aspects of Palestinian life, it is not surprising that the women's committees make great efforts to steer clear of controversial issues such as inequitable divorce and inheritance laws, and move into action only whenever the occupying power or its agents violate women's rights in the Occupied Territories. A case in point is the murder of a Palestinian girl by her father, a person known as a collaborator with the military authorities, in October 1985. According to reports published in the press, the sixteen-year-old girl had been locked in the basement of her father's house in al-Bireh for fifteen years. Discovered by chance in October 1985, she was killed by her father, who had briefly been detained by the police following the discovery and who apparently became enraged by the publicity the case was receiving in the media.[163] On 30 October, the UPWWC distributed a handbill denouncing the murder, blaming not so much the murderer as the military occupation: "It was not enough for the occupation just to release their spy without trial: they gave the girl [who was temporarily hospitalized following the discovery] back to him so that he could slaughter her and they [the occupation authorities] could tell the Israelis and the world about the barbarian savageness of our people, which gives them a justification for their fascism and their efforts to humiliate our people."[164] Thus, patriarchy has not been challenged; everything is neatly swept under the carpet of military occupation.

The UPWWC, imbued with a working-class ideology, has laid the emphasis on recruiting working women, whom it sees as oppressed on three levels: as women, as wage laborers, and as Palestinians under military occupation. The UPWWC therefore has made efforts to bring about women's liberation on these three levels. It has concentrated on bringing women out of their homes and into the production process, and organizing those who have joined the labor force. It has encouraged women to join trade unions, and has offered services to women where unions have proved inadequate or unwilling. In the words of one organizer: "The role of the committee is to encourage women and to tell them that they are not only working for money but also for themselves. . . . Women should know why they work: because it is one of their rights. We want them to be conscious of their condition as women. If they are conscious, they will know what their role is in society, even under occupation."[165] The UPWWC has lobbied actively with local employers to grant women a paid holiday on 8 March, International Women's Day. The committee reported in 1985 that 170 local institutions had paid heed to its call that year alone.[166]

The UPWC differs from the UPWWC and the FPWAC in its political position within the national movement (it identifies politically with the PFLP), and in the relative weight it assigns to the struggle for women's rights in the context of national oppression. In its view of itself as a women's committee it is quite similar to the FPWAC and UPWWC, however: the UPWC is "a popular and unionist women's framework that aims at recruiting the greatest number of women in the occupied nation and organizing them . . . to raise their national, economic, social, and cultural identity. Just like the other women's frameworks it aims at organizing women and pushing them to participate in the struggle to liberate themselves and their society."[167]

The UPWC holds that the PLO must encourage women to struggle against social oppression, and that women can join the struggle with the PLO against the Israeli occupation only once social liberation has been obtained.[168] According to the UPWC, "the social oppression, beside the class and political oppression, suffered by women in the Occupied Territories has made it an obligation for the UPWC to raise the social status of

Palestinian women in the towns, villages, and camps."[169] In interviews UPWC organizers have stressed the importance of the struggle for women's rights alongside the national struggle. Said one: "We are Palestinian women, so we are living the political circumstances here and must therefore take political positions."[170] Another activist explained:

> We place the women's question before the national question. We focus all our activities on bringing the women out of their homes to make them more self-confident and independent. Once they believe in themselves, they will know that they can become leaders in any field they choose, including the military field. So if a woman first gains her own rights by breaking down her internal barriers, then in the house, and then in society at large, then after that she will also be able to deal with the occupation. It depends completely on the woman herself, not on her father or brothers. A woman cannot fight the occupation if she is not even convinced that she has rights, for example the right to leave her house, for whatever reason.[171]

The UPWC has placed great emphasis in its official pronouncements on the need to organize working women, and has taken actions against Palestinian employers, as, for example, in 1985, when it carried out a boycott against the Imperial Cigarette Company in East Jerusalem after the owner fired twenty-five workers.[172] The majority of UPWC members, however, appear to be high-school and university graduates, who are usually highly committed and strong on ideology.

The fourth committee, the WCSW, comes closest to the model of the charitable societies. The WCSW was set up to take "a leading role in offering help for the needy." The committee "assumed the responsibility of easing the hard . . . conditions of people under occupation, particularly in refugee camps, in the absence of a national authority. Moreover, they assumed their role to resist all vicious attempts to eradicate the value of the Palestinian woman in the struggle for the Palestinian cause."[173] Unlike the other three committees, the WCSW has therefore focused on charitable work, including the distribution of clothes and medicine to the poor. At the same time, it has encouraged women to join men in the struggle for national liberation. It helped raise their consciousness through literacy classes and lectures, and by getting them out of their homes and involving them in economic and social activities. In the words of one organizer: "Because of the unusual situation of the occupation it is not enough for only men to be involved in the national struggle. Women have a role to play. . . . Women are half the population; they have the same rights as men to struggle for the liberation of their country. . . . The political and social struggle are interrelated: Fighting for women's rights will bring national rights and vice versa."[174]

In spite of the WCSW's stated recognition of the role of working women, there are scant references to workers and the particular problems they face in WCSW literature. No specific attempt is made to organize working women. Unlike the other committees, the WCSW has made reference to the Qur'an in its public statements. This is likely a reflection of its composition and constituency, and at the same time can be seen as an attempt to enhance the committee's mass appeal.[175]

The political content of the work of the women's committees mirrors conditions in which Palestinian women live in the Occupied Territories. The UPWC has explained the reasons for and nature of its political work as follows:

> The UPWC is not isolated from the reality of life of our people in the Occupied Territories. Last year, after the Lebanon War, we conducted a campaign to collect donations in order to give gifts and aid to those of our people who were injured in South Lebanon. We also paid visits to families of Palestinian prisoners and gave them presents, expressing our solidarity with them on Prisoners' Day, 17 April. During olive-picking time, we have helped farmers along with the voluntary work committees. Last month, when a curfew had been imposed on our camps, we participated with other societies and committees in collecting contributions and distributing them to our people, especially in the camps of Deheisha, al-Am'ari, and Jalazon.[176]

Similarly, the FPWAC has protested the attempted evacuation by the Israeli authorities of refugees from camps in the Gaza Strip, organizing a sit-in at the Jabalya camp in August 1984 "to prevent the Israeli military authorities there from bulldozing a number of refugee dwellings." The FPWAC has also protested land confiscations.[177] The UPWWC branch in Nablus reported the committee's participation in a sit-in at the Red Cross office in October–November 1985, and a visit to 'Ein Beit al-Ma' camp, where four houses were sealed by the military authorities in the summer of 1985. The visit was followed by a sit-in at the United Nations Relief and Works Agency office in the camp to protest Israeli measures.[178] In November 1983, the four committees organized a sit-in at Red Cross offices in Jerusalem in solidarity with women detained in Neve Tertza prison who were on hunger strike. The committees issued a joint statement calling for "the immediate release of all prisoners, the granting of prisoner-of-war status to all prisoners and an immediate end to the arbitrary measures against women prisoners in Neve Tertza."[179]

On a local level, politics often take second place to the struggle to solve the problems individual women face, for example in even joining a women's committee. According to one organizer: "Our work is based in the villages and camps because women are more oppressed by men there, and there are few facilities, and fathers don't allow their daughters to go to schools outside the village and so they remain uneducated and poor."[180] Social restrictions on women's right to be educated also extend to their right to join organizations such as women's committees. It has been one of the explicit aims of the committees to breach the social barriers prohibit-ing women in villages and camps from being organized. They must be-cause it is the women in the villages and camps, especially young, unmar-ried women, who contitute the committees' largest and most important pool of recruitable women.

Julie Peteet concludes from her research of Palestinian women in the refugee camps in Lebanon that "community consensus holds that unmar-ried activists are likely to engage in disreputable behavior as a conse-quence of political involvement which gives them fairly free access to men."[181] Activism also has the potential of exposing women to a particular group of men: the Israeli army and its interrogators. A FPWAC organizer in the village of Abu Dis, speaking about the difficulty of recruiting village women in the West Bank, said: "There are lots of problems. If a woman becomes active in a mass organization or a union, her parents fear she will be arrested, that she might be stripped or beaten, or even raped."[182] These fears are in part justified, as available evidence suggests that the Israeli internal intelligence service, the Shin Bet, uses sexual blackmail in prisons to extract confessions from women, and to turn women activists into informers.[183]

Organizers in the Occupied Territories have found that even when there are few overt objections from men, few women can be persuaded to make a decision of their own accord to join a committee. They have inter-nalized the restrictions imposed on them by their society. Said one activ-ist: "In terms of women's consciousness, we have to begin from nothing. Even though most women hold strong opinions regarding the national question, it is not easy for them, even if they are sixty, to take an inde-pendent decision."[184] A UPWC organizer argued that this "lack of con-sciousness" and this reluctance to "defend one's rights against the status quo" reflect "the underdeveloped social and economic situation in Pales-tinian society. It is a problem of objective conditions, not of the women themselves. Consequently, it is necessary to induce change in these con-ditions."[185] The organizers have therefore had to operate cautiously, with great sensitivity to the emotions involved. A UPWWC activist explained:

> Many fathers don't allow their daughters to go out. "X" here, for example, is from a village. Her father found out one day that she had become a member of the committee, so he began to make trouble. We went to talk to him and to her mother. Then we came to an agreement: it would be all right for her to work [full-time] in the committee office rather than in the sewing company [where she had been employed], because her father saw that we are real people.[186]

Another activist argued that if it could be made clear to a woman's fam-ily and community that the organization she was joining was exclusively for women, there would be no limit on the number of women who would join. "When we first established our committee, we were in the Textile Workers' Union [in Hebron]. But there we received a lot of criticism from the people [workers] who were around, and we were also denounced in the mosque. So then we arranged with the unionists to alternate using the office."[187] Eventually the committee moved to its own office. Another organizer in Hebron reported a problem of a similar kind. "Social values in this conservative society are a hindrance," she said. "Rumors are being spread about us that we are Communists, but we have overcome this simply through our activities. Two of our active members were forced to quit after people started telling their parents that they were members of a Communist group. When the mother of one of them became sick and needed blood, and there was nobody who offered any, it was our committee that offered blood. Then the whole family joined the committee; the men joined the union."[188]

As noted above, many young members of committees and unions "retire" from public life when they get married, or if not then, when they have their first child. "Most of our members are young and unmarried," said one activist. "We lose members as soon as they get married; it depends on the husband."[189] It is, however, not only the husband who reduces his wife's activism. According to Peteet,

Political activity has become an accepted part of "girlhood," the period just before the marriage when women are now active in the labor force and in politics. After marriage, commitment to and identification with domesticity tend to override political commitments. It is not always a simple matter of male opposition to a wife's activism. Domestic duties can be onerous and incompatible with sustained activism. Just as important, many women feel housewifery and motherhood are women's primary roles.[190]

Thus, the women's committees' members are typically young, unmarried women and older women whose duties at home can easily be taken over by their children. Equally typically, the committees' leadership consists predominantly of married women with children: the tradition they breached was so solid that their ability to breach it propelled them into leadership positions within the formal structure.

This is not to suggest, however, that there has been no progress. To the contrary, available evidence suggests that the traditional social obstacles to women's participation in public affairs have eroded steadily over the past ten years, as women have increasingly joined mass organizations in spite of the taboos associated with their doing so. The irony is that the social emancipation of women was not the committees' ultimate goal. The women's committees have sought to encourage the process of women's proletarianization, which had already begun in the 1970s because of economic needs, by smoothing the transition between home and workplace through the provision of child care and the teaching of necessary skills.

The committees did so primarily because they saw the need for the mobilization of women, as indeed of all sectors of the population, for the nationalist cause. In the process, however, women acquired new skills and new economic power, and therefore also, gradually, greater political power in their families and in their communities. A FPWAC organizer said:

> The liberation of women comes in stages, not overnight. It is important to get them out of the house first, then to get them together in one place where they work, then to discuss things with them—both the occupation and the traditional structures that keep them confined in the camp. The struggles for liberation from male oppression and national oppression are intertwined. They are one and the same struggle, because the occupation reinforces the structure of male oppression. By raising the consciousness of women, they will be able to join men in the struggle for national liberation while at the same time liberating themselves from male oppression in the process.[191]

Soraya Antonius has said of Palestinian women in the 1920s that their emancipation came "as an accidental consequence of their determination to carry out some political action, such as a demonstration, which entailed a flouting of conventional mores."[192] In the 1980s, essentially the same thing has happened, although women's public activities occur not only in the political but also in the economic sphere. In either case, however, these activities have entailed a break with the customs that hitherto had confined women to their homes. The example of the village of Kufr Na'meh in the Ramallah area illustrates the case. This is traditionally a highly politicized village; all the blocs in the national movement are present, and many are well organized. The FPWAC started mobilizing women in the village early on, and now has a considerable membership. During the uprising, Kufr Na'meh has been one of the more active villages, with women being prominent members in the local uprising committee set up to coordinate events in the village. What is significant in Kufr Na'meh is that many of the women of the FPWAC are also members of the local branch of the WUB-controlled Textile Workers' Union, which is based in Ramallah. Only a decade ago, that would have been difficult to imagine.[193]

Chapter Six

POPULAR ORGANIZATIONS
AND THE UPRISING

In December 1987, Palestinians spilled into the streets of towns, villages, and refugee camps in the West Bank and Gaza in mass protest over the military occupation, then in its twenty-first year. Two and a half years later, in the summer of 1990, the Palestinian uprising, the intifada, was continuing unabated, although its character had changed from the initial mass actions to a prolonged and institutionalized attempt to disengage Palestinian society from the structures of occupation. With a United States–sponsored "peace process" faltering in the face of Israeli intransigence, Palestinians had become used to taking the long view, contenting themselves with exhausting the occupying power rather than evicting it through a combination of local and international pressures.[1]

With hindsight, what is perhaps most remarkable about the uprising is not that it drew people from all sectors of the population. Palestinians had been involved in the resistance to the occupation *as a people*, directly or indirectly, actively or passively, previous to the uprising. What is remarkable is that the entire population could be mobilized simultaneously, and that a support structure needed to sustain the uprising's momentum came into being and functioned efficiently, with a leadership that was promptly accepted as legitimate by the population, in less than a month.

Ever since the outbreak of the uprising, journalists and academics have grappled with the question how the intifada really began: was it a spontaneous reaction by Palestinians to economic misery and political oppression, which the PLO in Tunis then turned to its own advantage? Or was it the culmination of many years of preparation at the popular level, occurring at a historic juncture when the requisite objective and subjective factors converged? This is not a trite debate. Answers to these questions help shape popular perceptions of the origins of the uprising, the conditions underlying it, and the forces propelling it. This in turn has an impact on policy, and since the Palestinians have succeeded in bringing the urgency of solving their predicament to the attention of the international community, states' policy will, in the decade to come, determine the shape of a future solution to the Palestinian-Israeli conflict.

THE ROOTS OF THE UPRISING

The notion most widely accepted in the West holds that the uprising began spontaneously in December 1987, catching by surprise not only the Israeli army, but even the PLO in Tunis, the avowed representative of Palestinians in the Occupied Territories and in the diaspora. Policymakers such as the Israeli defense minister, Yitzhak Rabin, and commentators such as Yehuda Litani saw it this way in December 1987, accusing the PLO of "trying to fuel the flames" of spontaneous revolt.[2] Israeli journalists Ze'ev Schiff and Ehud Ya'ari have reinforced this perspective in their book *Intifada: The Palestinian Uprising—Israel's Third Front* by referring, in a chapter titled "The Surprise," to Yasser Arafat's failure to understand the depth of the uprising during its first days. This, the authors say, "attested to an astounding degree of estrangement between the self-styled popular leader and the people he presumed to have led." The PLO had "misgauged the magnitude of distress in the territories, and just as they had never plumbed the depth of despair that had settled over the Palestinian masses, neither could they appreciate the great swell of energy that now surged up to the surface." Only toward the end of December did the PLO make "a desperate attempt to jump on the bandwagon that was already careening forward."[3]

An alternative view, current in sectors of the Israeli establishment at the outset of the uprising, holds that PLO agents were actively involved in inciting an otherwise docile population from the very beginning. Israeli chief of staff Dan Shomron said on 15 December 1987 that "although the area [Gaza] is not entirely quiet, the situation is already under control. Under no circumstances will we allow a small minority of inciters to rule over the vast majority, which is in general pragmatic and wants to live quietly."[4]

As Ibrahim Abu-Lughod has pointed out, both views, while virtual opposites, are premised on a single belief, a belief "in the fragility of the *intifada* and the efficacy of the countermeasures to be carried out by the Israeli army of occupation."[5] Both views derive from the profound conviction, nurtured in Israel and the West for many years, that there is no organic link between the Palestinian population and its chosen leadership, the PLO. These are views that do not permit the notion of a popular insurrection led and structured by indigenous leaders, even if they reside outside the country. One would have thought that the experiences of South Africa, Namibia, and Zimbabwe, among others in recent colonial history, would prove more educational than apparently they did.

Facts in the Occupied Territories suggest an entirely different picture. As should be clear from the previous chapters, grass-roots activists had been organizing and mobilizing sectors of the population for years prior to the outbreak of the uprising. They had a clear sense of strategy and tactics, and were astute in their evaluation of the conditions that would be necessary to sustain prolonged mass action. In June 1985, an ideologue of the Unity Bloc said in reference to trade unions:

> According to the [program of the] Unity Bloc, the end of the occupation can come about through a combination of forms of struggle: political, mass, and theoretical. By theoretical I mean instilling a working-class ideology in the masses. By political I mean diplomatic, propaganda, and armed struggle, where armed struggle is the highest form of political struggle. By mass struggle I mean the daily struggle for bread-and-butter issues, but on the highest level this would be demonstrations, rock-throwing, strikes, and commercial boycotts. A general strike/commercial boycott is the highest on the agenda of the union blocs, but the masses must first be convinced through their daily struggle that these tactics are beneficial to them. We should not be adventurous and declare a boycott while we are not ready to enforce it. This would betray weakness, not strength.[6]

In December 1987, following the reconciliation of the PLO factions at the eighteenth PNC session in Algiers in April and a year of escalating street confrontations with the army, activists were ready. When mass demonstrations broke out, spontaneously, throughout the Gaza Strip, spreading to areas of the West Bank, including East Jerusalem, and even to inside Israel for a day (20 December), activists could capitalize on their accumulated experience and credibility in the eyes of the masses, and deploy their organizations, including the trade unions and women's committees, to mobilize people further and channel the insurrection. As David McDowall has argued, the reconciliation of factions in the Occupied Territories as a result of the eighteenth PNC meeting made "the political ground far more propitious for united action than it had been for many years. When Gaza exploded in anger and frustration on 9 December 1987, the underground political leaders were ready."[7] One can quibble over the use of the word "united." "Coordinated" probably reflects the reality of 1987–88 more closely. However, the general assessment is sound. Equally perceptively, McDowall contends:

> The popular movement did not produce the Uprising, but its proven *modus operandi* was found to be essential to its success. By the end of 1987 not only had large numbers of people participated in community activities but many others were aware of the model. Furthermore, through the trade unions and the women's committees, the major political organizations were well aware of the potential political importance of the popular movement. Thus, while the health, agricultural and voluntary work committees remained social rather than political in their programmes, they blazed the trail that others widened

into a national highway. As a result, almost as soon as Israel tried to suppress the Uprising with curfews, blockades and violent policing, the community organized itself along the lines the popular movement had already prescribed.[8]

The examples of the labor and women's movements demonstrate the veracity of this assertion.

THE LABOR MOVEMENT DURING THE UPRISING

If it was the intent of labor organizers in the 1980s to organize and mobilize workers around a program of national action, and if the labor movement indeed became one of the pillars of the national movement, it is legitimate to ask whether the labor movement, when the uprising broke out, was prepared to participate and take the lead in the national struggle, and what role it played.[9] To answer these questions, it is useful to make distinctions among (1) the "working class," such as it was in the West Bank and Gaza; (2) the workers' organizations, the trade unions; and (3) the national movement and its leadership (the Unified National Leadership of the Uprising—UNLU—in the Occupied Territories and the PLO outside). All played, to a greater or lesser extent, a role in the uprising, and their actions intersected on important issues pertinent to labor, even if conflicts occurred and factionalism on a national level continued to divide the labor movement. Moreover, it will be useful for purposes of analysis to distinguish four separate stages of labor participation in the uprising: (1) mass action; (2) institutionalization; (3) retrenchment and consolidation; and (4) recognition and enduring factionalism.

Mass Action

During the first chaotic months of the uprising, Palestinians took to the streets to protest the military occupation, suffering high casualties as the army responded with live fire. Workers joined demonstrations as much as others did; given their relatively high numbers in the general population, it is no surprise that of all fatalities in the period from December 1987 to October 1988, approximately 50 percent were workers.[10] It is important to note that during the first month of the uprising, when no central leadership had yet emerged, no specific calls were made on workers to take action as members of the working class, and at no point later, when there was such leadership, did the UNLU summon workers to demonstrations. To the extent that workers demonstrated and were injured and killed, they participated in the uprising spontaneously as members of the general population.

The work of trade unions was largely suspended as soon as the insurrection spread to localities where trade unions were located. Moreover, the army was quick to shut down trade union offices, using the British Defense (Emergency) Regulations of 1945. Labor activists, however, used their standing in the community to lead the masses, alongside other community activists, helping bridge the gap between mass spontaneity and organized resistance. Many labor activists were instrumental in setting up popular committees in camps, villages, and neighborhoods. For example, in the village of Ya'bad near Jenin, trade unionists assumed a new role:

> A bare, cold hall in Ya'bad is full of life, as the local popular committee meets with [foreign] visitors in the wake of an army raid in the early morning hours of February 7 [1988]. The popular committee—young men, chainsmoking, with faces alive and powerful—comprises known village activists from the worker's union and youth groups in particular, but it is nonetheless a new formation, born of the uprising.[11]

The transition from open trade-union activities to illicit political work was smooth despite severe army repression, according to unionists, because "unions had been harassed before the uprising as well, and unions were therefore used to working informally. Unions were never bureaucracies. In Israel, for example, organizing in workers' committees was always done informally, and this simply continued during the uprising."[12] In the village of Yatta, south of Hebron, the local labor union was transformed into a workers' council shortly after the outbreak of the intifada and began to coordinate events in the village. According to local activists, the council used to "discuss the current situation, raise the political consciousness and press for the formation of popular committees."[13]

One of the functions of the popular committees was to classify workers according to their location of work and their economic needs, so as to determine which role each could and ought to play in the uprising. Volunteer blacksmiths, mobilized by the popular committees, fixed merchants' store locks that had been destroyed by the army in its (failed) attempt to break the commercial shutdown in the main towns in the West Bank and Gaza. During this period, the traditional work of trade unions—education, provision of health insurance and legal aid, and collective bargaining—was either reduced in scope or suspended altogether. In the words of one union leader, "after the intifada began, the national struggle aspect of the unions increased, while the social struggle aspect decreased proportionally; however, it did not end."[14]

Through their role in the trade unions before the uprising and in the popular committees from December 1987 on, labor leaders were particularly well positioned to play a wider political role. They placed themselves, according to one activist, "at the head of the national movement."[15]

There is considerable evidence that several labor leaders served as rotating members of the UNLU. Jamal Zaqout, a WUB unionist in the Commercial and Public Services Workers' Union in Gaza who had participated in the pathbreaking elections of April 1987, has claimed that he was instrumental in setting up the UNLU in Gaza. Representing the DFLP in the Gaza UNLU, he also served as UNLU liaison with the West Bank UNLU during the first months of the uprising.[16] Similarly, Muhammad al-Labadi, a WUB unionist in Ramallah, was accused by the Israeli authorities of having helped establish the UNLU in the Occupied Territories and having drafted the UNLU's first manifestos.[17] Several trade unionists, including Zaqout, Labadi, and his brother Majed al-Labadi, and the PWB unionist 'Adnan Dagher, were deported to Lebanon in 1988 and 1989.

The UNLU, which made its first public statement in the form of Communiqués nos. 1 and 2 (on 8 and 10 January, respectively), initially paid special attention to the role of workers in the uprising, alternately exhorting workers to take specific actions and showering them with praise for their contributions.[18] For example, in Communiqués nos. 1 and 2, the UNLU called on workers to participate in a general three-day strike planned for 11–13 January. Communiqué no. 2, allegedly cowritten by labor leaders Muhammad Labadi and Jamal Zaqout,[19] addressed the "valiant Palestinian working class," stating: "Let your arms of steel set to work to make the comprehensive general strike a success by stopping work on the designated days." And it promised, "Your pioneering proletarian role in our general uprising is the best answer to the threats and invective of the enemy authority and the best way to defeat its policy of racial discrimination and arbitrary action."[20] In Communiqué no. 3, issued on 18 January after the (successful) strike, the UNLU devoted one of its longest paragraphs during the entire uprising to the role of the working class, mixing Marxist and nationalist references so typical of the development of the Palestinian labor movement:

> To the Palestinian working class: Yes, the arms of steel have succeeded through their participation in the strike in stopping the machines in thousands of Israeli factories and workshops. Your role in this uprising is unique and special. Continue your strike against work in Israeli factories, oh heroic workers. We will not be frightened by the frantic threats uttered by the Zionist authorities, courts, and employers, for in this uprising we have nothing to lose but our chains and the oppression and exploitation befalling us. Let us paralyze the machine of Israeli production because enhancing the Israeli economic crisis is one of our weapons on the road to achieving our right to return, to self-determination, and to establish an independent national state.

The UNLU repeated its call to workers to stop working in Israeli factories regularly. It modified it, though: rather than asking workers to quit altogether, the UNLU called on workers to stay away on days of general strike only. However, the UNLU did urge workers employed in Israeli settlements in the Occupied Territories to look for alternative employment.[21]

It is not clear whether workers boycotted work in Israel on general-strike days consistently, or in all cases voluntarily. It appears that workers generally complied with UNLU calls, especially at the beginning of the uprising, but that local activists made a habit of enforcing strikes by blocking roads leading out of villages. In any case, evidence suggests that absenteeism in Israel was rampant in the first half of 1988. This was due not only to strikes but also to army curfews, which were frequent and prolonged during the first year of the uprising. In March 1988, the head of the Israeli Employment Service referred to the uprising as "traumatic" for the Israeli economy because of absenteeism, especially in the building industry and during the citrus harvest. Statistics showed that in March only about 58 percent of the Palestinian work force normally employed across the Green Line was going to work in Israel, including Israeli settlements in the Occupied Territories.[22] Official figures at the end of 1988 suggested that there had been a 20 percent drop in the number of Palestinian workers employed in Israel since the beginning of the uprising.[23]

Labor activists have suggested that many workers switched from jobs inside Israel or in settlements to agricultural production in their own villages. For example, of the sixty to seventy workers from Wadi Fukin near Bethlehem who used to work for Israeli employers, only fifteen continued to do so at the beginning of 1989. The nearby Israeli settlement of Hdar Betar had to hire Israeli workers to replace twenty Palestinian absentees. On the adjacent settlement of Beit Illit, building activity reportedly stopped altogether. Residents of Wadi Fukin say the workers went back to tilling their land.[24]

In response to the strikes, and to the uprising generally, the army launched a campaign of collective, including economic, punishments in an apparent attempt to exhaust the population. The authorities threatened, inter alia, to stop workers from entering Israel and replace them with workers from southern Europe. One Israeli official, for example, called on the government to institute a more flexible policy on entry of foreign workers.[25] Yet these were empty threats: the Israeli economy had simply grown too dependent on its cheap labor force from the Occupied Territories suddenly to cut all ties. But the army did on occasion carry out temporary bans on labor from particular camps or villages, usually as a punishment for nationalist activity in those locations.

Throughout the uprising, Israeli employers laid off workers who failed repeatedly to show up on strike days, usually after putting them on warning. To avoid losing their jobs and their income, growing numbers of workers began circumventing strike calls in the spring of 1988 by staying overnight in Israel. Although this is illegal under Israeli military law, which prohibits Palestinians access to Israel between one and five in the morning, unionists believe that the authorities closed an eye to the practice, both to protect the Israeli economy and to help undermine popular support for the UNLU.[26] Although there are no figures on workers' evasion of strike calls, interviews with labor organizers suggest that workers from refugee camps and nonagricultural villages (especially in the Hebron area) without alternative sources of income, as well as workers formally employed through the Israeli labor exchanges (who tend to have steady jobs), were more prone to working on strike days than the irregularly employed day laborers who hired themselves out on the "slave markets," or those who were able to fall back on agriculture.[27]

Institutionalization

During the second stage, which began, roughly speaking, in the spring of 1988, the UNLU began to concentrate its energies on institutionalizing the uprising by promoting the establishment of more popular committees. Thus, the UNLU encouraged workers to set up and "expand their workers' committees in their factories and in their places of residence, in order to organize themselves and consolidate their role in the struggle."[28] On the occasion of International Workers' Day (1 May), the UNLU called on workers to organize themselves and "to work for the unification of the labor movement."[29] Shortly thereafter, the UNLU urged workers "to complete the formation of unified workers' committees and to participate in existing unions."[30] The rationale appeared to be that so long as the proper structures were not in place, it would be impossible to support those workers who might be willing to strike but could not for lack of alternative sources of income or for fear of reprisals from the authorities.

At the same time, the UNLU softened its demand on workers to boycott work on "Israeli projects," aware of the economic difficulties workers faced and eager not to block the inflow of cash that could help sustain the uprising. So even while insisting on the importance of boycotting work in Israeli settlements,[31] the UNLU called on workers, in rather diplomatic language, "not to waste opportunities for [finding] alternatives to working across the Green Line."[32] In Communiqué no. 16 (13 May 1988), the UNLU urged workers to "intensify the boycott against work in Zionist settlements and to refrain from giving any services to the settlers."

However, if workers were to quit their jobs in the settlements, there had to be alternatives. The UNLU called repeatedly on Palestinian employers to absorb these workers, and not to fire workers or lower their wages in response to reduced sales resulting from the partial commercial strike. For example, the UNLU declared in March 1988, "Factories are requested to lower their prices, not to lower their workers' wages, and to open only during authorized periods."[33] A few months later, the UNLU urged "employers to refrain from dismissing workers, increasing their work hours, or deducting strike days from their salaries," in response to employers' attempts in the spring to shift the economic burden of the uprising onto the shoulders of the workers.[34] The UNLU then toned down its criticism of employers in July, affirming that "factories may work at full capacity and during hours agreed upon between management and workers' committees. Workers' rights should be protected, especially if there is overtime work."[35] This new position reflected the national leadership's growing confidence in the institutionalization of the uprising; they could now devolve a large degree of authority in handling day-to-day affairs to the popular committees.

Throughout 1988, the army saw its control over the population slipping as Palestinians refused to pay taxes, observed general strikes, and tried to avoid contact with the institutions of the occupation. The army responded with more arrests and deportations of perceived activists, and economic punishments against the population generally. In April, the authorities issued a deportation order against 'Adnan Dagher, an official in the PWB's large and active Construction and General Institutions Workers' Union in Ramallah, accusing him of UNLU membership; he was deported on 1 August. Five other unionists followed Dagher: Radwan Ziyadeh, Majed and Muhammad al-Labadi, 'Odeh Ma'aleh (all WUB activists), and Jamal Faraj, a PUAF unionist from the Deheisheh refugee camp.[36] Precise detention figures are not available. However, at least forty-four labor organizers who were members of executive councils in the three labor federations and affiliated unions were being held in the summer of 1988. At that time, the army had closed down at least thirty trade-union offices in the West Bank.[37]

When Jordan reneged on its claim to the West Bank in July, the army began to target the Palestinian infrastructure to ensure that the PLO would not fill the vacuum thus created. The popular committees were outlawed by military decree on 18 August. The definition of the term "popular committees" in the banning order was so vague as to allow the army considerable leeway in prosecuting anyone perceived as providing services at the grass-roots level.[38] Palestinian organizations continued operating, however, despite the ban, exposing themselves to the usual level of harassment, including the arrest of their leaders.

Some of the trade unions remained active. The GFTU-PWB opened offices in East Jerusalem (under Israeli law, therefore enjoying relatively greater protection), primarily to represent the labor movement vis-à-vis trade union delegations and journalists visiting from abroad. The federation convened a press conference in Jerusalem on 24 August to protest attacks on workers by Jewish extremists and army repression of unions.

Union leader Ibrahim Shuqeir claimed that "Israeli officials were doing everything possible to keep workers from organizing in the territories and demanding their economic rights."[39]

Despite the arrests and closure of union offices, labor organizers resumed union activities in the summer of 1988, but informally, operating on work sites rather than from union offices. Around this time, organizers also became more prepared to take on Palestinian employers for attempting to fire workers and lower wages. The first major action by workers at a Palestinian-owned factory since the beginning of the uprising took place at the Royal Crown Cola bottling plant in Ramallah in August. Workers organized in an impromptu workers' committee called for an end to exploitation and demanded basic rights. They were partially successful, gaining an eight-hour workday and the management's agreement to pay wages for UNLU strike days. The army, which traditionally allows labor disputes to run their course in the hope of dividing Palestinian from Palestinian, and intervenes only once a strong leadership emerges, promptly placed the committee's leader in administrative detention for six months.[40]

In the fall, union activists stepped up efforts to defend workers' rights in Palestinian workplaces in the Occupied Territories. One unionist explained that owners contended that because they were "national industries" it was imperative that they stayed in operation, even at the expense of their workers. According to the same logic, workers were not supposed to strike, because that might cause the employer's bankruptcy and attendant loss of jobs. Yet, the unionist said, unions were able to reach agreement with owners because "the bourgeoisie is happy as long as it stays on the safe side." Such agreements stipulated that owners could not penalize workers for observing general strikes by lowering their wages as long as they worked forty-eight hours a week, according to the law. Such an agreement was reached, for example, between workers and management at the Beit Sahour Plastics Company, following mediation by union organizers.[41]

In December, activists of the WUB's Construction and General Institutions Workers' Union in Ramallah, whose offices had been closed by the army, negotiated new collective agreements with local employers, adjusted to the exigencies of the uprising. The standard contract stated that the uprising had created new social conditions requiring a new basis for understanding between workers and management. It proposed that they should work together in a "spirit of understanding and cooperation . . . in the framework of national interests" to reach agreement on the following: stepped-up production to replace Israeli products with goods produced locally; dialogue between management and elected workers' committees; just wages per sector (specified in the contract); application of Jordanian labor law with regard to annual vacations, sick leave, and so on; a ban on layoffs except in limited circumstances (specified in the contract); continued payment of wages despite absenteeism due to army-imposed curfews; fair negotiations between management and workers' committees over health insurance and provident funds; and workers' right to organize.[42]

Retrenchment and Consolidation

Unionists were able to put their new willingness to address workers' concerns in the workplace at the end of the first year of the uprising to good use in the spring of 1989, the third stage of the uprising, the stage of retrenchment and consolidation. In the fall of 1988, the Jordanian dinar, which is the basic currency used in the West Bank, had started a slide downward, falling as low as 2.2 Israeli shekels to the dinar (from a previous 4.9 shekels) in January 1989, and stabilizing at 3.2 shekels in March. Because West Bank salaries are usually paid in dinars, workers suddenly found that their incomes, as well the value of their savings, had been cut in half. This, in addition to declining production and growing unemployment, led to a severe economic crisis in January 1989. In response, the labor movement decisively shifted the focus of its activity from nationalist to workers' social and economic concerns.

The UNLU took the lead in a leaflet in January, urging employers "to compensate their workers for the rising cost of living and the decline in the value of the dinar." The UNLU also encouraged employers "to expand the ranks of their employees, and to cease from singling out activists for special treatment and dismissal from their jobs."[43] Two weeks later, the UNLU called on employers to raise dinar wages by at least 40 percent and urged workers' committees to enforce this measure.[44] The UNLU issued repeated warnings to employers not to fire union organizers as unions began mediating labor disputes,[45] affirming "the necessity of resolving labor disputes on a nationalist basis," and calling for "the formation of national arbitration committees for this purpose."[46]

Strikes erupted in several Palestinian and foreign institutions in the West Bank in the following months. Employees of the United Nations Relief and Works Agency organized a sit-in, a partial (warning) strike, and eventually a full three-day strike at the beginning of February to demand a recalculation of their salaries, whose value, according to the Union of UNRWA Employees, had fallen by 70 to 80 percent. The union accused UNRWA, which is funded (in United States dollars) by member states of the U.N., of "making an unseen profit of about 50 percent off West Bank salaries as a result of the deterioration."[47] The union, which claims to represent 2,700 UNRWA employees, reached an interim agreement with UNRWA at the end of March, with UNRWA conceding a 30 percent salary increment for March pending a study of salaries by an ad hoc UNRWA committee.[48] The 214 employees at the Augusta Victoria Hospital in East Jerusalem, which is partly run by UNRWA, carried out a two-day strike in February and then continued with twice-weekly two-hour strikes to give force to their demand to be compensated for the fall of the dinar. A similar interim agreement was reached in this dispute.[49]

The economic crisis was exacerbated by what appeared to be a concerted Israeli attempt to punish Palestinians by economic means for continuing the uprising.[50] Aware of Palestinians' dependence on jobs in Israel, the authorities especially targeted the Palestinian work force employed across the Green Line. For example, the Israeli National Insurance Institute (NII), which pays out pensions, child allowances, and medical insurance to documented workers employed by Israeli companies, stopped payments to a number of residents of East Jerusalem in the fall of 1988. In March 1989, it became clear that at least 1,470 residents were affected by the cutoff. In defense of the measure, NII director-general Mordechai Zipori stated, inter alia, that "as long as they don't boycott our allowances, they shouldn't boycott our taxes either," suggesting political motives.[51]

Likewise, the Israeli Employment Service suddenly announced in March 1989 that it would start to "enforce the law" on employment of West Bank and Gaza residents in East Jerusalem, requiring them to be hired through the government's labor exchanges.[52] Unionists condemned the move, both because documented workers receive only limited services, compared with Israeli workers, on the basis of deductions made from their paychecks by the Employment Service (see chapter 2 above), and because, in the words of one unionist, "demanding West Bankers to get work permits to work in East Jerusalem is an attempt to enforce the illegal annexation of the city to Israel."[53]

The authorities also continued to regulate the daily flow of labor across the Green Line. The Palestinian press reported multiple incidents in which Israeli employers fired their Palestinian workers, usually because of repeated absenteeism.[54] In January 1989, Defense Minister Yitzhak Rabin issued a veiled threat to Palestinians, suggesting that denying work permits to workers might help the army put down the uprising.[55] In February, the military authorities in Gaza told vehicle owners there that they would need a special sticker if they wished to enter Israel. Stickers were provided only to owners who had a "clean record." In Israeli military parlance this means individuals who are not found to have committed regular "violations of public order." The local military commander, Yitzhak Mordechai, declared: "I don't want to punish anyone, but to grant those who deserve it the privilege of working in Israel."[56]

Gaza workers were already hit badly by army curfews, preventing them from reaching their jobs. During the first four months of 1989, for example, the army imposed a total of 210 curfews (lasting 627 days) in areas in the Gaza Strip.[57] The army introduced further restrictions on movement in the summer. In May, a military official was quoted as saying, "The Gaza population should know that we—and not some leaflet—decide when and how life is to be disrupted," a clear portent of things to come.[58] On 6 June, the army launched "Operation Plastic Card," requiring all Gazans who wished to enter Israel to obtain a special permit. While enabling the army to screen Palestinians entering Israel, the cards also constituted "one of a series of measures aimed at tying the individual to the central authority."[59] The cards cost ten dollars, and army officials said that part of the proceeds would be used to install protective windows on vehicles owned by Israeli settlers in Gaza. Referred to by the army as "honesty cards," they were issued only to those who had received a security clearance and had paid the taxes they or their relatives owed.[60] Despite repeated calls by the UNLU on workers to boycott "Operation Plastic Card" and attempts by local activists to confiscate and destroy as many cards as possible throughout the summer, it appeared by the fall that the army had won this battle.

Despite such measures, the UNLU continued to consolidate its hold over the Palestinian masses, including workers, throughout 1989, through specific gains on both local and international levels. Most important among these were the declaration by the PLO of an independent state and the opening of a dialogue between the PLO and the United States at the end of 1988. On this basis, the UNLU felt sufficiently strong to continue urging workers to boycott Israeli institutions, among other actions. In December 1988, the UNLU called on Palestinians "to escalate the struggle for the eviction of Israeli institutions from the state of Palestine, beginning with banks, agencies, labor exchanges, and the like."[61] In two examples, the Israeli labor office in the village of Attil was set on fire in January, and the labor office in Nablus was firebombed one month later.[62] Such attacks continued throughout the uprising.

Recognition and Continuing Factionalism

The fourth stage of the uprising pertaining to developments in the labor movement roughly covers the period from 1989 until the Persian Gulf crisis in 1990. This was a period of international recognition of Palestinian trade unions and their work, and of continuing factionalism inside the movement.

The uprising created vital political openings, not only on the international diplomatic level (most vividly manifested by the start of the United States–PLO dialogue), but also on an institutional level. European trade-union federations, which traditionally have had close links with the Histadrut, began establishing contacts with their Palestinian counterparts in 1988 and 1989. In January 1989, a delegation of the Dutch labor federation (FNV) tied a visit to trade unions in the Occupied Territories to an official visit to the Histadrut, much to the latter's dismay. The FNV mission was not the first by a European federation: Irish, French, Norwegian, and Italian federations had preceded it. But the FNV was the first federation affiliated to the powerful International Confederation of Free Trade Unions (ICFTU)—of which the Histadrut is an affiliate—to visit the Occupied Territories, and it paved the way for an official ICFTU mission later in 1989.

The FNV's two reports on the two parts of its mission are significant, because they set the framework of the debate on Palestinian worker and trade-union rights that ensued at the level of the ICFTU and the ILO in 1989 and 1990. In its report on Palestinian unions, the FNV expressed concern about Israel's violations of trade-union rights: "The impression is that the Israeli authorities . . . are using very harsh measures in a very loose way; on a number of occasions such measures appear prima facie totally unjustified." The report continued: "The position of the Histadrut that all trade unions in the Occupied Territories are front organizations for terror groups is highly disputable."[63] The report encouraged the Histadrut to pursue an independent role vis-à-vis the Israeli government, and called on the Histadrut to respect international norms regarding freedom of association. With regard to the problem of wages and wage deductions of Palestinians employed in Israel, the report argued for a more substantial Histadrut role in protecting these workers' rights, either directly (for example, by ensuring enforcement for Palestinians of collective agreements negotiated by the Histadrut) or indirectly (for example, by pressing the Israeli government to accept ILO mediation on the issue of wage deductions).

In its second report, the FNV took note of the Histadrut's ambivalent position regarding the status of the West Bank and Gaza, viewing the area both as foreign territory and as being in part owned and inhabited by Israeli Jews (including Histadrut members) who consider the area an inalienable part of the Jewish heritage. It criticized the Israeli federation for helping build Israeli settlements and settlement roads in the Occupied Territories (through its construction company, Solel Boneh), and for not opposing violations of Palestinian trade-union rights. In its conclusion, the FNV observed that the Histadrut position throughout the discussions was "extraordinarily politicized, i.e., everything is seen, analyzed, and evaluated in political and electoral terms. This leaves the impression that there is little room for autonomous trade-union policy." This is, ironically, of course the very same charge that the Israeli authorities and the Histadrut level routinely at Palestinian trade unions in the Occupied Territories.[64]

The two FNV documents rely heavily on the 1989 ILO report on the situation in the Occupied Territories, which is more critical of Israeli practices regarding Palestinian workers' rights than are previous reports. The ILO delegation noted, for example, that its observation made the year before "that a more acute and a more responsible trade-union spirit had developed, was even more in evidence this year." The report then went on to say that "interference by the army in the exercise of trade union activities has often taken place in an indiscriminate and exaggerated manner without any account being taken of the genuine trade union activity that exists," creating an "atmosphere of intimidation and a climate of violence which tend to draw workers away from trade unions and make their leaders' work more difficult."[65] As a result of the mission, the FNV proposed to offer financial support for trade-union projects in the Occupied Territories.

In June 1989, the ICFTU, a federation with an estimated membership of one hundred million in eighty countries, sent a large mission to Israel and the Occupied Territories. In a press conference at the conclusion of this unprecedented visit, delegates sharply criticized conditions in the refugee camps, Israel's deportation policy, and the exploitation of Palestinians employed in Israel.[66] Several top Palestinian trade unionists could not attend meetings with the ICFTU because they were in prison or had been deported, including two (Muhammad al-Labadi and Radwan Ziyadeh) who were expelled to Lebanon one day before the delegation arrived, on 29 June. Two of the three federations (the GFTU-WUB and the GFTU-WYM) submitted applications for ICFTU affiliation. In the summer of 1990, no decision had yet been taken on these applications, which were complicated by the fact that the official overarching Palestinian trade-union federation, the Palestinian Trade Union Federation (PTUF), which operates out of Tunis (and which is recognized in the Occupied Territories only by the WYM), is affiliated to the World Confederation of Labour in Prague.

The international missions had the result that for the first time in the history of the Palestinian labor movement, Palestinian trade unions were formally recognized as trade unions by the most powerful exponents of the international labor movement. This recognition will take time to translate into concrete support, although the ICFTU has made public statements in support of Palestinian worker and trade-union rights. In addition, financial support for trade-union projects is being considered.

The ICFTU started to press the Histadrut to open a dialogue with the Palestinian labor federations after the Histadrut mooted the possibility of such a dialogue in its meeting with the ICFTU delegation in July 1989. The Histadrut told the annual ILO mission early in 1990 that it was willing to recognize Palestinian unions, on the condition that "(1) they must be democratically elected unions; (2) they must deal with trade-union matters; and (3) they must not be involved in terrorist activities."[67] Unpublicized informal talks between the Histadrut and Palestinian trade unionists did in fact begin in the spring of 1990. After the Rishon Lezion massacre (in which an Israeli shot dead seven Palestinian workers from Gaza at a "slave market") in May, progressive forces in the Histadrut called on the federation's leadership to open a formal dialogue. A Histadrut official from the Labor Party said: "Until the intifada started, the PLO could be contained. Their unions in the territories were powerless and we were even able to organize in East Jerusalem. With the Rishon incident, there is a new focus on these workers and demands to take steps to protect them. Pressures inside and outside the Histadrut are moving us towards contact with the Palestinian unions."[68]

These developments on the international level were not matched by improvements in the labor situation on the ground. The economic situation, exacerbated by the devaluation of the dinar, deteriorated further in 1989 and 1990. Accurate figures are almost impossible to obtain, even for 1988. The Israeli Central Bureau of Statistics reported a drop in the gross domestic product in the Occupied Territories of 12 to 15 percent, not counting the results of the particularly prosperous olive harvest.[69] There also appeared to be a general trend toward growing unemployment and underemployment. The Israeli building industry has been marked by rampant absenteeism, largely caused by strikes and curfews in the Occupied Territories.[70] Palestinians seem to have lost jobs especially outside the building sector, in agriculture, textiles, and food, for example, and have been replaced to some extent by Israeli workers.[71] Generally, the ILO reports on the basis of its mission in 1990, "statistics indicate a major shift from full-time to part-time work and an upsurge in temporary absentees compared to the years before 1988. . . . The impact of the intifada is particularly evident from a sharp decline in the 1988 weekly work-hours of Palestinian wage-employees both in the Occupied Territories and in Israel." One of the results of this is that Palestinian workers "have apparently learned to 'get by' and their employment seems to have become more varied and at the same time less visible to the authorities in general and the statistician in particular."[72]

In one village that has been particularly dependent on the Israeli labor market in the past, Ya'bad in the Jenin area, labor activists reported an estimated increase in unemployment from 8 percent before the uprising to somewhere between 30 and 40 percent in 1989. Ninety percent of the local work force derives an income from jobs across the Green Line, but in 1989 only one-third of these workers made the daily journey to Israel, and not all of them found work every day. Those unemployed either relied on their extended families, received charity from relief committees, or resorted to agriculture if they had access to land.[73] In neighboring Arrabeh, unionists claimed that out of the eight hundred village workers employed in Israel, at most two hundred had retained their jobs or could still find day labor since the beginning of the uprising.[74] In the West Bank generally, the prolonged closure of schools and universities threw students into the labor market, causing exploitation of child labor and greater unemployment among adults as factories began to hire children. Examples of factories that engaged in this practice include, according to unionists, the Silvana and Diana sweets factories in Ramallah, the Star soap and detergent factory in Ramallah, and the Abdin plastics company in Bethlehem.[75] In Gaza, large numbers of workers reportedly lost their jobs in Israel because they could not obtain plastic cards from the military.

Unions made increasing attempts in 1989 and 1990 to address these problems. Activists reopened offices closed by the military even before the closure order had expired, or operated from other localities, especially at the work sites themselves, sometimes via workers' committees. By the end of 1989, concerted efforts were being made to negotiate collective agreements with Palestinian employers and to find work for the unemployed. A unionist in Ya'bad said that labor disputes were no longer being taken to court but were being resolved between employers and unions, strengthening the unions' role. Jordanian labor law, which for years served as the basis for resolving labor disputes, was largely being replaced by a sense of what is fair, evolving from a dialogue between employers and unions, encouraged by the UNLU.[76] In Bethlehem, unionists fought successfully for compensation for the devaluation of the dinar at Caritas Hospital, and continued negotiations over wages and general conditions with the owners of the Deheisheh stonecutting company and the Bandaq furniture and office equipment workshop in December 1989.[77] In Ramallah, unions negotiated new contracts (dinar wages pegged to the shekel, annual vacations, paid strike days, a forty-hour work week) in a number of factories and workshops, including at Diana sweets company, the Baqir plastic company, the Banjarat al-Sulh office furniture workshop, and the Samir Karam quarry. At Silvana, a local union gained an unprecedented wage rate for seventy women workers at the same level male workers had been earning, in addition to a 10 percent cost-of-living increase, sick leave, and the right to set up a workers' committee.[78]

In 1989, labor organizers came under growing pressure, both from the UNLU and from visiting international labor federations, to reunify the GFTU. Locally, unification was seen as crucial for coordinating labor activity in the face of the worsening economic situation and continuing army repression. Internationally, unification could help in mobilizing political and financial trade-union support for the Palestinian labor movement and Palestinian political objectives. This was easier said than done. Although on the level of the shop floor there has been a good deal of cooperation on

unionist issues between workers from different factions during the uprising, the unions' national leadership proved unable to bridge political differences on the federation level. The reason, one senior union official conceded, was bureaucratic: "All unionists speak the same language. But we
are dealing here with a matter of control, of who wants to be the leader."[79]

Coordinated labor action involving all four main union blocs took place
in Ramallah in February 1989, when activists jointly negotiated a workers'
agreement with the owners of the Star factory. WUB activists say this
effort gave birth to institutionalized coordination in the form of the Higher
Workers' Council, established in Ramallah in the spring of 1989, and na-
tionally in July 1989. Each bloc had one representative on the council,
which began to discuss possible reunification of the three federations with
the participation of the fourth, unaffiliated, bloc, the PUAF.[80] In December 1989, the WYM, the WUB, and the PUAF agreed to set up an executive committee for a reunified GFTU, with the WYM taking two seats,
and the others one each. The PWB rejected the undertaking, but negotiations over formal reunification continued.[81] In January 1990, the Tunis-
based PTUF organized a conference in Cairo to bring about the reunification, inviting the Higher Workers' Council. In the event, the PWB was
the only bloc present from the Occupied Territories, because its second-
in-command George Hazboun happened to be abroad already, while
Mahmoud Dweik, 'Adnan Natsheh, Sabri Safadi, Salah Qteish, and
Shaher Sa'ad, representing the other blocs, were prohibited from travel
by the army.[82] Following the Cairo conference, the PWB proposed an
arrangement for reunification that was adopted (after some wrangling) by
the WYM and others, except the WUB, in February. According to this
arrangement, the executive committee of the reunified GFTU would have
sixteen members: six from the WYM, three from the PWB, two from the
WUB, two from the PUAF, and three persons who identified with other
factions in the national movement.[83]

The WUB rejected this arrangement on the basis that it was "political,
not unionist: From a unionist viewpoint, the working class is not represented correctly. The workers are not represented [in the new GFTU],
and the representatives who are there are not workers."[84] WUB officials
claim that the three unaffiliated unionists were not labor organizers but
representatives of tiny political factions that basically kowtow to Fatah,
and that the entire arrangement was engineered by Yasser Arafat who
"wanted to take control of the institutions in the Occupied Territories by
letting Fatah's weight count."[85] The accusation has echoes from the split of
1981, when Fatah played its political weight against the unionist strength
of the PWB and WUB.

On 1 March, the GFTU was "reunified" on the basis described above.
An executive committee of fourteen members was established (with two
seats left open for the WUB, in case it changed its mind) for a maximum

period of two years, after which free general elections were to be held. In the intervening period, the GFTU was to develop new bylaws and a new program, to solve the problem of parallel unions (by reunifying them), to unify existing collective agreements, and to start developing a new labor law (in lieu of the Jordanian one) on the basis of international standards. Individual trade unions were to hold elections within a year.[86]

Since 1 March 1990, there have in effect been two parallel GFTUs, one controlled by the WUB and one incorporating all other blocs but effectively controlled by the WYM. Inability of the union blocs to resolve their differences underlines the depth of political rivalries inside and outside the Occupied Territories. The WYM has responded to the WUB's claim that not all the representatives on the executive committee are unionists by stating that elections will prove who represents workers and who does not. The WYM has given an identical answer to the WUB's complaint that it received one fewer seat than the PWB even though it is larger than the PWB.[87] The WUB has expressed no interest in further negotiations, and has also pinned its hope on future elections. One union official said, "The important thing is that we are organizing on the ground." He said the WUB would "step up its efforts so that the workers will get to know the unionists' faces." Once "real elections" ("not fake ones on paper") are held in individual unions, "the workers will press the GFTU to observe democratic procedures, and hold elections in the GFTU on the basis of proportional representation."[88]

From all appearances, the "unification" was engineered by the mainstream forces in the national movement to extend and facilitate their diplomatic maneuverings with Western governments and nongovernmental organizations. The new executive committee does not reflect the relative size of the four union blocs in the Occupied Territories, and includes members who are not known as labor organizers. The GFTU's "reunification" is therefore a continuation of the factionalism that has beset the labor movement since the late 1970s, but in a different guise. Typically, the conflict between the new GFTU and the GFTU-WUB began to reverberate locally when, in March, the GFTU canceled a collective agreement reached between the Higher Workers' Council and the Nabil Jidde' workshop in Ramallah in February (before the "reunification"), and replaced it with a new one, resurrecting the specter of parallel unions.[89]

Factionalism also entered into attempts to settle a serious labor dispute at the Malhis shoe factory in Nablus, which employs over three hundred workers, in the spring of 1990. The workers' committee at the factory had approached the management in January to negotiate a new contract. The committee consisted of five Shabbibe activists linked to the WYM. The WYM was brought in, and negotiations took place in February after workers had carried out a four-day warning strike. On 20 March, the WYM recommended that workers go on strike since the negotiations had

yielded no results. Following an eight-day strike and intervention by outside mediators, the WYM and Malhis management agreed to settle the
conflict, accepting only one of the workers' thirteen demands, a pay raise
of twenty-five dollars a month. The workers rejected the accord and in-
structed the workers' committee to establish contacts with other union
blocs to see if they could resolve the conflict. The WUB then intervened
with the WYM, but the WYM's general secretary, Shaher Sa'ad, proceeded to sign a new contract with the Malhis management. Soon slogans
signed by Fatah activists appeared on walls in Nablus, denouncing Sa'ad's
action. Malhis declared the strike illegal and deducted strike days from
the workers' paychecks. Because it was the end of the month, most workers decided to go back to work, but the workers' committee, supported by
some thirty workers, continued to press for the original demands. Malhis
then "terminated the services" of a total of twenty-nine workers, including
the five members of the workers' committee, "for economic reasons."[90]
Similar problems occurred at the Nablus municipality, which owed its
employees five months' back salary in June 1990.

In the face of such problems, the ILO's assessment of the situation of
trade unions in the Occupied Territories in 1990 leads to mixed reactions:

> The ILO remains convinced that a genuine trade union structure exists with
> which it would be desirable to enter into dialogue. The recent trade union
> unification seems to indicate the Palestinian organisations' wish to develop a
> professional approach in order to enhance their collective bargaining capacity
> and thereby improve the conditions of work and life of the Palestinian work-
> ers. The Israeli authorities should recognise this development as well as the
> credibility of these trade union organisations.[91]

On the one hand, recognition of the Palestinian labor movement is a positive development; it will make possible new projects, and will provide
needed protection for workers. On the other hand, continuing factionalism, which is being encouraged by the new international interest in the
Palestinian labor movement, has the potential to alienate workers from
the movement, and may therefore lead to the delegitimation locally of a
movement that has just received legitimacy on an international level.
This, and not the repressive actions by the Israeli military authorities, is
the greatest threat to the future of the Palestinian labor movement.

THE WOMEN'S MOVEMENT DURING THE UPRISING

The early days of the uprising yielded striking images of women marching
in the street, schoolgirls throwing stones at soldiers, older women carrying baskets of stones on their heads to supply younger demonstrators,
women arguing and tussling with soldiers to win the release of an arrested

boy, and so on.[92] Women assumed a profile they had not had on such a scale in public before, at least not as part of the resistance to the occupation. Soon commentators were referring to the intifada not only as a "shaking off" of military rule, but as a social revolution in its own right, in which the younger generation was rebelling against the older one, street activists were challenging the authority of the PLO, and women were casting off the yoke of gender oppression.

In the third year of the uprising, the above interpretation of women's role in the revolt seemed increasingly premature: despite women's activism, their social and political position in Palestinian society had hardly changed. Yet to write off the intifada as a total loss for women's rights would be wrong: women made important progress in raising consciousness of their rights in society, and more women were mobilized than ever before in organizational structures that channeled their energies toward satisfying, beyond demonstrations, the needs of a society under siege. Perhaps most importantly, they began to address in a serious manner the sensitive subject of the rights and role of women in the struggle for national liberation, a subject to which only a handful of committed activists had paid lip service before the uprising.

Young women demonstrators, usually affiliated with the women's committees, set the tone of this debate in the very first days of the uprising in December 1987, when Gaza was in flames but the West Bank, except for a few isolated refugee camps such as Balata, was still quiet. They claim they were the first to be out in the streets of Ramallah, Nablus, and elsewhere, challenging not only the occupation, but men: "On 11 December, we were out in the streets of Ramallah shouting 'Where are you, men of Ramallah?!'" one activist recalled.[93] The tone was defiant, the action self-assertive. Following this, relations between men and women were never quite the same.

As in the case of the labor movement, it is legitimate to ask whether the women's movement, which emerged from the youthful activism in schools and universities in the 1970s, was sufficiently prepared in December 1987 to convert mobilization, its proven strength, into collective action, and to transform itself from a mobilizational framework into an institution that could become part of the future Palestinian state. I will address this question by surveying three aspects of women's participation in the uprising: women's actions, women's organizations, and women's discourse.

Women's Activism

What set the uprising apart from the preceding years in terms of women's activism was that those who participated in direct confrontations with soldiers were no longer only students and longtime activists, but women of all ages and from all sectors of society, especially in the villages and refugee camps. These were women who had been courted by the women's committees for several years, through nationalist-oriented literacy and skill-training programs, but who, despite their sympathies, had not joined any formal frameworks. The uprising provided the occasion for these women to leave their homes and act for the national cause in a situation of real emergency that required the energies of all. "Because our program [before the uprising] was explicitly political, economic, and cultural, women were afraid to join," one Nablus activist explained. "But during the uprising, our program addresses reality. Now women are more eager to join, because they want to address problems in their real lives."[94]

From the early days of the uprising, women's activism was part spontaneous, part organized by the women's committees, which seized the occasion to mobilize their own members and sympathizers, and absorb new recruits. "We were not surprised by the intifada," said another Nablus activist, "and we were quick to adjust our activities. . . . Many young women came to us at the beginning of the uprising saying they wanted to do something, and the framework was there."[95] The committees deployed their strongest resources: child-care centers extended their schedules to accomodate women who were active in the uprising; health-education classes were put to good use as casualties mounted in neighborhoods, especially as a result of beatings and tear gas. The FPWAC reported: "Our members in villages, camps and cities have taken in the injured and administered first aid whenever possible in an attempt to prevent the inevitable arrests at hospitals." And: "The day-care centers are open seven days a week now rather than the usual five and one-half day schedule, and are keeping late hours."[96] Whereas before the uprising the committees had to organize lectures or film screenings to recruit new members, the uprising made it possible for unorganized women to involve themselves directly in the committees' activities, and become members.[97]

The women's committees lent their experience and leadership to the new structures that emerged during the first weeks of the uprising, especially the popular committees in neighborhoods, villages, and refugee camps. In the beginning, the work of the women's committees and popular committees became indistinguishable, as women activists deployed their energies fully in the service of the uprising and its specific requirements. In the towns, neighborhood committees sought "to pinpoint problems in the community and to find ways to solve them, to disseminate information on daily activities and to encourage the residents' participation in mass activities."[98] Committee members would fan out through the neighborhood after an army raid to survey the human and material damage, and draw emergency services to where these were needed. They would pay solidarity visits to the families of martyrs and detainees, and provide material assistance whenever necessary. In the villages and camps, popular committees had a similar function, though women played a lesser role in them.[99]

For example, activists from the women's committee of Arrabeh in the Jenin district joined the local popular committee and became active in working on behalf of prisoners and their families (contacting lawyers, sending clothes to prison, arranging prison visits via the Red Cross), producing food and handicrafts (including Qur'ans) to promote the domestic market, and teaching children in their homes. In addition, women demonstrated and distributed leaflets, discussing politics openly (for the first time) with villagers who remained unconvinced. The committee reported an increase in active membership from twenty before the uprising to over one hundred at the end of 1989.[100]

Throughout the uprising, the women's committees organized marches, while activist women (and many schoolgirls) participated in demonstrations and confrontations with the army. The level of participation differed from locality to locality. Ramallah residents claim that the women's march on International Women's Day 1988 (8 March) was the largest in the town's history.[101] In Hebron, a fairly religious and conservative town in the southern West Bank, it has been much more difficult to draw women into the street: "If a hundred women turn out for a march, that's very good," one activist said.[102] Slogans included not only demands for an independent state, but demands for women's liberation as well. In Ramallah on 8 March, "women unfurled banners, posters and flags and began their silent procession to the center of town. The banners and slogans called for women's liberation, for an independent state with the P.L.O. as its leadership, for an end to the occupation, and for an end to Israeli brutality."[103] It is remarkable that despite the prominence of women in such actions, the number of casualties among women remained relatively low.[104]

As the uprising evolved, new situations created new demands, which were articulated by the UNLU and then translated into specific calls to action by the women's committees. In a landmark joint program of the four committees on 8 March 1988, the committees called on women to participate in popular committees and trade unions, to boycott work on strike days, to teach children despite the closure of schools, to confront soldiers and settlers, and to promote a "home economy" of locally produced food and clothes.[105] When some merchants tried to circumvent the commercial strike by selling wares on the side for a higher price, popular committees were charged with the task of monitoring prices, and of initiating a boycott if the merchant did not comply with UNLU directives. Women were prominent in this effort. Likewise, when the UNLU's calls for a boycott of Israeli-produced goods intensified early in 1989, the committees were active in enforcing the measure. When schools were shut by the army in 1988, the popular committees provided alternative education to children, teaching in homes, churches, and mosques. And in response to the food shortages caused by army curfews and the boycott of Israeli products, women's committees began to set up production cooperatives, manufacturing relatively simple food products for the local market.

Although women were active in popular committees, it is not clear that they made any gains in their rights as women through their involvement in the popular struggle. On the positive side, one could argue that women for the first time engaged in collective political action in the streets, occupying a space usually reserved only for men. Participants included a wide range of women from all sectors of society. Their politicization is bound to have a long-term impact on their role in society. On the negative side, as Islah Jad has argued, the "essential goal" of the popular committees was merely "to find new members for the mass organizations of each faction," and "women's role in the popular committees became an extension of what it traditionally had been in the society: teaching and rendering services," without ever going beyond that.[106]

In the only clear effort to transcend the strictures on women's role in Palestinian society, the women's committees began to establish women's production cooperatives. The cooperatives constitute one of the more significant achievements of the uprising, although they have not nearly accomplished the goals that were envisioned. Neither are the goals very clear. UPWC pamphlets assert that the objective of the committee's "Our Production Is Our Pride" project was "to build the basis for women's emancipation by constructing economic projects."[107] Of the project's five main aims and principles, two pertain to women: "the transformation of women's traditional role in the domestic economy into a positive role in the national economy," and "the provision of opportunities for the participation of women in economic enterprises as a basis for economic independence and social emancipation."[108] However, the UPWC has not explained how a "positive role in the national economy" will enhance women's social and political status in society and lead to social emancipation, nor how the cooperatives can contribute to this transformation. Summing up the project's achievements after only a few months of operation, the UPWC noted that "more and more women [had become] involved in the social and economic process. This qualitative level of participation makes women an integral part of the development of our national economy and society."[109] The UPWC's main cooperatives are in Beitillo near Ramallah, Sa'ir in the Hebron district, and in the Jabalya refugee camp in Gaza.

Other committees set up cooperatives of their own. The establishment of the UPWWC's cooperative in the village of Idhna, near Hebron, "helped bring the issue of women onto the agenda," claimed one activist.

Participation in the cooperative "increased women's social consciousness. Women realized that they had the same abilities as men. It helped them get out of the family circle, and help out in the bad economic situation, as men were either in jail or unemployed."[110] Women are in charge of all stages of the productive process, including marketing, and distribute the profits among themselves. Where marketing is a problem, the women's committees make their own outlets available for sales. The various co-ops have produced food (fruit juices, pickled vegetables, jams), clothes, embroidery, and picture frames. The number of co-ops remains fairly limited. More commonly, women affiliated with the committees produce goods in their homes, which are then sold by the committees through their regular outlets in the urban centers. Needless to say, such production does result in a measure of economic independence for women, but does not provide the stimulus for women to leave their homes and become more active in the life of their community rather than their immediate families. As Islah Jad has argued about the cooperative effort, "setting up a women's production cooperative in the countryside does not automatically lead to changes in the gender-based division of labor, nor to an upward reevaluation by men of women's work."[111]

The women's committees, the main engines behind the activism of women in popular committees and other frameworks, were enormously successful during the first months of the uprising. Building on their grass-roots experience, they took advantage of the relative protection they enjoyed from military oppression by providing services to communities in crisis, even during army curfews. Although necessity forced this activism, the committees' traditional focus on education and training suffered during the first year of the uprising. After the nineteenth PNC session and the declaration of a Palestinian state in November 1988, the committees, as well as other grass-roots organizations, began a critical self-evaluation. It was then decided to keep the work of the women's committees completely separate from that of the popular committees, and to return to the committees' original program. The rationale behind this shift lay in the consideration that the women's committees were not just vehicles for popular action—a role filled anyway by the popular committees—but were well-developed networks that could contribute to the building of the infrastructure for the future independent state. Organization then became the main theme.

Women's Organization

The daily struggle in the streets brought activists from the various factions in the national movement closer together. In the words of one activist, "because of neighborhood work, women from the different blocs are now blending, developing strong personal relationships, and struggling side by side."[112] In the women's movement this led to greater formal cooperation, and eventually crystallized in the establishment of the Higher Women's Council (HWC) in December 1988, which united the four committees in one forum. The roots of this new and close collaborative effort lay in the move toward coordination between the committees in 1984, well before the uprising, and the reconciliation of PLO factions at the eighteenth PNC meeting in Algiers in April 1987, a few months before the uprising.[113] During the first year of the intifada, the committees issued joint statements, such as the one published on the occasion of International Women's Day in March 1988, quoted above, or the communiqué denouncing the deportation of nine (male) political activists issued in October 1988.[114] The HWC, formed on the first anniversary of the intifada, issued its first joint statement only three months later, on the occasion of International Women's Day, 8 March 1989.

The four committees each sent one representative to the HWC. The council's aim was to unify the women's movement around the twin themes of women's social and people's national struggle, and to find a proper balance between the two in order to prevent the return of women to their traditional social roles after the national victory, as occurred—so activists remind their constituents again and again—in Algeria in the 1960s. Women leaders felt that only through joint efforts could such crucial questions as education and the legal situation created by the religiously based family law be addressed effectively.[115] The HWC was also more suited than women's committees individually to interpret and carry out the directives of the UNLU, which itself reflected the same four political tendencies. The HWC decentralized by encouraging women's committees throughout the Occupied Territories to set up regional "unified women's councils." The latter coordinated women's activities locally, distributing UNLU leaflets and issuing leaflets of their own, either interpreting UNLU directives or articulating positions pertaining to conditions prevailing in their own regions. The Unified Women's Council in the Jenin area, for example, unites three of the four blocs—the FPWAC, UPWC, and WCSW (the UPWWC having little activity in the north)—and has coordinated the committees' regional activities.[116]

The HWC was later renamed the "Unified Women's Council," reportedly after it became a branch of the GUPW, the official women's organization of the PLO outside the Occupied Territories. Differences inside the council occurred, usually reflecting political conflicts at the level of the national movement. The UPWC, for example, has at times frozen its membership on the council, which has proven a handicap to the council's work. The UPWC claims that, among other matters, it has called for more than coordination: it wants a common program for the four committees, but they cannot agree on one.[117]

While unifying the women's movement, coordination did not amount to formal unification of the four committees. The committees continued operating side by side, following their separate programs according to their own separate bylaws. Some regional committees claim to have held elections, while others clearly have not. The UPWWC branch in Nablus did not hold elections in the first two years of the uprising.[118] One UPWWC leader said that because of army raids on committee offices, the committee no longer kept membership records, and that this had also made elections difficult.[119] The UPWC has claimed that its branch committees have held local and regional elections,[120] and so has the FPWAC.[121]

The women's movement has been relatively insulated from military repression, in all likelihood because of the authorities' traditional view of women. Several women activists have spent time in jail, including administrative detention, or have been restricted in their movement. Maha Mustaqlem-Nassar of the UPWC went on a hunger strike in prison in October 1989 after being subjected to physical and psychological abuse, she told her attorney. She was released without charges shortly afterward.[122] The FPWAC's Fadwa al-Labadi and Amal Wahdan have related similar experiences.[123] Activists also report army raids on committee offices, including the UPWWC office in Salfit in March 1988 (in which the army damaged two knitting machines, chairs, and doors) and Beit Dajan in September 1989 (in which the army confiscated three sewing machines).[124] In a raid on the FPWAC office in Arrabeh in August 1988, soldiers damaged two sewing machines, windows, and benches.[125] The UPWC claims the army closed three of its kindergartens, each for the period of one year, during the uprising.[126] Generally, however, women took advantage of the army's reluctance to detain women and harass women's committees by stepping up their efforts, both individually in the street, and organizationally.[127]

The active participation of the women's committees in the uprising and the consolidation of the women's movement did not translate into women activists taking a prominent role in the leadership of the national movement. Although it is likely that women at one point or another have made up part of the UNLU, generally the UNLU's members have been men, as the language of UNLU communiqués (discussed below) and the pattern of arrests and deportations suggests.[128] To what extent women have been integrated into the leadership of the PLO factions is impossible to say because the factions are illegal and therefore operate underground. In terms of public leadership, women have, with one exception, acted only as representatives of the women's movement. The exception is the representation of the four political tendencies in Non-Governmental Organization (NGO) meetings at the United Nations. In the June 1990 conference on Palestine at the U.N. in New York, for example, the FPWAC's Zahira Kamal and the UPWC's Maha Mustaqlem represented their political factions, the Unity Bloc and the Action Front, respectively.[129]

Women's Discourse

When women challenged men to join them in street demonstrations during the first days of the uprising in the West Bank, and when they raised joint slogans for women's liberation and the establishment of an independent state during marches on 8 March 1988 and afterwards, they placed the issue of women's status firmly on the Palestinian nationalist agenda. Because of the uprising, women could no longer be ignored: coming out of their homes for reasons both economic (male breadwinners being in jail) and political (protection of their families and communities), they created the opportunity and obtained leverage to press for issues of their own collective concern. In the third year of the uprising, these steps forward had not translated into concrete gains.

On the positive side, Rita Giacaman and Penny Johnson argue, despite the fact that women "have enlarged or extended their traditional role rather than adopting a completely new role," aspects of their role in the uprising "have become a source of resistance because women have transformed their family responsibilities to encompass the entire community."[130] An activist in the village of Kufr Na'meh (Ramallah) reported that women participate in marches, demonstrations, and confrontations with the army, and get injured or killed; that they go to town to sell produce in the market, visit relatives in prison, and join political events in Ramallah and Jerusalem; and that they have strengthened their role in the family, often have control over money, can refuse to obey certain orders, and can decide which school their children will attend. She called the role of women "outstanding" compared with the years before the uprising.[131]

A UPWWC activist said, however, that although women's participation in the uprising had put the issue of women on the agenda and women for the first time began to discuss their status in society, these changes were meeting stiff resistance. "Our position in the political struggle has changed," she said, "but our position in social life has not."[132] A Nablus activist complained that "men are still making the decisions. If a woman is active, the neighbors start talking. So it will take a long time of struggle, and we won't automatically get our rights as women when we get our state."[133]

On the political level it appears also that although women have made certain strides forward, they still have a distance to go. A perusal of UNLU communiqués reveals not only a shocking disregard for women's issues and the role of women in the uprising, but also an attitude toward women that is profoundly traditional, patriarchal, and condescending. For example, when the UNLU addresses the participants in the intifada, it invariably refers to "our sons," "brother doctors," "brother workers," and "brother businessmen and grocers."[134] When women are mentioned, it is usually as "mothers," in relation to someone else—their sons; or else they are bunched in with children and old men, all people "who are suffering."[135] Women are commended for their "steadfastness," for "standing firm," and for "protecting the uprising" (not for participating in it).[136] In Communiqué no. 21, the UNLU invites "students, workers, merchants, peasants, and strike forces" to carry out acts of civil disobedience. Women are notably excluded, despite the obvious activism of the women's committees.

Thus women's roles are marginalized; women are cast as protectors of the uprising and of those who supposedly carry out the uprising: their male relatives. There are, however, slight departures from this general pattern. In Communiqué no. 5, the UNLU called on "mothers, sisters, and daughters to work side by side with their husbands, sons, and brothers." But again here, despite the call to action, it is not a given that women would "work side by side" with men, nor is it recognized that in fact they had been doing so from the beginning of the uprising.[137] In August 1988, when the UNLU tried to fill the institutional vacuum created by King Hussein's formal withdrawal of his claim to the West Bank by reinforcing the popular committees and other grass-roots organizations, it for the first time made a strong appeal to the women's committees, among others. The UNLU reminded the women's committees that they had to "shoulder a special responsibility in organizing sit-ins and other appropriate activities" in solidarity with male and female prisoners. After all the committees had been doing during the preceding eight months, this must have seemed a puny, if not offensive, reminder to women organizers.[138]

International Women's Day proved to be the only occasion when the UNLU devoted any attention to women's participation in the uprising, but again the record is mixed. In 1988, the UNLU included a call for demonstrations on 8 March as part of its weekly schedule of events.[139] In 1989, the UNLU went so far as to "salute the Palestinian woman" and to declare its "admiration for her heroism in the national struggle." The UNLU referred to women's organizations, urging a "strengthening [of] the unity of the women's movement in the state of Palestine within the framework of the Unified Women's Council." But again, all references were made in the context of the UNLU's weekly schedule.[140] In 1990, the

UNLU finally went so far as to name its communiqué "The Woman's Call," and reserved a special section to women, but made sure they were referred to in the "proper" context, in relation to men:

> Progressive nations celebrate International Women's Day on 8 March as a day of struggle for the world's women's masses. While celebrating this great day, in the name of all the sons of our people, we congratulate the world's women's masses and the masses of the Palestinian women's movement and its vanguard organizations, hailing every working woman, woman struggler, and housewife, and especially our imprisoned strugglers. We also pay tribute to the struggling role of the Palestinian uprising's women's movement, to every mother who has lost a son, daughter, husband, or brother, and to every woman who meets with a struggling daughter or a heroic son from behind the Bastille of the Zionist enemy.

The UNLU then moved on to congratulate mothers on Mother's Day, calling their "sufferings and pain the source of our strength and determination." Almost in the same breath, the UNLU exhorted "our sons at school to adhere to school times," and praised Palestinians for making history "through the blood of their sons."[141]

The Palestinian leadership in the diaspora has shown itself scarcely more astute. The Palestinian declaration of independence first makes the lofty pledge that "governance will be based on principles of social justice, equality, and nondiscrimination in public rights on grounds of race, religion, color or sex," and then proceeds to define women's status in Palestinian society, stating: "We render special tribute to the brave Palestinian woman, guardian of sustenance and life, keeper of our people's perennial flame."[142] Clearly, the only roles assigned to women in the new state are to protect, preserve, and procreate.

Palestinian women activists do not appear to have publicly challenged the leadership's approach to the question of women. To the contrary, one occasionally stumbles on interesting rationalizations of the approach. An activist in Arrabeh (Jenin) contended that the UNLU preferred not to focus on women in its communiqués because it did not want to draw attention to them, with a view to protecting them, because it understood women's important role in the uprising.[143] On the other hand, the women's movement has sought to capitalize on the declaration of independence by reminding women that they were "entitled to preserve all the gains already achieved on the national level," but that they "must also continue fighting for their liberation and for a radical and comprehensive solution to their economic, social, and gender problems." Most important, perhaps, women were told that they "must participate in developing legislation and a constitution, which will give women equal rights with men."[144] Use of the word "entitled" suggests a certain defensiveness, but the overall tone is assertive, as the committees seek to translate political gains into concrete steps toward furthering women's rights.

In the second year of the uprising, the UPWWC put the following questions to its membership:

> Has the intifada changed the perception of women's role in Palestinian society? Has it changed the way women themselves perceive their roles? These questions have to be reckoned with by the Palestinian women's movement to enable it to keep pace with the fast-moving events of the intifada. The intifada has confronted the women's movement with a number of challenges. How do we safeguard the achievements of Palestinian women and maintain the prominence of the political status they have achieved in the popular uprising by virtue of their active participation in the struggle and in the confrontation with the army? What are the safeguards against a recession of the post-intifada role of women? What assurances do women have that they will not be asked to return to their traditional, domestic roles if and when national independence is achieved?[145]

The UPWWC reports that members in branch meetings frequently raise the question, "When can we have birth control?"[146] The UPWWC concludes that "if the Palestinian women's movement is to grow and develop, it must address itself to women's issues."[147]

The other two progressive committees have echoed such sentiments. In lectures, meetings, and publications, women activists set off a lively debate on the relationship between the women's struggle and the national struggle. One UPWWC representative said:

> We haven't had a feminist agenda. We have been preoccupied with political concerns, and as a result we often became traditional in our approach, because we didn't want to become alienated in our society. We weren't necessarily aware that we were not on the right track. Recently, we have come to realize that this approach doesn't work. We realize that if we don't raise issues now, we won't be able to push them later on, and we'll be abused by the national movement. We are struggling for independence, but we don't want to compromise our role as women. The issue has come up now because we have realized through our work in the intifada how important our role really is. This has given us confidence.[148]

The UPWWC therefore started holding lectures about early marriages, divorce, personal status law, the division of labor at home, and other social problems relevant to the lives of women. The FPWAC has also stressed the importance of addressing women's issues, and proposed concentrating efforts on unifying the women's movement, intensifying recruitment of new members, offering skill training, getting women involved in production cooperatives, providing practical health education, revising the existing personal status laws, promoting literacy and secondary education, and encouraging women to participate in committees supporting the national struggle.[149]

Committees report that when women seek their advice about problems they face at home, activists will attempt to mediate, either as women's committees or individually. One activist said members of her committee had intervened on behalf of women who had been beaten by their husbands on more than one occasion, but not in name of the committee for fear of being evicted from the village.[150] Another organizer said, however, "Our committee will visit families if women are beaten or prevented from leaving the home. But the point is that women have to change their ideas about themselves so that they can solve their problems themselves. So all we do is to exchange with other women our own experiences."[151] Discussions in the homes of women are also the first step in the process of bringing women out of their homes and, eventually, it is hoped, into the women's committees. Education of men as well as women is key, as is encouraging emulation. Activists talk with the fathers of prospective members, using an "approach of respect," according to organizers in Hebron. "Families in the villages eventually see what the committee is doing, and we gain their respect. We convince them by the way we are. Often the men themselves are involved in the uprising, but they feel that it's a shame for women to participate and they are concerned for their safety."[152] One young activist said, "In the beginning, I felt a certain timidity from the young men who ideologically believe women should take a more active role, but who also hold traditional social values. But I think this interaction between men and women will become more natural."[153]

In 1988 and 1989, women in the Occupied Territories came under growing pressure from the new Islamic movement to don a head-scarf (hijab) in public. Many secular women, especially community activists, resisted such pressures, but by the end of 1989, the campaign had succeeded in the Gaza Strip to the point where women could no longer appear in public without headscarves, and it had made major inroads in the West Bank as well. Neither the UNLU nor the women's committees themselves excelled in countering the practices of the Islamic Resistance Movement (HAMAS), and this may have contributed to the defeat in Gaza.[154] Some female activists later tried to explain the national leadership's and their own inaction by claiming that

> we couldn't act earlier in Gaza, because the time was not right. The intifada was at its height, and we didn't want to create internal differences while fighting the occupation. Because HAMAS will throw stones at us, we will throw stones at them, and the army meanwhile can take a break. Only now that the intifada has a solid grounding is it possible to address these issues. It is late now to act against this religious coercion, but not yet too late.[155]

Such setbacks, however, do not augur well for the prospects of achieving further gains for women, and have undermined the credibility of the women's movement. The status of women in the intifada and in Palestinian society in general will therefore to a large extent depend on whether the women's committees, as the vanguard of the women's movement, will be able to match their important objectives, which they have articulated with growing vigor after the declaration of independence in November 1988, with concrete action.

A Preliminary Assessment

The UPWC has described the uprising as the "historical embrace" of the objective factor of forty years of occupation, dispossession, and repression, and the subjective factor of political consciousness, popular mobilization, and active resistance: "The popular uprising was not the result of a one-day struggle, but it is the climax of continuous Palestinian struggle, a struggle rooted in and supported by political awareness and mobilization in popular committees, [mass] organizations, [labor] unions, etc."[156] The FPWAC claims that its "ten years as a grass-roots organization of women—where all are viewed as potential leaders—has given it an effective role in the current uprising, itself a grass-roots movement of all sections of the Palestinian population."[157]

These appear to be fair assessments of the role that the popular organizations existing before the uprising have played during the insurrection that began in 1987. As Giacaman and Johnson note, "while not the generators of women's mass participation in the uprising, the [women's] committees played a major role in shaping that participation."[158] So, of course, did the trade unions and other grass-roots organizations, such as the medical relief committees. The individual performances of these organizations during the uprising differ, however, as the cases of the labor and women's movements illustrate.

What trade unions and women's committees have in common is that each forsook the routine of its trade-unionist and educational work for direct political action during the first year of the uprising. Each lent its infrastructure, experience, and leadership to help the national movement take control of the streets and shepherd mass action according to the directives of the UNLU-PLO. At the end of the first year, when popular committees had proven their skills in mobilizing the masses and sustaining the revolt, and after the PLO had declared an independent state and urged further institutionalization of the intifada, trade unions and women's committees reverted to their original tasks. They were able to expand their programs and infuse them with new ideas and energies, reflecting the gains made by the national leadership on the political level.

The trade unions made a halfhearted attempt at reunification and began to negotiate new collective contracts with employers, taking into account the new conditions created by the uprising. They also began looking into the possibility of developing a new labor law, and started to seek protection for Palestinian workers from the Histadrut and international labor federations. The women's committees expanded their educational programs, opened production cooperatives, and started a crucial debate about the role and status of women in Palestinian society before and after independence. They also made new contacts abroad, and likewise began looking into the possibility of changing the existing personal status law, which has been a major stumbling block to the attainment of women's rights.

There are important differences between the trade unions and women's committees, however, suggesting that they were not equally prepared to deal with the uprising once it burst forth in December 1987. From the very beginning, the women's movement was much more intimately involved in the daily affairs of the uprising than was the labor movement. A number of factors explain this. First, the Palestinian working class could not afford to expend most of its energies on demonstrations and civil disobedience, because families needed incomes to buy food. The role of workers, therefore, was to carry out the instructions of the UNLU as well as they could, while continuing to work and sustain their families and, by implication, the uprising. In the words of one trade unionist: "The uprising equals life. This means that it is the task of workers to bring in money for others who are active in resistance to the occupation."[159] The UNLU, for its part, was careful, especially after the first three or four heady months of the uprising had passed, to assume a pragmatic approach toward workers, making only demands that they could satisfy.

Second, many trade-union offices were closed by the army at the beginning of the uprising, while unionists became active intifada coordinators in the popular committees, leaving labor organizing temporarily behind. And third, once these labor activists returned to their unionist duties, interfactional rivalries continued to mar such effective trade-union work as collective bargaining, since employers were able to play one bloc against another. In sum, despite their solid framework, popular base, accumulated experience, and credible leadership, trade unions have played a relatively limited role in the uprising.

By contrast, the women's movement delivered a remarkable performance, acting in those areas where the labor movement was weak. Given the low percentage of women in the labor force, the participation of women in the uprising did not lead to a significant loss of income for most Palestinian families. The army paid scant attention to the activities of the women's movement, resorting to no more than the usual harassments. Although more women activists were imprisoned during the uprising than before, their numbers were still limited. Women's committee offices therefore continued to serve as centers for mass mobilization. Finally, the women's movement was able to consolidate dialogue and cooperation among the four main committees in the form of a coordinating higher council. Even though differences of opinion have occurred among the factions, they did not have the debilitating effects witnessed in the labor movement. Indeed, it is a surprise, given the success of the informal coordinating apparatus set up by the women's movement, that the labor movement continues to insist on reunifying the GFTU (which requires a single structure and elections), whereas it could perhaps function much more smoothly through an informal higher workers' council emphasizing coordinated action rather than uniformity in structure.

In short, in the third year of the uprising, the labor and women's movements had proven their worth. Not only did they survive the changes wrought by the uprising; they deployed their considerable resources to sustain the intifada and then were actually able to capitalize on the uprising's political accomplishments, at least to some extent—the women's committees more so than trade unions. Yet in one respect the women's movement was still lagging behind the labor movement: political representation. Clearly, several top union officials have been leaders in their political factions and have represented these in the UNLU. The same cannot be said for the women's movement, despite its great activism and achievements on the ground. This can be explained in part by the conservative mood that swept the Occupied Territories beginning in 1989, which is expressed in the emergence of the Islamic Resistance Movement. By the summer of 1990, the nationalists had not succeeded in forging a proper strategy to counter this tendency, and in fact seemed to prefer to avoid a battle with the Islamists even as they appeared to be losing ground. A second reason for women's limited political representation probably lies in the domination of the national movement by forces that, as Islah Jad has pointed out, have indicated little interest in social issues, including the rights of women, and have generally held that all Palestinians should galvanize their energies to struggle for an independent state, and that women will obtain their rights (almost automatically, it is suggested) after independence.[160]

These, then, were the challenges the popular organizations were facing as the intifada approached the end of its third year: to overcome factionalism, to counter organized bigotry effectively, to devise new strategies to sustain collective resistance to the occupation, to build the institutions that would carry the revolt to independence, and to be prepared to fight for workers' and women's rights now—and then.

Chapter Seven

CONCLUSION

THE PALESTINIAN UPRISING should not have been a surprise to anyone. A particular conjunction of forces is required for mass mobilization to occur in any social situation, and for mobilization successfully to culminate in collective action. This conjunction of forces was present in the West Bank and Gaza in 1987. The population of the Occupied Territories was disaffected with military rule, as were the Dutch under German occupation, the Namibians under South African rule, the Afghans under Russian occupation, and the Algerians under French colonial rule, to give only a few examples from the sorry record of twentieth-century history. In the West Bank and Gaza a peculiar combination of settler-colonialism and military rule engendered a process of integration of the Occupied Territories into Israel that entailed parallel drives of administrative takeover, economic exploitation, and increasing land alienation and the settlement of Jews in the area. The effects of Israeli actions were felt by Palestinians in their everyday lives, as the economic pinch hurt landowners, shopkeepers, wageworkers, high school and university graduates, and entrepreneurs across the board. In addition, those who stood up to protest the unfolding occupation were silenced by the military authorities. In that kind of situation it is impossible not to have a heightened awareness of one's own objective predicament. On the level of consciousness, therefore, nationalism found a fertile breeding ground in the population of the Occupied Territories.

On a structural level, too, nationalism could be a powerful force for change, as the economic and political violence perpetrated by the occupier affected all sectors of the population regardless of their class base (with the possible exception of a small group of commercial importers), which facilitated the forging of a broad alliance of classes against the occupation. In this alliance the petite bourgeoisie of small merchants and professionals and the growing wage-labor force played the most important roles in the early and mid-1970s, where the professionals provided the leadership for the national movement while the unions organized the masses and raised their national consciousness. What was missing, however, was the impetus from the outside that could give direction to the movement inside the Occupied Territories.

Palestinians in the West Bank and Gaza Strip were well aware, after all, that they constituted only a part of the total Palestinian population, the majority of which has been scattered over refugee camps and slums throughout the Arab world. The PLO, which emerged as a unifying nationalist movement for Palestinians in the late 1960s, from the outset represented all Palestinians, inside and outside Palestine, and although it had a decisive influence for that reason on nationalist activity inside the Occupied Territories, its disjointed nature and initial preoccupation with organizing its constituency in the diaspora left the nationalist forces inside the West Bank and Gaza essentially rudderless for almost a decade after the defeat of 1967.

In the mid-1970s, the PLO shifted its focus and gave the green light to activists in the Occupied Territories to start building institutions and organizing the Palestinian masses, ostensibly to prepare the population to receive the "national authority" the PLO intended to constitute in any part of Palestine from which Israel could be made to withdraw. The following years saw a flurry of activity in the Occupied Territories as Palestinians intensified efforts to organize their own society to ensure, however, that, in the words of Salim Tamari, "when a Palestinian state arrives it will not arrive in a vacuum. It will already have an infrastructure of political and civic institutions to support it."[1]

The work of local organizers was facilitated by the very structure of the military occupation itself, as the authorities had consistently proven themselves negligent in the provision of basic services to the population, and as important sectors, such as the workers, continued to be deprived of their most basic rights, especially in the Israeli workplace. The infrastructure of organizations that emerged was born, therefore, from the womb of colonialism itself, as Palestinians began to fill in the gaps left by the occupying power. Institution building had as its purpose not only preparing Palestinian society for a state system, but also, on a very basic level, securing the society's survival.[2] In this sense the Palestinian experience runs closely parallel to the anticolonial struggles that took place in Africa and Asia earlier in this century.

The most successful maneuver, approved and encouraged by the outside leadership, was the drive to unionize the migrant workers employed across the Green Line. The particular experience of discrimination along ethnic and national lines that characterized the lives of those who were employed in Israel made this group of people exceptionally prone to being inducted into the national movement. This too has its parallels elsewhere, as Jeffery Paige has convincingly shown in his comparative work on migrant-labor estates. The infusion of the existing trade unions with new recruits who represented and reinforced the growing influence of nationalism in the Occupied Territories led to a radical transformation of the labor movement, as the unions' agenda was altered from a unionist to a nationalist one.

In short, a vast network of institutions and organizations emerged in the late 1970s and 1980s whose dual aim it was (1) to provide services to the local community, and (2) to substitute for the missing state system. These organizations generated their own leaders, elected routinely in the democratic process, who would promptly pledge their allegiance to the PLO. By the mid-1980s these organizations had succeeded in extending their activities throughout the Occupied Territories through branches set up in refugee camps and in villages, however remote. The occupied had started to outadminister the occupier. According to Tamari, this "strategy of informal resistance . . . or institutional resistance, was actually far more successful than even its own designers envisioned. By the late 1970s, it had established the complete political hegemony of Palestinian nationalism and the PLO as the single articulator of Palestinian aspirations."[3]

Aware of their success, activists began to adjust their goals in the 1980s, emphasizing the organizations' role, actual and potential, in the nationalist resistance. However, objective conditions still prohibited the organizing of a combined general workers' strike and commercial boycott, which some activists envisioned would be the necessary next step in resistance to the occupation. The factionalism that marked the national movement from the early 1980s on made any form of across-the-board joint action impossible. A number of factors, including a protracted Syrian assault on Palestinian camps in Lebanon in 1985–86, finally led to a reconciliation of the Palestinian national movement at the eighteenth PNC session in Algiers in April 1987. Unity in the overall national movement led to a reconciliation among the various factions of the PLO on all levels of organization, including in the Occupied Territories. In addition, the Palestine Communist Party was formally drawn into the movement for the first time in its history, making a larger degree of cooperation between the Communists, who controlled a considerable segment of the popular organizations in the Occupied Territories, and the other PLO factions possible. Thus the road was cleared for joint action on a mass level.

All that was needed at this point was a series of catalysts that would pull people out of their homes and into the streets. A number of events took place throughout 1987, and with increasing frequency in the fall of 1987, that might be seen as catalysts for the uprising. Through numerous demonstrations during the year, usually triggered by particular repressive acts by the Israeli army or events in Lebanon, Palestinian youths accumulated insurrectionary experience in the streets, and transformed their fears into bravery. The arrest and deportation of several prominent leaders of Fatah and the Islamic Jihad in the Gaza Strip in particular roused people's emotions. The Arab governments' shifting interest from the Palestinian question to the Iran-Iraq war, manifested in the Arab Summit conference in Amman at the beginning of November, drove home the point to Palestinians that they could not count on outside support for their cause, and that they would have to take matters into their own hands. A hang glider attack by a lone Palestinian commando on an army camp in northern Israel at the end of November 1987, an event in which six Israeli soldiers were killed, punctured for many Palestinians the myth of Israeli invincibility. Finally, a relatively banal road accident involving an Israeli truck and taxis ferrying Palestinians from their work in Israel to their homes in the Gaza Strip at the beginning of December sparked the fuse that started the uprising. At that point, any such incident would have had the same effect.

In December 1987, Palestinians took to the streets en masse to protest the military occupation, despite the very severe repression to which they had been subjected. Popular committees sprang up spontaneously in neighborhoods and villages and began to coordinate the local resistance. Within a month a national leadership committee was formed, the Unified National Leadership of the Uprising in the Occupied Territories (UNLU), which issued directives to the population through leaflets. Palestinians followed the UNLU's directives to the extent they were able, given the authorities' attempts at counteracting the UNLU's sway through massive military repression and an administrative crackdown. Mass compliance with the UNLU's directives underlined the local leadership's legitimacy in the eyes of the population. The UNLU made it clear from the beginning that it saw itself as the arm of the PLO in the Occupied Territories, and not as an alternative leadership. In the ensuing division of labor, the PLO outside the West Bank and Gaza provided the strategic framework for the resistance in the Occupied Territories (though, some would argue, not very effectively); the UNLU coordinated day-to-day activities in the Occupied Territories; and local groups, both existing committees and newly constituted ones, supervised the implementation of the UNLU's directives in the streets. The immediate deployment by the women's and medical relief committees of their resources to serve the population in locations most severely affected by the military response to the uprising stand as shining examples of how years of hard work at the mass level paid off when the chips were down.

The type of repression, as well as the particular impact the military occupation has had on people's everyday lives, helps explain the form the uprising has taken. First, the all-encompassing nature of repression and exploitation implicated all Palestinians in the struggle. Second, the lack of channels for political expression of just grievances, the lack of accountability on the part of the military authorities, and the mass organizations' inability to find legal redress for violations committed by the military forced Palestinians to respond to injustice by resorting to a combination of violence and withdrawal through nonparticipation in the institutions of the occupier. Third, the ongoing process of economic and administrative integration prompted, because of its long-term political implications for the status of the Occupied Territories, a deliberate effort to disengage from the structures of occupation. Finally, the military repression that traditionally targeted the Palestinian community's leadership compelled Palestinians to decentralize and spread their leadership so that the impact of detentions and deportations would not adversely affect the functioning of the movement, and leaders could be replaced immediately.

Other factors as well account for the particular form the uprising has taken, and for the peculiar phenomenon that although the uprising has moved in a definite direction, it has not had clear and concrete goals. The international constellation of forces, which finds the United States firmly behind Israel, offering unwavering and uncritical political, military, and economic support, and which finds the Arab world hopelessly divided, has essentially destroyed the possibility of Palestinians gaining their independent state anytime soon. Deprived of the prospect of accomplishing its goal, the Palestinian national movement is left to drift aimlessly on the waves of contemporary history, being thrown back and forth between opposing currents, a leaf in gusty political winds. Unlike movements of national liberation in other settings, the movement in the Occupied Territories, which is only a wing of the larger Palestinian movement, is thus truncated.[4]

This is what sets the Palestinian national movement apart from other movements of national liberation. Although the Palestinian case is not an anomaly in the twentieth century insofar as it shares its essential features with other anticolonial movements, the Palestinian case differs from all other major historical examples: this is a liberation movement that has been successful in mobilizing its people in a powerful resistance against dispossession and occupation, but it has been frustrated in its goal of establishing an independent state out of the ruins of colonialism. It could be argued that there are other cases where national liberation has not yet been achieved, such as South Africa. The emphasis is on "yet," however. In 1990, the African National Congress stood a much better chance than the PLO of liberating its nation from the yoke of white settler rule, primarily because of the international balance of forces and the different roles played by South Africa and Israel in the international capitalist political and economic system. Israel is not a crumbling vestige of Western colonialism: it plays an integral role in Western imperialism today, virtually as America's fifty-first state, firmly ensconced in a divided Arab world, supplying arms to those countries crucial to United States strategic designs that the United States, because of congressional or other restrictions, cannot do business with, such as Guatemala and Iran. It is in this respect, then, that Jeffery Paige's theory of social movements in migrant-labor estates does not apply to the Palestinian case, and it is for this reason that the developments sketched by Immanuel Wallerstein in the case of colonial Africa have not culminated in similar success in Palestine.

The Palestinian national movement has had to lower its sights. The uprising cannot aim in the first instance at establishing a Palestinian state, but only at raising the cost of the military occupation to Israel by reducing Palestinians' dependence on the Israeli infrastructure and replacing it with one of their own, in short by effectively outadministering the Israeli system of control and by making the Occupied Territories ungovernable, by redrawing the Green Line between Israel and the Occupied Territories. The two goals are not the same, because even if structural disengagement eventually leads to a dismantling of the military occupation, this does not mean that Palestinians will be able to set up their own state. Alternatives that are deemed acceptable by the United States and some circles in Israel include some form of Palestinian autonomy; Israeli-Jordanian joint rule; or a Jordanian-Palestinian federation—the worst-case scenario in the eyes of the United States and the Israeli left; but in no case independence.

Given the limited options currently open to Palestinians, the uprising constitutes a watershed in the history of the Palestinian movement for national liberation. After all, the world has been jolted into the realization that a Green Line does exist between the state of Israel and the Occupied Territories, and that a vibrant Palestinian nation exists and strives to set the course of its own history. These are momentous achievements in and of themselves. For Palestinians a psychological barrier has been broken: they are now aware of their own collective strength, and they have seen the vulnerabilities in their opponent's armor, previously deemed impenetrable.

The organizational work of trade unions, women's committees, and other grass-roots organizations over the past fifteen years has accounted for Palestinians' ability to sustain the intifada beyond the highly visible but relatively unproductive (and in human terms very costly) street demonstrations. Activists in the popular organizations were able to deploy their resources at a moment when these were most in need. If certain organizations, such as trade unions, were not fully equipped to participate in the uprising within their formal frameworks, their cadres would still form the core of the committees that sprang up spontaneously in villages and neighborhoods in towns and refugee camps.

However, despite the accomplishment of local organizers in sustaining the popular uprising, and given the probability that the military occupation will not end soon, a word of caution about the limitations of the mass-based organizations in the Occupied Territories is called for. There are two main threats to the survival of the popular organizations in the West Bank and Gaza: internal contradictions within these organizations themselves, and military repression.

The problems with the organizations themselves are that they are ideologically ambivalent, that they do not necessarily practice what they preach, and that, because they cannot really deliver what they promise, their members may become disaffected and demoralized, and leave the movement. The labor movement is a prime example. It is, in essence, a workers' movement, but the environment of military occupation and colonial exploitation has provoked an overriding nationalist current. Generally speaking, the workers of even those unions that proclaim themselves to be Marxist-Leninist in ideology—to be fighting for workers' rights in a continuing struggle with the bourgeoisie, with their ultimate goal the establishment of a socialist state—have subordinated, consciously and explicitly, the class struggle to the national struggle. The nationalist stance of the major union blocs has effectively rallied workers to the all-consuming national cause, while their attempt to address bread-and-butter issues in their union work has helped cement the unions' base. But it has been argued that the unions' strong penchant for nationalist concerns has distracted them from the long-term work of securing workers' basic rights.

Trade unions exist purely by the grace of their members, and although the articulation of nationalist sentiments and aspirations constitutes an attraction of considerable force to most Palestinians, the more prospects and hopes for the attainment of a Palestinian state recede, the more likely it is that unions will collapse if they fail to provide their members with tangible benefits of enduring value. One Palestinian critic warned, for example: "As the national movement gains in strength, the unions' membership will increase. When the national movement ebbs, so will the unions' membership. Only the core will remain, because the unions will not be able to produce direct benefits for the workers."[5] Another critic said: "I think it is a mistake to look at the national struggle and at social issues as divided into stages. National liberation may be part of workers' liberation, but socialist liberation is not a part of national liberation. . . . You find yourself in a trap: social issues will explode one way or another. If they are ignored by the union leadership, the workers will either end up completely demoralized, or they will go with an antinational leadership instead."[6]

A similar argument can be made for the women's movement. Suad Joseph has said that "women often do not choose the moment and the context for their political involvement [in movements]. Their political participation may be evoked by the state, by rulers, and by politicians or others in authority. Women become a subject of mobilization, targets of political action programs, a mass to be welded into citizens or political followers."[7]

In other words, women are used to bolster social movements, including nationalist movements, but depending on their role and power in these movements, they may not easily transcend the restrictions traditionally imposed on them. If a feminist agenda exists, it is subordinated to the more pressing nationalist concern.

In the Palestinian case, the position of women in the West Bank and Gaza did advance due to their participation in the national movement by sheer virtue of the role they played in their communities. It may have changed their consciousness and their identity of themselves as women, and their participation may have given them legitimacy as social actors rather than as homemakers and preservers of culture. One could see, in the streets during the uprising, who was making decisions, and who was coordinating the resistance behind the barrage of rocks. Women played an increasingly important role, especially since many of the men were imprisoned.

But the point should not be overstated. Women have not been liberated from existing constraints; it is simply that the constraints, at a time of national crisis, were temporarily suspended. Julie Peteet has argued, in the case of Palestinian women in Lebanon, according to Suad Joseph, that the Palestinian national movement "gave women's participation in informal communal politics a national context and legitimacy. But this diluted a commitment to women's issues because the movement has carefully avoided challenging patriarchal structures, thus deflecting the emergence of feminist consciousness."[8] Rita Giacaman has said of the women's movement in the Occupied Territories:

> The problem is the imbalance among the various components of the women's liberation formula. The progressive women's committees movement's attempts to deal with the three contradictions that subjugate Palestinian women [the oppression of women as women, as workers, and as Palestinians] led to the national political struggle being afforded supremacy and to the other contradictions being relegated to secondary positions. Although the conceptual framework espoused by the progressive women's movement takes these problems into consideration, the movement's practices reflect the two-stage revolution theory: national liberation now and women's liberation later appears to be the working formula.[9]

Giacaman concludes that "the national question is a major factor which both supports the movement for women's liberation and simultaneously limits its further development. It supports liberation by calling on women to move beyond the household realm and to face the occupation 'side by side' with men. But it deters further development by emptying it from its feminist and class content and limiting it to the confines of the national liberation struggle."[10]

What will happen when the uprising peters out, men return from prison, enthusiasm dies down? Will the traditional division of labor be resumed? Most likely. And what if the uprising, against all odds, succeeds in bringing about national liberation, and a Palestinian state is created? Will women be forced to resume their traditional roles of supporters, cheerleaders in the game of national politics? Palestinians would do well to draw a lesson from the experience of the Algerian revolution. Rosemary Sayigh refers to Algerian sources who note that the Algerian National Women's Union "was the last to mobilize against the reactionary Family Code of 1981," two full decades after independence, which supposedly had brought a fundamental transformation of women's traditional roles thanks to their activism in the resistance against French colonial rule.[11]

As for the second threat to the grass-roots movement in the Occupied Territories, repression by the military authorities: the authorities have consistently sought to suppress any form of organized activity in Palestinian society. They have been particularly weary of the trade unions because of their great potential for transformation into vehicles of nationalist struggle. After the launching of the Iron Fist policy in August 1985, the unions were singled out by the military, which has created an atmosphere of fear through a systematic policy of harassment and intimidation in an effort to force members to withdraw and to deter potential members from joining. In addition, through arrests and deportations of unionists and other community activists, the authorities have systematically skimmed off any incipient Palestinian leadership in the West Bank and Gaza. Such practices may indeed cripple the unions and other popular organizations. Still, it seems, and organizers claim, that the movement has grown too large and amorphous to be destroyed by Israeli repression. The intifada has proven this.

On the Israeli side, however, repression of popular organizations in the Occupied Territories will do little to solve Israel's problem of what to do with the area and the indigenous Palestinian population living there. Given the continuing effort to decapitate the Palestinian leadership, the oft-repeated Israeli claim that, its own desire for peace notwithstanding, no meaningful negotiations can be carried out because there supposedly is no one with whom to negotiate on the Palestinian side is disingenuous. This policy, in addition to the continuing refusal of the Israeli authorities to deal directly with the Palestinians' chosen representative, the PLO, is perpetuating the occupation of the West Bank and Gaza indefinitely, with benefits accruing to no one. Worse, the withholding of legal venues for political expression from Palestinians easily leads to violence as the only available option for the Palestinians to assert their rights, and indeed their existence.

Here too it is instructive to draw a parallel with the Algerian experience. In the words of Eqbal Ahmad:

> The Algerian Revolution . . . was actually crushed militarily while it had won politically by the time de Gaulle negotiated independence. The French military effort in Algeria was formidable. A total of some 800,000 troops . . . in a population of nine million Muslims . . . were tied down by a guerrilla force whose number did not exceed 35,000 regular combatants. . . . In 1958, the construction of the Morice and Challe electrified fences, guarded by a military cordon across the frontier, had turned the flow of arms and men to trickles. More than two million people were moved into "regroupment centers" (read concentration camps); torture and napalming of villages were widely practiced. By 1961, the inside guerrillas had been reduced to some 5,000, and their ability to engage the French at will had markedly declined. But France faced a sullen Algerian population that it had conquered but could not rule. It had outfought the FLN but the latter continued to outadminister and "illegitimize" the French. [12]

One must hope that Palestinians will be spared such a fate. As for Israel, it too would do well to take to heart the lessons of the Algerian experience.

NOTES

CHAPTER ONE

1. For a useful analysis of the events in the Gaza Strip before and during the first days of the uprising, see Vitullo, "Uprising in Gaza."

2. For an elaboration of the above arguments, see chapter 6.

3. Tamari, "Palestinian Demand," 31–32.

4. For an excellent review of three recent Zionist revisionist interpretations of the events of 1947–49, see Lockman, "Original Sin."

5. For analyses of the Palestinian national movement, see Sayigh, *Palestinians*; Lesch, *Arab Politics in Palestine*; Cobban, *Palestinian Liberation Organisation*; and Quandt, Jabber, and Lesch, *Politics of Palestinian Nationalism*.

6. Paige, *Agrarian Revolution*.

7. As explained by Charles Tilly in *From Mobilization to Revolution*, 199–200.

8. Paige, *Agrarian Revolution*, 66–67.

9. Ibid., 59.

10. Ibid., 68.

11. Ibid., 256.

12. Ibid., 257–58.

13. Simon, *Gramsci's Political Thought*, 24.

14. Wallerstein, *Africa*, 42–43.

15. Ibid., 51–53.

16. Friedland et al., *Revolutionary Theory*, 111.

17. Simon, *Gramsci's Political Thought*, 25–26.

18. Iliffe, "Creation of Group Consciousness," 49–50.

19. B. A. Khoapa, quoted by Dekker et al., "Case Studies," 234.

20. Friedland et al., *Revolutionary Theory*, 30.

21. Moore, *Injustice*, 472–73.

22. Tilly, *From Mobilization to Revolution*, 69.

23. Friedland, et al., *Revolutionary Theory*, 128.

24. Ibid., 156.

25. Moore, *Injustice*, 462.

26. Ahmad, "Revolutionary Warfare," 145.

27. Ibid., 142.

28. Ibid., 164.

29. Ibid., 167.

CHAPTER TWO

1. See especially Shehadeh, *Occupier's Law*.

2. Ryan, "Israeli Economic Policy," 6.

3. Graham-Brown, "West Bank and Gaza," 16.

4. Hilal, "Class Transformation," 9.

5. Budeiri, "Changes," 49.

6. Dakkak, "Development and Control," 76.

7. Rekhess, "Employment in Israel," 396.

8. Ibid., 392.

9. Cited in Ryan, "Israeli Economic Policy," 9.

10. Rekhess, "Employment in Israel," 392. To Palestinians, who have suffered for more than two decades under a ruthless and ubiquitous military occupation, these proclaimed objectives of "nonpresence," "noninterference," and "open bridges" must sound like a poor joke.

11. Ministry of Defense, *Thirteen-Year Survey*, 2.

12. Benvenisti, *1986 Report*, 25. See also Shehadeh, *Occupier's Law*, and Mansour, *Palestine*, 34–42.

13. See Budeiri, "Changes"; Mansour, *Palestine*; Gharaibeh, *Economies*, 59–82; Roy, *Gaza Strip*; and Frisch, *Stagnation and Frontier*.

14. See Stephens, *Taxation*. See also International Center for Peace in the Middle East, *Research on Human Rights*.

15. For example, on the issue of health, see Giacaman, "Disturbing Distortions." See also Roy, *Gaza Strip*.

16. Benvenisti, *1986 Report*, 25.

17. Central Bureau of Statistics, *Statistical Abstract*, 723. In 1986, the Occupied Territories had an active labor force of 269,200 (West Bank: 173,600; Gaza: 95,600). Approximately 25 percent of the workers employed in the Occupied Territories themselves in 1986 worked in the agricultural sector, 16 percent were employed in industry, 11 percent worked in construction, and the remaining 47 percent were employed in other branches of the economy, mostly in the service and public sectors.

18. Benvenisti, *1986 Report*, 10. The Gaza figure for 1983 is 9.9 percent, according to Roy, *Gaza Strip*, 58.

19. Central Bureau of Statistics, *Statistical Abstract*, 736–37.

20. *Jerusalem Post*, 15 February 1985.

21. Benvenisti, *1986 Report*, 11.

22. Frisch, *Stagnation and Frontier*, 12.

23. Central Bureau of Statistics, *Statistical Abstract*, 722.

24. Rekhess, "Employment in Israel," 393.

25. Semyonov and Lewin-Epstein, *Hewers of Wood*, 12–13.

26. Rekhess, "Employment in Israel," 394.

27. International Labour Office, "Report [1989]," 16–17.

28. Central Bureau of Statistics, *Statistical Abstract*, 724. The figure (in 1986) for the West Bank is 30.7 percent, and for Gaza, 46.1 percent.

29. Excluded from official statistics are a large number of undocumented workers who find work through the informal labor markets and who are therefore not counted by the official labor exchanges. In addition, women and children working irregularly in agriculture, who are easily skipped in household surveys, also tend to remain uncounted. Finally, residents of East Jerusalem are excluded from West Bank statistics since Israel considers East Jerusalem to be part of Israel.

30. *Jerusalem Post*, 22 May 1989.

31. Central Bureau of Statistics, *Statistical Abstract*, 723.

32. Farjoun, "Palestinian Workers in Israel," 121.

33. Semyonov and Lewin-Epstein, *Hewers of Wood*, 28.

34. Greenberg, *Race and State*, 368.

35. Metzger, Orth, and Sterzing, *This Land Is Our Land*, 92.

36. International Labour Office, "Report [1989]," 26–27.

37. Greenberg, "Indifferent Hegemony," 35.

38. *Al-Fajr Jerusalem Palestinian Weekly*, 2 December 1983.

39. International Center for Peace in the Middle East, *Research on Human Rights*, 76.

40. Ibid., 76–77, 94–95. Only Israeli citizens are eligible to receive benefits granted by the National Insurance Law. This could include migrant workers unless, as in the case of Palestinian workers, they return home every night. See Ben Israel, "On Social Human Rights," 148. This is a typical catch-22, since Palestinian workers, especially those from Gaza, generally prefer to stay overnight in Israel, but are in most cases not permitted to do so by the authorities. See also International Labour Office, "Report [1989]," 28.

41. International Center for Peace in the Middle East, *Research on Human Rights*, 96.

42. Ibid., 76.

43. Ibid., 90. See also Benvenisti, *1986 Report*, 11–12, and International Labour Office, "Report [1989]," 28–29.

44. Farjoun, "Palestinian Workers in Israel," 138. For the wage situation of Gaza workers, see Roy, *Gaza Strip*, 33–37.

45. See Greenberg, *Race and State*, chap. 16.

46. Undated memo signed by Yeruham Meshel (obtained from the Histadrut). It should be noted that the Histadrut is not only a trade union but also one of Israel's largest employers, and that Histadrut companies, like the Solel Boneh construction company, operate in Israeli settlements in the Occupied Territories. How this squares with the Histadrut's official position opposing annexation remains a mystery.

47. International Labour Office, "Report [1989]," 31.

48. Information provided by Al-Haq, Ramallah.

49. International Center for Peace in the Middle East, *Research on Human Rights*, 79. See also Rekhess, "Employment in Israel," 397.

50. See, for example, Joshua Brilliant, "Histadrut, Gov't Trade Blame for 'Inadequate Protection': Arabs Kept Out of Works Committees," *Jerusalem Post*, 3 February 1984.

51. Benvenisti, *1986 Report*, 13. On the same case, see Michael Shalev, "Winking an Eye at Cheap Arab Labour," *Jerusalem Post*, 7 January 1986.

52. See, for example, Robert Rosenberg, "At One Histadrut-Owned Factory, the Workers Are Holding On," *Jerusalem Post*, 5 February 1986.

53. *Jerusalem Post*, 22 May 1989.

54. Metzger, Orth, and Sterzing, *This Land Is Our Land*, 94.

55. Farjoun, "Palestinian Workers in Israel," 137.

56. *Jerusalem Post*, 20 January 1989.

57. *Al-Fajr Jerusalem Palestinian Weekly*, 25 November 1983 (translated from

Ha'Aretz). See also Ilan Chaim, "Katsav to Industrialists: 'Organized Israeli Workers Should Get Job Preference,'" *Jerusalem Post*, 30 November 1984. See also *Jerusalem Post*, 20 November 1984.

58. *Jerusalem Post*, 6 December 1984.

59. International Labour Office, "Report [1989]," 26.

60. Greenberg, "Indifferent Hegemony," 29.

61. Ibid., 33–34.

62. Semyonov and Lewin-Epstein, *Hewers of Wood*, 114.

63. Benvenisti, *West Bank*, 4–5.

64. Migdal, "Effects of Regime Policies," 67–68.

65. Rockwell, "Palestinian Women Workers," 121. Studies in other Arab countries bear out this claim. In Egypt, migration of male workers in many cases increased the work load, especially in agriculture, of women in the family. See Taylor, "Egyptian Migration," 7–8, and Khafagy, "Women and Labor Migration," 18–19. See also Hammam, "Labor Migration," 11.

66. See, for example, the case of North Yemen in Myntti, "Yemeni Workers Abroad," 15.

67. Samed, "Proletarianization," 12.

68. WWC, "First Social Field Study," 12–13.

69. Rockwell, "Palestinian Women Workers," 119–20.

70. Siniora, "Palestinian Labour," 85.

71. Rockwell, "Palestinian Women Workers," 119.

72. Central Bureau of Statistics, *Statistical Abstract*, 718. (The percentage is higher in the West Bank—approximately 16 percent of the labor force—than in Gaza, where only about 5 percent of the labor force consists of women.) This is almost certainly a severe underestimate. According to Budeiri, it "ignores the thousands of women who work on domestic plots or who are employed by labour contractors in small spinning mills in their own villages. It also ignores those who are involved both in seasonal labour such as fruit picking, and partial employment such as selling fruits and vegetables in markets." Budeiri, "Changes," 51.

73. Samed, "Proletarianization," 14–15.

74. Interview, Ramallah, 8 December 1985.

75. Samed, "Proletarianization," 14.

76. Cited in Flavia Pesa, "Women's Work and Women's Pay: Super-Exploitation in the Sewing Industry," *Al-Fajr Jerusalem Palestinian Weekly*, 19 April 1985.

77. Rockwell, "Palestinian Women Workers," 120. See also chaps. 3 and 4 of the excellent study by Siniora, "Palestinian Labour."

78. WWC, "First Social Field Study," 14–18. These conclusions are supported by Siniora's study on women employed in the West Bank garment industry, "Palestinian Labour."

79. Pesa, "Women's Work," (see n. 76 above).

80. Ibid.

81. Siniora, "Palestinian Labour," 91.

82. Ibid., 87.

83. Ibid., 88.

84. Samed, "Proletarianization," 11.

85. This is a point elaborated by Hammam, "Labor Migration," 5–6.

86. Kimmerling, *Zionism and Economy*, 59, 61–62. See also Benvenisti, *1986 Report*, 18. Benvenisti says that according to Israeli statistics, the Occupied Territories have already become a part of Israel from an economic point of view (5).

87. Ryan, "Israeli Economic Policy," 22.

88. Benvenisti, *1986 Report*, 7.

89. See Shehadeh, *Occupier's Law*, and Greenberg, "Indifferent Hegemony," 14.

90. Arkadie, *Benefits and Burdens*, 40.

91. Ibid., 45.

92. Greenberg, "Indifferent Hegemony," 8.

93. Arkadie, *Benefits and Burdens*, 138.

94. Benvenisti, *West Bank*, 10.

95. Kimmerling, *Zionism and Economy*, 61.

96. See, for example, Greenberg, "Indifferent Hegemony," 57–65.

97. Ehrlich, "Oriental Support for Begin," 43.

98. Ibid., 44.

99. Benvenisti, *1986 Report*, 18.

100. Tamari, "Building," 33–34.

101. Arkadie, *Benefits and Burdens*, 42.

102. Tamari, "Building," 50.

103. Lesch, *Political Perceptions*, 103.

104. Interview, Jerusalem, 18 November 1985.

105. See, for example, Giacaman, "Palestinian Women," 21–22.

106. Peteet, "Women and the Palestinian Movement," 20.

107. Tamari, "Building," 62.

108. Peteet, "Women and the Palestinian Movement," 24.

109. Samed, "Proletarianization," 14.

110. Layne, "Women in Jordan's Workforce," 23.

111. Siniora, "Palestinian Labour," 96–98, 113–20.

112. Ibid., 98.

113. FPWAC, "Fighting Woman," 17.

114. Ibid., 18–19.

115. Peteet, "Women and the Palestinian Movement," 20.

116. Roy, *Gaza Strip*, 86. The same argument can be made for the West Bank.

CHAPTER THREE

1. Dakkak, "Back to Square One," 68.

2. Lesch, *Political Perceptions*, 39. See also Abraham, "Development," 40.

3. Lesch, *Political Perceptions*, 33.

4. Ibid., 40.

5. The National Guidance Committee of 1967 later became known as NGC-I, to set it apart from the more famous NGC of the late 1970s.

6. Dakkak, "Back to Square One," 71.

7. Lesch, *Political Perceptions*, 38. See also Dakkak, "Back to Square One," 75.

8. Quandt, "Political and Military Dimensions," 145.

9. Lesch, *Political Perceptions*, 41.

10. For the legal arguments, see Playfair, "Legal Aspects."

11. Palestine Focus, "Interview with Rita Giacaman," 3.

12. Lesch, *Political Perceptions*, 41.

13. Fasheh, "Education," 161–62.

14. Ibid., 171–72.

15. See Taraki, "Mass Organizations."

16. Tamari, "Building," 58.

17. Ibid., 59.

18. Palestine Focus, "Interview with Rita Giacaman."

19. Ma'oz, *Palestinian Leadership*, 114.

20. Lesch, *Political Perceptions*, p. 46.

21. MERIP, "Interview with the Palestine National Front [1974]," 21. See also Dakkak, "Back to Square One," 75–78.

22. Lesch, *Political Perceptions*, 53. For a summary of the manifesto, see MERIP, "Palestinian National Front," 22.

23. MERIP, "Interview with the Palestine National Front [1976]," 17.

24. Lesch, *Political Perceptions*, 54.

25. Dakkak, "Back to Square One," 76. See also MERIP, "Palestinian National Front," 22–23.

26. Abraham, "Development," 413.

27. Dakkak, "Back to Square One," 79.

28. Tamari, "Palestinian Demand," 29.

29. Interview, San Francisco, 22 April 1988.

30. Ma'oz, *Palestinian Leadership*, 116.

31. Awwad and Qawwas, "Resistance," 165.

32. *Palestine Human Rights Newsletter*, no. 2 (March–April 1986): 4.

33. Ibid.

34. Quoted in Rifkin, "Notes from the Occupation," 5.

35. MERIP, "Interview with the Palestine National Front [1976]," 18. See also MERIP, "Open Door in the Middle East," 10.

36. Dakkak, "Back to Square One," 76. See also MERIP, "Abd el-Jawad Saleh," 27, for an account of Arafat's maneuvering.

37. Lesch, *Political Perceptions*, 75–76.

38. Dakkak, "Back to Square One," 84–85.

39. Ma'oz, *Palestinian Leadership*, 166. See also Cobban, *Palestinian Liberation Organisation*, 175.

40. *Jerusalem Post*, 11 October 1979, reported in MERIP, "Israeli Military Authorities," 12.

41. Tamari, "Palestinian Demand," 34.

42. See, for example, Ma'oz, *Palestinian Leadership*, 163–64, 188–212.

43. Lesch, *Political Perceptions*, 84.

44. Dakkak, "Back to Square One," 86.

45. Tamari, "Palestinian Demand," 30. The late 1970s in fact saw the emergence of new, more activist-oriented women's committees, and a revival and radicalization of the trade-union movement, as will be described in greater detail in chapters 5 and 4, respectively.

46. Ibid., 33. For a PLO view in support of the funding, see MERIP, "Khalid al-Hassan," 12–14. For a DFLP critique, see MERIP, "Abu Leila," 16–17.

47. Interview with an activist, Ramallah, November 1987.

48. Interview with Lisa Taraki, Ramallah, 8 March 1988.

49. Dakkak, "Back to Square One," 90.

50. Tamari, "Palestinian Demand," 34.

51. Quoted in Graham-Brown, "Report," 4.

52. Quoted in MERIP, "Hussein Hangover," 20.

53. Interview with a Palestinian activist, Ramallah, 3 March 1985.

54. See the Index of Organizations for an overview of the chief political actors in the Palestinian national movement.

55. Graham-Brown, "Report," 5.

56. Tamari, "In League with Zion."

57. MERIP, "Hussein Hangover," 17.

58. Khalidi, "PNC Strengthens Palestinian Hand," 38.

59. Interview, Ramallah, 8 March 1988.

60. This argument was previously made in Hiltermann, "Mass Mobilization," 57–59. For a more detailed analysis, see Hiltermann, "Human Rights."

61. See, for example, the various publications of Al-Haq in Ramallah.

62. For documentation on Israel's repression of the intifada, see Al-Haq, *Punishing a Nation* and *A Nation under Siege*.

Chapter Four

1. Hopstaken, "Bi-National Railway Workers' Union," 50.

2. Greenberg, *Race and State*, 370.

3. Lesch, "Frustration," 161.

4. Budeiri, *Palestine Communist Party*, 54.

5. Taqqu, "Peasants into Workmen," 271.

6. Lesch, "Frustration," 162.

7. Hopstaken, "Bi-National Railway Workers' Union," 82.

8. Budeiri, *Palestine Communist Party*, chap. 7.

9. Hopstaken, "Bi-National Railway Workers' Union," 98–101.

10. Ibid., 97.

11. Beinen, "Palestine Communist Party," 13. See also, Hazboun and al-Salhi, "Workers' and Trade-Union Movement," part 1. For an interesting account of union organizing during the immediate prewar years, see also Sayigh, *Palestinians*, 54–56.

12. See Hazboun and al-Salhi, "Workers' and Trade-Union Movement," parts 1 and 2.

13. Cohen, *Political Parties*, 29.

14. Hazboun and al-Salhi, "Workers' and Trade-Union Movement," part 2, 27.

15. Cohen, *Political Parties*, 33–34.

16. Hazboun and al-Salhi, "Workers' and Trade-Union Movement," part 2, 35.

17. Hourani, *Stages of the Struggle*, 4–5.

18. Cobban, *Palestinian Liberation Organisation*, 169.

19. Hourani, *Stages of the Struggle*, 8–9.
20. Ibid., 11.
21. Hazboun and al-Salhi, "Workers' and Trade-Union Movement," part 2, 29.
22. Ibid., 38.
23. Interview with Majed al-Labadi, Jerusalem, 20 May 1985. Al-Labadi himself was deported to Lebanon by the Israeli military authorities on 27 August 1989.
24. Hazboun and al-Salhi, "Workers' and Trade-Union Movement," part 3, 40.
25. Ibid., 41.
26. Ibid., 41–42.
27. Ibid., 39.
28. Interview, Nablus, 14 December 1985.
29. Hazboun and al-Salhi, "Workers' and Trade-Union Movement," part 4, 9.
30. Ibid., 10.
31. Ibid.
32. Ibid.
33. Interview with Majed al-Labadi, Jerusalem, 20 May 1985.
34. Hazboun and al-Salhi, "Workers' and Trade-Union Movement," part 4, 10.
35. For a list of repressive measures in this period, see ibid., 15–17.
36. Ibid., 11.
37. Interview with a Palestinian historian, Ramallah, 7 December 1985.
38. Interview with Palestinian sociologist Salim Tamari, Berkeley, California, 21 April 1988.
39. Interview with a representative of the WUB, Jerusalem, 27 May 1985.
40. WUB, *Workers' Unity Bloc*, 5.
41. "Provisional Labour Law," articles 68–69.
42. CGIWU, *Bylaws*, part 5, articles 32–34.
43. Ibid., parts 8 and 10.
44. Ibid., part 12.
45. GFTU, *Bylaws*, article 22.
46. Ibid., parts 5 and 6.
47. Ibid., article 5.
48. WUB, *Workers' Unity Bloc*, 8–9. Unlike trade unions, which are governed by Jordanian law, the union blocs operate solely according to their own bylaws. The blocs are active in both the West Bank and the Gaza Strip, though organized labor activity has been minimal in Gaza since 1967, and even before.
49. Interview with a WUB unionist, Ramallah, 8 December 1985.
50. Interview with a Palestinian historian, Ramallah, 7 December 1985.
51. WYM document about the 1981 split in the West Bank union movement (in Arabic; undated; obtained from the WYM).
52. Ibid.
53. Unofficial (draft) WYM document about the 1981 split in the labor movement, provided by a WYM unionist (in Arabic; undated).
54. *Al-Fajr Jerusalem Palestinian Weekly*, 23–30 August 1981.
55. WYM document (see n. 51 above).
56. *Al-Fajr Jerusalem Palestinian Weekly*, 23–30 August 1981.
57. Ibid.
58. Ibid.

59. Interview with Shehadeh al-Minawi, secretary-general of the WYM-controlled GFTU, Nablus, 15 December 1985.

60. Interview with a PWB unionist, Ramallah, 24 October 1985.

61. Interview with Adel Ghanem, secretary-general of the PWB-controlled GFTU, Nablus, 14 December 1985.

62. Interview with a PWB unionist, Ramallah, 24 October 1985.

63. According to an opinion poll conducted by the weekly *Al-Fajr*, ABC (Australia), and *Newsday* (New York) in the Occupied Territories in the summer of 1986, 93 percent of the population supported the PLO in general, and 71 percent supported Arafat in particular. *Al-Fajr Jerusalem Palestinian Weekly*, 12 September 1986.

64. WYM document (see n. 51 above).

65. Interview with a PWB unionist, Ramallah, 24 October 1985.

66. Interview with Adel Ghanem, secretary-general of the PWB-controlled GFTU, Nablus, 14 December 1985.

67. WUB, *Workers' Unity Bloc*, 4.

68. Interview, Ramallah, 8 December 1985.

69. Interview, Nablus, 14 December 1985.

70. Interview, Hebron, 2 December 1985.

71. MGIWU, "Statement."

72. Interview, Ramallah, 8 December 1985.

73. Interview, Ramallah, 2 November 1985.

74. CGIWU, *Bylaws*, part 5, articles 32–34.

75. Interview, Nablus, 14 December 1985.

76. Interview, Ramallah, 2 November 1985.

77. Interview with a union official, Jerusalem, 12 September 1985.

78. Interview with a union official, Hebron, 7 December 1985.

79. Interview with a union official, Nablus, 21 December 1985.

80. Interview, Nablus, 14 December 1985.

81. Interview, Jerusalem, 20 May 1985.

82. Interview with a PWB unionist, Ramallah, 2 November 1985.

83. Interview, Ramallah, 8 December 1985.

84. Interview with a PWB unionist, Hebron, 2 December 1985.

85. Interview, Nablus, 15 December 1985.

86. Interview with a WUB unionist, Jerusalem, 3 June 1985.

87. Interview, Hebron, 7 December 1985.

88. Interview, Ramallah, 8 December 1985.

89. Interview with a WUB official, Ramallah, 1 December 1985.

90. Interview with a WUB unionist, Ya'bad, 30 January 1986.

91. Ibid.

92. Interview with a WYM unionist, Hebron, 7 December 1985, and with a WUB unionist, Hebron, 25 November 1985.

93. Interview with a WUB unionist, Nablus, 14 December 1985, and with a WYM unionist, Nablus, 21 December 1985.

94. Interview with a PWB unionist, Ramallah, 24 October 1985.

95. Interview, Nablus, 15 December 1985.

96. Interview with a PWB unionist, Ramallah, 24 October 1985.

97. Interview, Abu Dis, 20 June 1985.

98. Interview, Abu Dis, 13 June 1985.

99. Interview, Nablus, 14 December 1985.

100. Interview, Ramallah, 24 October 1985.

101. From interviews with unionists and workers, 1985–87. See also Tamari, "Building,"

102. Interview with a WUB unionist, Jerusalem, 20 May 1985.

103. Interview with officials and members at the union office, Hebron, 9 November 1985.

104. Interview, Nablus, 14 December 1985.

105. Interview, Nablus, 21 December 1985.

106. Interview with a PWB unionist, Nablus, 26 January 1986.

107. Interview, Hebron, 2 December 1985.

108. Copies of collective contracts obtained from unions (in Arabic).

109. Interview, Ramallah, 24 October 1985.

110. Interview with one of the union's officials, Nablus, 26 January 1986.

111. Ibid.

112. Interview with a WUB unionist, Nablus, 14 December 1985.

113. Presentation, Jerusalem, 8 April 1986.

114. Interview with a PWB unionist, Nablus, 26 January 1986.

115. Interview with a PWB unionist, Ramallah, 2 November 1985.

116. Interview with a WYM unionist, Hebron, 7 December 1985.

117. Interview, Jenin, 31 January 1986.

118. Interview, Nablus, 14 December 1985.

119. Interview with a PWB unionist, Ramallah, 24 October 1985.

120. Taggert, *Workers in Struggle*, 39.

121. Interview with a PWB unionist, Ramallah, 24 October 1985.

122. "JEC Workers Strike; Israel Grabs Company Funds," *Al-Fajr Jerusalem Palestinian Weekly*, 6 June 1986. See also the interview with the head of the JEC union, Nabil 'Azza, *Al-Fajr Jerusalem Palestinian Weekly*, 5 December 1986.

123. Interview with an official of the union, Jerusalem, 20 May 1985.

124. Interview with a member of the union, Ramallah, 8 March 1988.

125. Interview, Jerusalem, 27 May 1985.

126. Interview, Jerusalem, 3 June 1985.

127. Interview with a WUB unionist, Nablus, 14 December 1985.

128. Interview with a PWB unionist, Ramallah, 24 October 1985.

129. Interview, Hebron, 2 December 1985. Jamil al-'Amla announced his resignation as the leader of the local Village Leagues and declared that he was joining the national movement during the early months of the intifada.

130. Interview, Abu Dis, 20 June 1985.

131. Interview, Ya'bad, 30 January 1986.

132. Interviews conducted in January and February 1986 with some of the very few lawyers, both Palestinian and Israeli, who claimed to have had schooling in labor law showed, by the contradictory answers they gave to simple legal questions, that even these few experts knew very little on this subject.

133. Presentation at a panel discussion, West Jerusalem, 8 April 1986.

134. Ibid.

135. Ibid.

136. Presentation at a panel discussion, West Jerusalem, 8 April 1986.

137. Interview with a unionist, Ya'bad, 30 January 1986.

138. Interview with a PWB unionist, Hebron, 2 December 1985.

139. Interview with a PWB unionist, Ramallah, 28 June 1986.

140. Interview with a unionist, Ya'bad, 30 January 1986.

141. Interview with a WUB unionist, Abu Dis, 20 June 1985.

142. Ibid.

143. Interview with a unionist, Jerusalem, 27 May 1985.

144. Interview with a unionist, Ya'bad, 30 January 1986.

145. Interview with a WYM unionist, Jerusalem, 12 September 1985.

146. Ibid.

147. Shalev, "Winking an Eye" (see chap. 2, n. 51 above).

148. Interview with a unionist, Nablus, 14 December 1985.

149. International Labour Office, "Report [1987]," 34.

150. Ibid.

151. Interview with a unionist, Jerusalem, 3 June 1985.

152. *Al-Fajr Jerusalem Palestinian Weekly*, 18 November 1983.

153. Ibid.

154. Interview, Jerusalem, 3 June 1985.

155. Interview, Jenin, 31 January 1986.

156. "Provisional Labour Law," article 83.

157. Israel Defense Forces, "Military Order 825."

158. Israel Defense Forces, "Military Order 101."

159. Israel Defense Forces, "Military Order 378."

160. Interview with a unionist, Ramallah, 2 November 1985.

161. "Censorship in the West Bank," *International Labour Reports*, no. 24 (November–December 1987): 14.

162. Interview, Jenin, 31 January 1986.

163. Al-Haq/Law in the Service of Man, "Raid on Jenin Trade Unions," *Newsletter*, no. 18 (March–April 1987): 9.

164. Interview, Ramallah, 28 June 1986.

165. Interview, Hebron, 2 December 1985.

166. Interview, Ramallah, 2 November 1985.

167. Interview with a WUB official, Ramallah, 20 April 1987. The two union leaders who were not arrested were 'Adnan Natsheh, who holds a Jerusalem identity card and therefore enjoys a margin of protection under the law, and 'Amneh Rimawi, the WUB's second-in-command, who as a woman is less likely to be detained during a roundup.

168. Research of military court records commissioned by Al-Haq, Ramallah.

169. Affidavits obtained by Al-Haq, Ramallah.

170. Interview, Ramallah, 28 June 1986. 'Adnan Dagher was deported to Lebanon during the uprising in 1988.

171. Files of Al-Haq.

172. *Al-Fajr Jerusalem Palestinian Weekly*, 12 July 1985.

173. Files of Al-Haq.

174. *Jerusalem Post*, 3 May 1987.

175. One unionist in 'Arrabeh said in December 1989 that his union was no longer recording anything because of escalating army raids. Interview, 16 December 1989.

176. Interview, Nablus, 14 December 1985.

177. Interview, Nablus, 15 December 1985.

178. Presentation, West Jerusalem, 8 April 1986.

179. He was deported to Jordan at the end of January 1986.

180. *Al-Mithaq*, 11 September 1985.

181. "Memo from the WUB."

182. Interview, Nablus, 14 December 1985.

183. Interview, Nablus, 26 January 1986.

184. Interview, Ramallah/al-Bireh, 8 December 1985.

185. Interview, Ramallah, 20 January 1986.

186. See *Jerusalem Post* from 21 May until the end of July 1985. See also, Hiltermann, *Israel's Deportation Policy*, 81–87.

187. See Moffett, *Perpetual Emergency*.

188. See Playfair, *Administrative Detention*. In the fall of 1989, a new military order permitted the military commander to issue one-year administrative detention orders. Review is minimal, and they can be renewed at the end of the term.

189. *Jerusalem Post*, 5 August 1985.

190. GCGST, "Statement."

191. Amnesty International, *Amnesty International Report, 1987*, 351–52.

192. Ibid., 351. The report refers erroneously to Majed al-Labadi's town of residence as al-Bireh. It is Abu Dis, a village on the outskirts of Jerusalem. Majed's brother Muhammad al-Labadi, also a trade unionist, was under town arrest in al-Bireh on more than one occasion after the summer of 1985. The brothers were both deported to Lebanon during the intifada, in the summer of 1989. Muhammad al-Labadi has been fingered as one of the main instigators behind the intifada by Ze'ev Schiff and Ehud Ya'ari in their superficial and seriously flawed analysis of the uprising, which is based to a large extent on Shin Bet files. See Schiff and Ya'ari, *Intifada*.

193. Files of Al-Haq.

194. See PCA and PU, "Statement."

195. Affidavits obtained by Al-Haq.

196. "Case No. 1390: Complaint against the Government of Israel Presented by the Palestine Trade Unions Federation and the World Confederation of Labour," in Committee on Freedom of Association, *251st Report*, 46–51.

197. Ibid., 50–51.

198. Letter signed by David Yahav, legal advisor to the military government in the West Bank, in Al-Haq files. See also, Al-Haq, "Closure of the Nablus Trade Union Federation," *Newsletter*, no. 17 (January–February 1987): 6–7.

199. Rishmawi, "Finding Security."

200. Al-Haq/Law in the Service of Man, "Protection of Trade Union Rights," *Newsletter*, no. 15 (September–October 1986): 1.

201. International Labour Office, "Report [1987]," 32.

202. Hazboun was released one month early, on 3 August 1987.

203. "Unionist Movement Should Unify Its Ranks to Contribute to National Struggle," *Al-Fajr Jerusalem Palestinian Weekly*, 26 April 1987.

204. *Al-Fajr Jerusalem Palestinian Weekly*, 9 August 1987.

205. Interview with a unionist, Ya'bad, 15 June 1990.

206. Interview, Ramallah, 3 July 1987.

207. Hazboun and al-Salhi, "Workers' and Trade-Union Movement," part 3, 32.

208. Ibid.

209. Taggert, *Workers in Struggle*, 19.

210. Hazboun and al-Salhi, "Workers' and Trade-Union Movement," part 3, 33.

211. Interview with Gaza unionists at the Gaza Federation office, Gaza City, February 1986.

212. International Labour Office, "Report [1985]," 43–44.

213. Interview with Gaza unionists in the Gaza Federation office, Gaza City, February 1986.

214. International Labour Office, "Report [1986]," 33–34.

215. *Middle East International*, 12 September 1987.

216. *International Labour Reports*, no. 24 (July–August 1987).

217. *Al-Fajr Jerusalem Palestinian Weekly*, 27 February 1987.

218. Ibid.

219. See also Frances X. Clines, "Gaza Carpenters Defy the Israelis: A Union Votes," *New York Times*, 22 February 1987.

220. Al-Haq, "West Bank Trade Unions."

221. I personally observed the elections of the Commercial and Public Services Workers' Union in Gaza City on 4 April 1987.

222. GBWCU and GCPSWU, "Violations."

223. Ibid.

224. *Jerusalem Post*, 17 June 1987.

225. "Case No. 1414," in *Committee on Freedom of Association, 256th Report*.

CHAPTER FIVE

1. Giacaman, "Reflections," 5.

2. Peteet, "Women and the Palestinian Movement," 20.

3. Ghada Talhami, "Women in the Movement: Their Long, Uncelebrated History," *Al-Fajr Jerusalem Palestinian Weekly*, 30 May 1986.

4. Antonius, "Fighting," 63.

5. Giacaman, "Reflections," 4.

6. Interview with an activist, Ramallah, November 1987.

7. Usama Khalid, "A Palestinian History of Woman's Struggle," *Al-Fajr Jerusalem Palestinian Weekly*, 8 March 1985.

8. Giacaman, "Reflections," 6.

9. Ibid., 7.

10. See In'ash Al-Usra, *Society*.

11. Interview, al-Bireh, 11 December 1985.

12. Sayigh, "Encounters," 12.

13. Giacaman, "Reflections," 8.

14. Giacaman, "Palestinian Women," 11.

15. Interview with a (female) unionist, Nablus, 26 January 1986. See also the section on women in trade unions in this chapter.

16. According to Rita Giacaman, "the group was composed of those who were ideologically motivated and politically committed and those who were well-educated, nationalistic, socially aware and already fairly active in social and political life." Giacaman, "Palestinian Women," 16.

17. WWC, "First Social Field Study" and "Second Social Field Study." According to Rosemary Sayigh, this was the first research study done by any women's group. "Encounters," 18.

18. Interview with a UPWC activist, Hebron, 9 December 1985.

19. Interview with a UPWWC activist, Nablus, 26 January 1986. A member of the Textile Workers' Union in Nablus, she was one of the two women in the West Bank ever to assume a top leadership position in one of the GFTUs, the GFTU-PWB.

20. Sayigh, "Encounters," 18.

21. Interview, al-Bireh, 11 December 1985.

22. Interview, Hebron, 9 December 1985.

23. Kazi, "Palestinian Women," 34.

24. Interview, Ramallah, 31 October 1985.

25. Interview, al-Bireh, 22 November 1985.

26. Interview, Hebron, 9 December 1985.

27. Giacaman, "Reflections," 12.

28. *Al-Fajr Jerusalem Palestinian Weekly*, 27 June 1986.

29. Interview with a UPWWC activist, Nablus, 26 January 1986.

30. Interview with a WCSW activist, Nablus, 15 December 1985.

31. Interview with an activist, Hebron, 9 December 1985.

32. UPWC, *May*, 8.

33. Ibid., 8–9.

34. "Women Organize in Gaza," *Outwrite* (London), no. 46 (April 1986).

35. *Al-Fajr Jerusalem Palestinian Weekly*, 6 March 1987.

36. *Al-Fajr Jerusalem Palestinian Weekly*, 15 March 1985.

37. Interview, al-Bireh, 22 November 1985.

38. Interview, al-Bireh, 20 January 1986.

39. Palestine Focus, "Interview with Rita Giacaman," 3.

40. Giacaman, "Palestinian Women," 25.

41. Interview with a UPWWC activist, Nablus, 26 January 1986.

42. Interview with a WCSW activist, Nablus, 15 December 1985.

43. Interview, Nablus, 26 January 1986.

44. Interview, Abasan (Gaza), 1 February 1986.

45. FPWAC, "Women's Work Committee," 3. Full documentation on Ms. Kamal's case is also available in the files of Al-Haq, Ramallah.

46. *Al-Fajr Jerusalem Palestinian Weekly*, 19 July 1985.

47. Interview with Amal Wahdan, al-Bireh, 20 January 1986.

48. For the text of the 1980 resolution, see *Al-Fajr Jerusalem Palestinian Weekly*, 5 July 1985.

49. "Evaluating Nairobi," *Al-Awdah Weekly*, 18 August 1985.

50. PFWAC, *Newsletter*, no. 5 (August 1986): 1.

51. Interview, Ramallah, 14 November 1985. In 1987, the UPWWC reported having expanded to sixty-three branches. See UPWWC, *Union*.

52. Interview with an activist, Ramallah, 31 October 1985.

53. UPWC, "March," 22. A UPWC spokesperson that same year gave the much lower figure of eight hundred members, but she excluded "those who would support us when necessary but are not formal members." Interview, Jerusalem, 27 June 1985.

54. Interview with an activist, Nablus, 21 December 1985.

55. Interview with an activist, Hebron, 4 December 1985.

56. Interview with an activist, Abasan, 1 February 1986.

57. Interviews with an activist, Nablus, 26 January 1986, and in Hebron, 9 December 1985.

58. Interview with an activist, Hebron, 9 December 1985.

59. Interview with an activist, Nablus, 15 December 1985.

60. FWCSW, *Bylaws*, article 5, 6–7.

61. Ibid., article 7, 7.

62. Interview, al-Bireh, 22 November 1985.

63. Interview, Ramallah, 31 October 1985.

64. Giacaman, "Palestinian Women," 20–21.

65. Ibid., 21–22.

66. Interview with a UPWWC activist, Ramallah, 14 November 1985. In 1987, the UPWWC still claimed that working women made up 65 percent of its membership. See UPWWC, *Union*.

67. Interview with a UPWWC activist, Nablus, 26 January 1986.

68. Interview with a UPWC activist, Jerusalem, 27 June 1985.

69. UPWC, "Pioneering Experiment," 12.

70. Interview with a FPWAC activist, Abasan, 1 February 1986.

71. FPWAC, "All Efforts," 27.

72. Ibid.

73. Interview, al-Bireh, 22 November 1985.

74. Interview with a UPWWC activist, Jerusalem, 12 January 1988.

75. Giacaman, "Palestinian Women," 18.

76. Interview with a WCSW activist, Ramallah, 31 October 1985.

77. Interview with a WCSW activist, Nablus, 15 December 1985. In Nablus, however, rules are clearly laid down and elections are reported to take place. The activist explained: "One member has to nominate another before the latter can run for election. The most recent elections took place in May 1985: five members were elected to the administrative committee, one of whom will represent the committee in the federation in Ramallah."

78. UPWC, "What Is the Federation," 3.

79. FPWAC, *Amended Bylaws*, article 6(B), 7–8.

80. Interview with a UPWWC activist, Ramallah, 14 November 1985.

81. FPWAC, "Basic Committees," 17.

82. Interview with a FPWAC activist, Nablus, 21 December 1985, interview with a FPWAC/WUB activist, al-Bireh, April 1986, interview with a FPWAC activist, al-Bireh, 22 November 1985, and *FPWAC Bylaws*.

83. "Woman Power in Palestine," *Al-Fajr Jerusalem Palestinian Weekly*, 7 March 1984.

84. Interview, Hebron, 4 December 1985.

85. Interview, al-Bireh, 22 November 1985.
86. FPWAC, "Working Women and the Law," 6.
87. UPWWC, *Union* 7. See also UPWWC, "Kindergartens," 27.
88. Interview with an activist, Ramallah, 31 October 1985.
89. UPWC, "March," 23.
90. FPWAC, *Amended Program*, 2–3.
91. UPWC, "March," 23.
92. Interview, al-Bireh, 22 November 1985.
93. Interview with an activist, Hebron, 9 December 1985.
94. Interview with an activist, Ramallah, 31 October 1985.
95. UPWWC, *Union*, 5.
96. Interview, Hebron, 9 December 1985.
97. FPWAC, "Abassan Biscuits," *Newsletter*, no. 5 (August 1986): 5, 7.
98. UPWWC, *Union*, 4.
99. Debus and Spieker, "'We Do Not Only Want a Liberated Land,'" 6.
100. UPWWC, *Union*, 7.
101. Interview with a UPWWC activist, Jerusalem, 12 January 1988.
102. Interview, al-Bireh, 22 November 1985.
103. FPWAC, "Women's Work Committee," 2.
104. Interview with a PWB unionist, Nablus, 26 January 1986; interview with Samar Hawash, Nablus, 26 January 1986. For the election of Ms. Hawash to the GFTU, see *al-Tali'a*, 30 April 1987.
105. Interview with an activist, Hebron, 9 December 1985.
106. Interview, Ramallah, 8 December 1985.
107. WWC, *On the Condition*.
108. Interview, al-Bireh, 20 January 1986. Note that this is not only a construction workers' union but also a general services workers' union—in other words, a catchall union for the irregularly employed or for those who have no other union. Palestinian women are generally not employed in construction. Secretaries, however, are likely recruits in a general services workers' union.
109. Interview, 1 December 1985.
110. Ibid.
111. Libby Fillmore and Sharry Renn, "Palestinian Woman Unionist Finds Organizing Tough Going," *Al-Fajr Jerusalem Palestinian Weekly*, 7 March 1986.
112. Interview with a WUB unionist, al-Bireh, 15 March 1986.
113. FPWAC, "All Efforts," 28.
114. UPWWC, "The Federation," 17.
115. Interview, Ramallah, 1 December 1985.
116. Interview, al-Bireh, 20 January 1986.
117. Ibid.
118. Interview, Ramallah, 1 December 1985.
119. Ibid.
120. Manar Said, "The Ramallah Sewing Union Going Strong," *Al-Fajr Jerusalem Palestinian Weekly*, 19 April 1985.
121. Interview, Ramallah, 8 December 1985.
122. Interview, Ramallah, 1 December 1985.
123. Ibid.

124. Quoted in Said, "Ramallah Sewing Union" (see n. 120 above).

125. Ibid.

126. Interview, Ramallah, 1 December 1985.

127. Said, "Ramallah Sewing Union" (see n. 120 above).

128. Interview with a WUB unionist, Ramallah, 1 December 1985.

129. Ibid.

130. Interview, Ramallah, 8 December 1985.

131. Interview, al-Bireh, 20 January 1986.

132. Interview, Ramallah, 8 December 1985.

133. Interviews, Ramallah, 1 and 8 December 1985.

134. UPWC, *May*, 7.

135. Interview with an activist, Jerusalem, 27 June 1985. See also UPWC, "March," 22–23.

136. Quoted in Fillmore and Renn, "Palestinian Woman" (see n. 111 above).

137. Interview with an activist, al-Bireh, 22 November 1985.

138. FPWAC, "Palestinian Working Woman," 16.

139. FPWAC, "Working Women," 5–7.

140. FPWAC, "Palestinian Working Woman," 16.

141. Interview with a FPWAC activist, Abasan (Gaza), 1 February 1986.

142. FPWAC, "Fourth General Conference," 9.

143. UPWWC, *Union*, 4.

144. UPWWC, "Federation."

145. Interview, Nablus, 26 January 1986.

146. UPWWC, "Statement of the Palestinian Women," 28–33.

147. Giacaman, "Palestinian Women," 20.

148. Interview, Hebron, 9 December 1985.

149. Interview, Hebron, 4 December 1985.

150. FPWAC, *Amended Program*.

151. FPWAC, "Spotlight," 3–6.

152. See, for example, FPWAC, "PUWWC: No to State Terrorism," *Newsletter*, no. 5 (August 1986): 6–7; and Zahera Kamal, "Israel Attempts to Paralyze Palestinian Power," *Al-Fajr Jerusalem Palestinian Weekly*, 7 March 1986.

153. Quoted in "Sawt al-Mara'a: Women's Issues Find Their Voice," *Al-Fajr Jerusalem Palestinian Weekly*, 24 June 1983.

154. Quoted in Fillmore and Renn, "Palestinian Woman" (see n. 111 above).

155. Quoted in Nadia Hijab, "Arab Women Find Their Voice," *The Middle East* (London), no. 131 (September 1985): 31–33.

156. FPWAC, "Women under Occupation," *Newsletter*, no. 3 (April 1985): 3.

157. FPWAC, "All Efforts," 27.

158. FPWAC, *Amended Program*.

159. UPWWC, *Union*, 1.

160. Ibid.

161. Ibid.

162. Quoted in *The Middle East* (London), September 1985.

163. "Army, Police Protect Ramallah Murderer," *Al-Fajr Jerusalem Palestinian Weekly*, 1 November 1985.

164. UPWWC handbill (in Arabic), 30 October 1985.

165. Interview, Nablus, 26 January 1986.

166. "Local Women's Groups Celebrate March 8," *Al-Fajr Jerusalem Palestinian Weekly*, 15 March 1985.

167. UPWC, "What Is the Federation."

168. Ibid.

169. UPWC, "March," 23.

170. Interview, Jerusalem, 27 June 1985.

171. Interview, Hebron, 9 December 1985.

172. Ibid.

173. WCSW, *Association Bulletin No. 2*.

174. Interview, Nablus, 15 December 1985.

175. "Local Women's Groups Celebrate March 8" (see n. 166 above). See also *Al-Fajr Jerusalem Palestinian Weekly*, 21 March 1984.

176. UPWC, *May*, 9.

177. FPWAC, *Newsletter*, no. 3 (April 1985): 8.

178. Interview, Nablus, 26 January 1986.

179. *Al-Fajr Jerusalem Palestinian Weekly*, 4 November 1983.

180. Interview, Nablus, 21 December 1985.

181. Peteet, "Women and the Palestinian Movement," 22.

182. "We Are Political Prisoners," 98.

183. Interview with a lawyer, Ramallah, November 1987.

184. Interview, Nablus, 26 January 1986.

185. Interview, Jerusalem, 27 June 1985.

186. Interview, Nablus, 26 January 1986.

187. Interview, Hebron, 9 December 1985.

188. Interview, Hebron, 9 December 1985.

189. Interview with a UPWWC activist, Nablus, 26 January 1986.

190. Peteet, "Women and the Palestinian Movement," 22.

191. Interview with a FPWAC activist, Nablus, 28 December 1985.

192. Antonius, "Fighting," 63.

193. Interview with a Palestinian sociologist, Ramallah, 11 March 1988.

CHAPTER SIX

1. On this period, see "Intifada: Year Three."

2. Quoted by Baumgarten, "'Discontented People,'" 207.

3. Schiff and Ya'ari, *Intifada*, 46-47.

4. *Jerusalem Post*, 16 December 1987.

5. Abu-Lughod, "On Achieving Independence."

6. Interview, Jerusalem, 6 June 1985. The idea of mass civil disobedience is a relatively old one in the Occupied Territories. One of the main features of the famous Revolt of 1936–39, which remains deeply embedded as a heroic event in the memories of today's Palestinians, was a prolonged commercial strike. The PNF and the NGC (see chapter 3) both called for strikes and boycotts in their heyday. Nonpayment of taxes was considered an option of resistance to the occupation from the moment the value-added tax was imposed in 1976. Such actions never

amounted to much, however, precisely because there was no infrastructure to support mass civil disobedience.

7. McDowall, *Palestine and Israel*, 36. This argument is supported by Jamal Zaqout, an activist from Gaza deported to Lebanon by the army in 1988. Zaqout says that the reconciliation of PLO factions at the eighteenth PNC session was "of crucial importance" because at the beginning of the uprising, "all the factions had one direction." The four factions' first joint leaflet was issued *before* the uprising, in October 1987, against the visit by United States Secretary of State George Shultz to the area. Interview, Cairo, 19 June 1990.

8. Ibid., 117–78.

9. Parts of this section appeared, in a somewhat different form, in Hiltermann, "Work and Action"; "Worker's Rights"; and "Sustaining Movement."

10. These figures, calculated for only the West Bank by Al-Haq, the Palestinian affiliate of the International Commission of Jurists in Ramallah, are not exhaustive, but they approximate reality. During this eleven-month period, 104 workers were killed in the West Bank, as opposed to 101 nonworkers. Included in the category "workers" are the unemployed and self-employed, such as drivers and barbers, as well as white-collar workers, such as teachers. Workers constituted approximately 50 percent of the monthly fatality toll as well, except for March 1988, when twenty-eight workers were killed as opposed to sixteen nonworkers. Figures for the Gaza Strip can be assumed to be similar. Al-Haq files.

11. Johnson, O'Brien, and Hiltermann, "West Bank Rises Up," 40.

12. Interview with a labor leader, Ramallah, 15 December 1988.

13. "Yatta Diary," In Facts Information Committee, *Towards a State of Independence*, 30.

14. Interview with a labor leader, Ramallah, 15 December 1988.

15. Interview with a union leader, Ramallah, 18 December 1989.

16. Interview with Jamal Zaqout, Cairo, 19 June 1990.

17. See chap. 7 in Schiff and Ya'ari, *Intifada*, 188–219.

18. The UNLU was set up as the Palestinian leadership in the Occupied Territories, linked organically to the PLO. DFLP officials have claimed responsibility for establishing the UNLU, but were upstaged, they contend, when a faction inside Fatah distributed a communiqué signed by the "Palestinian Nationalist Forces" in some areas of the West Bank (Hebron, Ramallah, and parts of East Jerusalem) on 8 January 1988, despite Fatah assurances to the DFLP earlier that day that no decision had been reached on putting out such a leaflet. The DFLP then issued a similar manifesto, naming it Communiqué no. 2 and signing it with the hitherto unknown name "Unified National Leadership of Escalation of the Uprising," on 10 January, reportedly after reaching agreement with Fatah. Further communiqués were coordinated by Fatah and the DFLP, and were signed by the Palestine Liberation Organization/Unified National Leadership of the Uprising. The PFLP joined the UNLU after Communiqué no. 3 a few days later, and the PCP joined after Communiqué no. 11 in March. As the uprising progressed, it became clear that the UNLU was less a leadership committee than a regular meeting attended by representatives from the four main factions of the PLO in the Occupied Territories: Fatah, the DFLP, the PFLP and the PCP. These represen-

tatives were often second-level cadres, not leaders, in their factions. This has meant that when the army "arrested the UNLU," as it claimed to have done on more than one occasion, it may have arrested that period's representatives of the PLO factions to the UNLU, who were easily replaced because they were rotating members anyway. Interviews with Jamal Zaqout, a DFLP trade unionist deported for membership in the UNLU by Israel in 1988, Cairo, 19 June 1990, and Salim Tamari, a sociologist at Bir Zeit University, Ramallah, 26 June 1990; Schiff and Ya'ari, *Intifada*, chap. 7, also has an interesting, though highly distorted, take on the matter.

19. Interview with Jamal Zaqout, Cairo, 19 June 1990.

20. The UNLU communiqués, distributed on the streets in the Occupied Territories throughout the uprising, are not publicly available, and can usually only be found in private archives. Due to difficulties in communication between the various authors of the UNLU's leaflets, sometimes more than one version of the same leaflet can be found, with slightly differing content. The leaflets have been broadcast throughout the uprising by two radio stations: the "Al-Quds" station in Damascus, and the "Voice of the PLO" in Baghdad. "Al-Quds" is known to have changed the contents of leaflets it broadcast, reflecting its political agenda, which varies from that of the PLO. A number of English translations have been published, including in Lockman and Beinin, *Intifada*, and in Facts Information Committee, *Towards a State of Independence*. Most have also appeared in the daily installments of the Foreign Broadcast Information Service (FBIS).

21. For example, in UNLU Communiqué no. 6, 3 February 1988.

22. *Jerusalem Post* (international edition), 26 March 1988.

23. *Jerusalem Post*, 21 December 1988. The figures available are contradictory. The Bank of Israel reported in May 1989 that there had been a 25 percent decrease in the effective supply of workers from the West Bank and Gaza in 1988. *Jerusalem Post*, 1 June 1989.

24. Interview with a resident of Wadi Fukin, Jerusalem, 18 March 1989.

25. For a record of repeated threats issued by various Israeli goverment officials, see the *Jerusalem Post*, 15 and 22 December 1987; 12 and 13 January 1988; and 1 and 4 March 1988. See also the *New York Times*, 17 May 1989, for later threats.

26. Interview with a trade unionist, Jerusalem, 9 January 1989.

27. Interview with a labor activist, Jerusalem, 18 March 1989.

28. UNLU Communiqué no. 13, 12 April 1988.

29. UNLU Communiqué no. 15, 30 April 1988.

30. UNLU Communiqué no. 19, 8 June 1988.

31. For example, in Communiqués nos. 13 (10 April 1988) and 14 (20 April 1988).

32. UNLU Communiqué no. 15, 30 April 1988.

33. UNLU Communiqué no. 10, 10 March 1988.

34. UNLU Communiqué no. 19, 8 June 1988.

35. UNLU Communiqué no. 22, 21 July 1988.

36. Al-Haq, *Punishing a Nation*, 318–19.

37. Ibid., chap. 9.

38. Ibid., 322–23.

39. Quoted in the *Jerusalem Post*, 25 August 1988.

40. Memos written by the Interim Workers' Committee at the Royal Crown Cola Factory, August 1988 (in Arabic).

41. Interview with a unionist, Jerusalem, 9 January 1989. See also the article by Muhammad Manasreh in *Al-Tali'a*, 27 October 1988.

42. Copy of contract obtained from the Construction and General Institutions Workers' Union (WUB), Ramallah, December 1988 (in Arabic).

43. UNLU Communiqué no. 32, 9 January 1989.

44. UNLU Communiqué no. 33, 24 January 1989.

45. UNLU Communiqués nos. 32 (9 January 1989) and 34 (11 February 1989).

46. UNLU Communiqué no. 36, 16 March 1989.

47. Quoted in *Al-Fajr Jerusalem Palestinian Weekly*, 13 February 1989.

48. *Al-Fajr Jerusalem Palestinian Weekly*, 10 April 1989.

49. *Al-Fajr Jerusalem Palestinian Weekly*, 27 February and 10 April 1989.

50. See Al-Haq, *Punishing a Nation*, chap. 7.

51. *In Jerusalem* (special section in the Friday issue of the *Jerusalem Post*), 17 February 1989; and *Jerusalem Post*, 15 March 1989.

52. *Jerusalem Post*, 14 February 1989.

53. *Al-Fajr Jerusalem Palestinian Weekly*, 6 February 1989; 19 February 1989.

54. See, for example, *Al-Tali'a*, 14 July 1988.

55. *Jerusalem Post*, 25 January 1989.

56. *Jerusalem Post*, 26 February 1989.

57. Figures provided by Al-Haq, Ramallah, July 1989. Some of the detail on this four-month period is telling: The Shabura section of the Rafah refugee camp was under curfew 120 days, or 57 percent of the time during January–April, which were relatively quiet months. There were more and longer curfews in 1988, and the situation deteriorated again sharply in May and June 1989.

58. *Jerusalem Post*, 16 May 1989.

59. Army source quoted in the *Jerusalem Post*, 4 September 1989.

60. *Jerusalem Post*, 13 June 1989.

61. UNLU Communiqué no. 31, 22 December 1988.

62. *Jerusalem Post*, 11 January 1989; 24 February 1989.

63. FNV, *Report of the FNV Mission*. The report did not provide evidence to support its implicit suggestion that some Palestinian unions might not be bona fide trade unions, thereby parroting standard, unproven claims by the Israeli military authorities.

64. FNV, *Report of the FNV Visit*.

65. International Labour Office, "Report [1989]," 33–34.

66. *Jerusalem Post*, 5 July 1989; *Al-Fajr Jerusalem Palestinian Weekly*, 10 July 1989.

67. International Labour Office, "Report [1990]," 32.

68. Jacob Wirtschafter, "Histadrut Grapples with Legacy of Rishon," *Jerusalem Post*, 25 May 1990.

69. For a summary of the findings of the Israeli Central Bureau of Statistics on the economic situation in the Occupied Territories in 1988, see "Economic Activity in Areas Drops Sharply," *Jerusalem Post* (international edition), 20 January 1990.

70. David Rosenberg, "Building Worker Shortage Worsens," *Jerusalem Post* (international edition), 30 December 1989.

71. Shlomo Maoz, "Trade with Territories Continues to Drop," *Jerusalem Post*, 1 June 1990.

72. International Labour Office, "Report [1990]," 19–21.

73. Interview with an official of the Construction and General Institutions Workers' Union, Ya'bad, 16 December 1989.

74. Interview with an official of the Construction and General Institutions Workers' Union, Arrabeh, 16 December 1989.

75. Interview with a WUB official, Ramallah, 18 December 1989.

76. Interview, Ya'bad, 16 December 1989.

77. Interview with a PWB unionist, Bethlehem, 15 December 1989.

78. Interview with a WUB unionist, Ramallah, 18 December 1989.

79. Interview with a PWB unionist, Jerusalem, 9 January 1989.

80. Interview with a WUB official, Ramallah, 18 December 1989.

81. Interview with unionists at the WUB's Labor Studies Center, Ramallah, 6 June 1990, and with a WYM unionist, Jerusalem, 24 June 1990.

82. *Jerusalem Post*, 7 January 1990.

83. Interview with a WYM unionist, Jerusalem, 24 June 1990. Originally, the unionists offered the Islamic Resistance Movement (HAMAS) a seat as well, but HAMAS expressed no interest in participating.

84. Interview with a WUB official, Ramallah, 6 June 1990.

85. Interview, Ya'bad, 15 June 1990. The three factions, which have hardly any following in the Occupied Territories, are: the Popular Struggle Front (Samir Ghosheh), the Arab Liberation Front, and the Palestinian Liberation Front.

86. Interview with a WYM unionist, Jerusalem, 24 June 1990.

87. Ibid.

88. Interview, Ya'bad, 15 June 1990.

89. Interview with a WUB official, Ramallah, 6 June 1990.

90. Interview with an official of the Institutions Workers' Union, Nablus, 16 June 1990.

91. International Labour Office, "Report [1990]," 47.

92. A shorter version of this section appeared in Hiltermann, "Women's Movement." Some additional quotes appeared previously in Hiltermann, "Sustaining Movement."

93. Interview with a UPWWC activist, Ramallah, 20 December 1989.

94. Interview with a FPWAC activist, Nablus, 17 December 1989.

95. Interview with a UPWWC activist, Nablus, 17 December 1989.

96. PUWWC, *Newsletter* (8 March 1988): 11.

97. Interview with a UPWWC activist, Ramallah, 20 December 1989.

98. Palestinian Union of Women's Work Committees (currently FPWAC), *Newsletter* (8 March 1988): 10.

99. Reported by Islah Jad, who interviewed women in villages and refugee camps, "Salons," 135.

100. Interview with a FPWAC activist, Arrabeh, 16 December 1989.

101. From personal observations and interviews, March 1988. The FPWAC reports that six hundred women participated. *Newsletter* (8 March 1988): 9. Other estimates exceed one thousand.

102. Interview with a UPWC activist, Hebron, 13 June 1990.

103. FPWAC, *Newsletter* (8 March 1988): 9.

104. Al-Haq reported at the end of the first year of the uprising that 15 women had been killed by the army, compared with 189 men. Al-Haq, *Punishing a Nation*, 12.

105. Quoted by Jad, "Salons," 134.

106. Ibid., 135.

107. UPWC, "Our Production Is Our Pride" (undated; available from the UPWC).

108. Pamphlet by Kathy Glavanis and Eilene Kuttab, Department of Sociology, Bir Zeit University (undated; available from the UPWC).

109. From a speech given by a UPWC representative at a Palestinian-Italian women's conference, Jerusalem, August 1988 (available from the UPWC).

110. Interview with a UPWWC activist, Ramallah, 20 December 1989.

111. Jad, "Salons," 136.

112. Interview with a UPWWC activist, Ramallah, 20 December 1989.

113. This point was emphasized by a UPWWC activist interviewed in Nablus, 17 December 1989.

114. Referred to in Jad, "Salons," 133. Several of the deportees were husbands of prominent women activists.

115. See for example FPWAC, "The Unified Women's Councils: Pressing Women's and National Concerns" (in Arabic), *Newsletter* (March 1989): 6.

116. Interview with a FPWAC activist, Arrabeh, 16 December 1989.

117. Interview with a UPWC activist, Ramallah, 5 June 1990.

118. Interview with a UPWWC activist, Nablus, 17 December 1989.

119. Interview, Jerusalem, 21 October 1989. The UPWWC has contradicted itself on this matter, though. Another leader said that every branch committee has elected an administrative committee during the uprising. She cited elections in the village of Burhan near Ramallah in December 1989 as the most recent example. She added that no national elections have been held, but that some of the activity committees (as opposed to the district committees) had elected representatives to the national executive committee. Interview, Ramallah, 20 December 1989.

120. Interviews with UPWC activists in Hebron, 13 June 1990, and Ramallah, 5 June 1990.

121. Interview with a FPWAC leader, Jerusalem, 21 October 1989.

122. UPWC, "Maha Nassar on Hunger Strike."

123. FPWAC, *Newsletter* (October 1988): 3–5.

124. Interview with a UPWWC activist, Ramallah, 20 December 1989.

125. From personal observations during visit to Arrabeh, 16 December 1989.

126. Interview with a UPWC activist, Ramallah, 5 June 1990.

127. Al-Haq's second annual report describes a litany of abuse against women's committees and their cadres. *A Nation under Siege*, chap. 15.

128. This assessment is shared by Giacaman and Johnson, "Palestinian Women," 165. The Israeli authorities arrested what they referred to as members of the UNLU on several occasions in 1988 and 1989. All were men.

129. The other two NGO representatives are Mustapha Barghouthi for the Progressive Bloc and Faisal Husseini for the Youth Movement.

130. Giacaman and Johnson, "Palestinian Women," 161.

131. Interview with a FPWAC activist, Kufr Na'meh, 12 June 1990.

132. Interview, Ramallah, 20 December 1989.

133. Interview with a UPWWC activist, Nablus, 17 December 1989.

134. For examples of references to "sons," see UNLU Communiqués nos. 3 ("O brave sons of our people"), 9 ("We address a militant greeting to the sons of Qabatya"), and 23 ("We have no choice but to depend on ourselves to educate ourselves and our sons"). For references to "brother," see Communiqués nos. 1 and 14. Yasser Arafat is referred to as "the father symbol" Abu Ammar (Communiqué no. 28).

135. For examples of references to women as "mothers," see UNLU Communiqués nos. 8 ("Our love for all mothers of this homeland"), 29 ("Mother of the martyr"), and 53 (celebrating Mother's Day). For references to women in the context of victims of the occupation, see Communiqué no. 24, which intones, "In the name of our people under curfews and in prisons, the bereaved, children, women, and the elderly who are suffering from the repressive measures of occupation. . . ." Communiqué no. 7 or 8 (this is not clear from Lockman and Beinin, *Intifada*, which reproduces it) calls on "women and old men" to organize protest marches to Red Cross headquarters and prisons. Is this supposed to be a demonstration of the invalids?

136. See UNLU Communiqués nos. 12 ("Our children, women, men, and youths stand firm against the ruthless Zionist military machine") and 32 ("The UNLU also values the role of the Palestinian woman in furthering steadfastness, uplifting the morale of our people, and in protecting the uprising").

137. Similarly, in Communiqué no. 7 or 8 (unclear from Lockman and Beinin, *Intifada*), schoolgirls are urged to go to school every day and organize demonstrations, despite the fact that they had been doing so for at least a year prior to the uprising, often taking the initiative, at least from my own observations in Ramallah.

138. UNLU Communiqué no. 23, 5 August 1988.

139. Communiqué no. 9 (2 March 1988) calls on women to "go to the streets in tumultuous demonstrations announcing their rejection of the occupation and setting the most splendid examples of how to confront the Zionist army."

140. UNLU Communiqué no. 35, 26 February 1989.

141. UNLU Communiqué no. 53, 6 March 1990.

142. "Proclamation of the Independent Palestinian State," issued by the nineteenth PNC session, Algiers, 15 November 1988. Reproduced in Lockman and Beinin, *Intifada*, 395-99.

143. Interview with a FPWAC activist, Arrabeh, 16 December 1989.

144. These are quotes from an editorial published in the FPWAC *Newsletter* of March 1989. They reflect the position of all three of the progressive women's committees, however.

145. UPWWC, "The Intifada and the Role of Palestinian Women," *Voice of Women* (UPWWC newsletter) 1, no. 2 (September 1989): 1.

146. Ibid., 4.

147. Ibid., 10.

148. Interview with a UPWWC activist, Jerusalem, 21 October 1989.

149. FPWAC, "The Tasks Required from the Women's Movement to Capitalize on the Intifada" (in Arabic), *Newsletter* (April 1989), 3–6. See also, UPWC, "The Palestinian Woman Breaks Her Fetters," 5–8.

150. Interview with a UPWC activist, Ramallah, 5 June 1990.

151. Interview with a FPWAC leader, Jerusalem, 21 October 1989.

152. Interview with UPWC activists, Hebron, 13 June 1990.

153. FPWAC, "Neighborhood Committees: Organizing for Self-Reliance," *Newsletter* (30 June 1988): 8.

154. See the excellent article by Rema Hammami, "Women, the Hijab and the Intifada."

155. Interview with a UPWC activist, Ramallah, 5 June 1990.

156. "Women in the Uprising" (pamphlet available from the UPWC, 1988).

157. FPWAC, *Newsletter* (8 March 1988): 10.

158. Giacaman and Johnson, "Palestinian Women," 159.

159. Interview with a unionist, Jerusalem, 9 January 1989.

160. Jad, "Salons," 139.

CHAPTER SEVEN

1. Tamari, "What the Uprising Means," 26.

2. Ibid.

3. Ibid.

4. Some of the movements of national liberation in Africa were able to take advantage of the diminishing strength of the colonial powers in the international balance of forces. The example of the Angolan struggle against Portuguese colonialism is instructive in this regard. The Palestinian movement, by contrast, faces rather different odds.

5. Interview, Jerusalem, 18 November 1985.

6. Interview, Jerusalem, 9 June 1985.

7. Joseph, "Women and Politics," 3–4.

8. Ibid., 5.

9. Giacaman, "Reflections," 11.

10. Ibid., 15.

11. Sayigh, "Looking across the Mediterranean," 24.

12. Ahmad, "Revolutionary Warfare," 148–49.

BIBLIOGRAPHY

BOOKS AND ARTICLES

Abraham, Sameer Y. "The Development and Transformation of the Palestine National Movement." In *Occupation: Israel over Palestine*, edited by Naseer H. Aruri. Belmont, Mass.: Association of Arab-American Graduates Union, 1983.

Abu-Lughod, Ibrahim. "On Achieving Independence." Introduction to *Intifada: Palestine at the Crossroads*, edited by Jamal R. Nassar and Roger Heacock, 1–11. New York: Praeger Publishers, 1990.

Ahmad, Eqbal. "Revolutionary Warfare and Counterinsurgency." In *National Liberation: Revolution in the Third World*, edited by Norman Miller and Roderick Aya, 137–213. New York: Free Press, 1971.

Al-Haq. *A Nation under Siege: Al-Haq Annual Report on Human Rights in the Occupied Palestinian Territories, 1989.* Ramallah: Al-Haq, 1990.

———. *Punishing a Nation: Human Rights Violations during the Palestinian Uprising, December 1987–December 1988.* Ramallah: Al-Haq, 1988; Boston: South End Press, 1990.

———. "West Bank Trade Unions under Israeli Occupation." Internal report prepared for the Australian government, 1987.

Amnesty International. *Amnesty International Report, 1987.* London: Amnesty International Publications, 1987.

Antonius, Soraya. "Fighting on Two Fronts: Conversations with Palestinian Women." In *Third World—Second Sex: Women's Struggle and National Liberation—Third World Women Speak Out*, compiled by Miranda Davis, 63–77. London: Zed Books, 1983.

Arkadie, Brian Van. *Benefits and Burdens: A Report on the West Bank and Gaza Strip Economies since 1967.* Washington, D.C. and New York: Carnegie Endowment for International Peace, 1977.

Awwad, Arabi, and Jiryis Qawwas. "Resistance in the Occupied Territories." *Journal of Palestine Studies* 3, no. 4 (Summer 1974).

Barghouthi, Mustafa, and Rita Giacaman. "The Emergence of an Infrastructure of Resistance: The Case of Health." In *Intifada: Palestine at the Crossroads*, edited by Jamal R. Nassar and Roger Heacock, 73–87. New York: Praeger Publishers, 1990.

Baumgarten, Helga. "'Discontented People' and 'Outside Agitators': The PLO in the Palestinian Uprising." In *Intifada: Palestine at the Crossroads*, edited by Jamal R. Nassar and Roger Heacock, 207–26. New York: Praeger Publishers, 1990.

Beinen, Joel. "The Palestine Communist Party, 1919–1948." *MERIP Reports*, no. 55 (March 1977): 3–16.

Ben Israel, Ruth. "On Social Human Rights for Workers of the Administered Areas." *Israel Yearbook on Human Rights* 12 (1982).

Benvenisti, Meron. *Israeli Rule in the West Bank: Legal and Administrative Aspects*. Jerusalem: West Bank Data Base Project, 1983.

——. *1986 Report: Demographic, Economic, Legal, Social, and Political Developments in the West Bank*. Jerusalem: West Bank Data Base Project, 1986.

——. *The West Bank Data Project: A Survey of Israel's Policies*. Washington, D.C.: American Enterprise Institute, 1984.

Budeiri, Musa K. "Changes in the Economic Structure of the West Bank and Gaza Strip under Israeli Occupation." *Labour, Capital, and Society* 15, no. 1 (April 1982).

——. *The Palestine Communist Party, 1919–1948: Arab and Jew in the Struggle for Internationalism*. London: Ithaca Press, 1979.

Carmi, Shulamit, and Henry Rosenfeld. "The Origins of the Process of Proletarianization and Urbanization of Arab Peasants in Palestine." *Annals of the New York Academy of Sciences* 220, no. 6 (11 March 1974): 470–85.

Central Bureau of Statistics, *Statistical Abstract of Israel, 1987*, no. 38. Jerusalem: Central Bureau of Statistics, 1987.

Cobban, Helena. *The Palestinian Liberation Organisation: People, Power, and Politics*. Cambridge: Cambridge University Press, 1984.

Cohen, Amnon. *Political Parties in the West Bank under the Jordanian Regime, 1949–1967*. Ithaca and London: Cornell University Press, 1982.

Committee on Freedom of Association. *251st Report of the Committee on Freedom of Association*. Geneva: ILO, 1987.

——. *256th Report of the Committee on Freedom of Association*. Geneva: ILO, 1988.

Dakkak, Ibrahim. "Back to Square One: A Study in the Re-Emergence of the Palestinian Identity in the West Bank, 1967–1980." In *Palestinians over the Green Line: Studies on the Relations between Palestinians on Both Sides of the 1949 Armistice Line since 1967*, edited by Alexander Schölch, 64–101. London: Ithaca Press, 1983.

——. "Development and Control in the West Bank." *Arab Studies Quarterly* 7, nos. 2, 3 (Spring, Summer 1985).

——. "Survey of the Attitudes of Palestinian Wage-Earners on Both Sides of the 1949 Armistice Line." In *Palestinians over the Green Line: Studies on the Relations between Palestinians on Both Sides of the 1949 Armistice Line since 1967*, edited by Alexander Schölch, 117–46. London: Ithaca Press, 1983.

Debus, Barbara, and Maria Spieker. "'We Do Not Only Want a Liberated Land': The Palestinian Women's Movement in the West Bank." Manuscript, Ramallah, 1984.

Dekker, L. Douwes, et al. "Case Studies in African Labour Action in South Africa and Namibia (South West Africa)." In *The Development of an African Working Class: Studies in Class Formation and Action*, edited by Richard Sandbrook and Robin Cohen. London: Longman Group, 1975.

Ehrlich, Avishai. "The Oriental Support for Begin: A Critique of Farjoun." *Khamsin*, no. 10 (1983).

Facts Information Committee. *Towards a State of Independence: The Palestinian Uprising, December 1987—August 1988*. Jerusalem: Facts Information Committee, 1988.

Farjoun, Emanuel. "Palestinian Workers in Israel—A Reserve Army of Labour." *Khamsin*, no. 7 (1980).

Farsoun, Samih K., and Jean M. Landis. "The Sociology of an Uprising: The Roots of the *Intifada*." In *Intifada: Palestine at the Crossroads*, edited by Jamal R. Nassar and Roger Heacock, 15–35. New York: Praeger Publishers, 1990.

Fasheh, Munir Jamil. "Education as Praxis for Liberation: Birzeit University and the Community Work Program." Ph.D. Diss., Harvard University, 1987.

Fawzia, Fawzia. "Palestine: Women and the Revolution." In *Sisterhood Is Global*, edited by Robin Morgan, 539–48. Harmondsworth, Middlesex: Penguin Books, 1985.

Federatie Nederlandse Vakverenigingen. *Report of the FNV Mission to the Israeli Occupied Territories, 15–18 January 1989* (in Dutch). Amsterdam: FNV, 1989.

————. *Report of the FNV Visit to the Israeli Trade Union Federation Histadrut, 18–22 January 1989* (in Dutch). Amsterdam: FNV, 1989.

Friedland, William H., et al. *Revolutionary Theory*. Totowa, N.J.: Allanheld, Osmun and Co., 1982.

Frisch, Hillel. *Stagnation and Frontier: Arab and Jewish Industry in the West Bank*. Jerusalem: West Bank Data Base Project, 1983.

Fuller, Graham E. *The West Bank of Israel: Point of No Return?* Santa Monica, Calif.: RAND Corporation, 1989.

Gansekoele, Heleen, and Claartje van Well, "I Fight a Lot, But So Does Everyone Else. . . : A Description of the Life of Palestinian Women" (in Dutch). Doctoraalscriptie culturele anthropologie, University of Nijmegen, Netherlands, 1979.

Gharaibeh, Fawzi A. *The Economies of the West Bank and Gaza Strip*. Boulder and London: Westview Press, 1985.

Giacaman, Rita. "Disturbing Distortions: A Response to the Report of the Ministry of Health of Israel to the Thirty-Eighth World Health Assembly on Health and Health Services in the Occupied Territories, Geneva, May 1983." Paper, 1983.

————. "Palestinian Women and Development in the Occupied West Bank." Manuscript, Bir Zeit University, West Bank.

————. "Reflections on the Palestinian Women's Movement in the Israeli-Occupied Territories." Manuscript, Bir Zeit University, West Bank, May 1987.

Giacaman, Rita and Penny Johnson. "Palestinian Women: Building Barricades and Breaking Barriers." In *Intifada: The Palestinian Uprising against Israeli Occupation*, edited by Zachary Lockman and Joel Beinin, 155–69. Boston: South End Press, 1989.

Graham-Brown, Sarah. "Report from the Occupied Territories." *MERIP Reports*, no. 83 (December 1979).

————. "The West Bank and Gaza: The Structural Impact of Israeli Colonization." *MERIP Reports*, no. 74 (January 1979): 9–20.

Greenberg, Stanley, B. "The Indifferent Hegemony: Israel and the Palestinians." Manuscript, Yale University, 1985.

————. *Race and State in Capitalist Development: Comparative Perspectives*. New Haven and London: Yale University Press, 1980.

Hammam, Mona. "Labor Migration and the Sexual Division of Labor." *MERIP Reports*, no. 95 (March–April 1981).

Hammami, Rema. "Women, the Hijab, and the Intifada." *Middle East Report*, nos. 164–65 (May–August 1990): 24–71.

Hazboun, George, and Bassam al-Salhi. "The Workers' and Trade-Union Movement in the Occupied Territories: 1967–1983" (in Arabic). Part 1: *Al-Kateb*, no. 49 (May 1984): 6–16. Part 2: *Al-Kateb*, no. 50 (June 1984): 23–35. Part 3: *Al-Kateb*, no. 51 (July 1984): 32–51. Part 4: *Al-Kateb*, no. 52 (August 1984): 9–17.

Heller, Mark. "Politics and Social Change in the West Bank since 1967." In *Palestinian Society and Politics*, edited by Joel S. Migdal, 185–211. Princeton: Princeton University Press, 1980.

Hilal, Jamil. "Class Transformation in the West Bank and Gaza." *MERIP Reports*, no. 53 (December 1976): 9–15.

Hiltermann, Joost R. "The Emerging Trade Union Movement in the West Bank: Mass Mobilization under Occupation." *MERIP Reports*, nos. 136–37 (October–December 1985): 26–31.

———. "Human Rights and the Palestinian Struggle for National Liberation." *Journal of Palestine Studies* 18, no. 2 (Winter 1989): 109–18.

———. *Israel's Deportation Policy in the Occupied West Bank and Gaza*. 2d ed. Ramallah: Al-Haq, 1988.

———. "Mass Mobilization and the Uprising: The Labor Movement." In *The Palestinians: New Directions*, edited by Michael C. Hudson, 44–62. Washington, D.C.: Center for Contemporary Arab Studies, 1990.

———. "Sustaining Movement, Creating Space: Trade Unions and Women's Committees." *Middle East Report*, nos. 164–65 (May–August 1990): 32–53.

———. "The Women's Movement during the Uprising." *Journal of Palestine Studies* 20, no. 3 (Spring 1991): 48–57.

———. "Work and Action: The Role of the Working Class in the Uprising." In *Intifada: Palestine at the Crossroads*, edited by Jamal R. Nassar and Roger Heacock, 143–57. New York: Praeger Publishers, 1990.

———. "Workers' Rights during the Uprising." *Journal of Palestine Studies* 19, no. 1 (Autumn 1989): 83–91.

Hopstaken, Korrie. "From Bi-National Railway Workers' Union to Arab Workers' Congress: International Influences on the Origin and Development of the Palestinian-Arab Trade-Union Movement during the British Mandate, 1920-1948" (in Dutch). Doktoraalscriptie Politikologie, University of Nijmegen, Netherlands, 1982.

Hourani, Hani. *Stages of the Struggle of the Working Class and the Trade-Union Movement in Jordan, 1950–1971* (in Arabic). Pamphlet. Ramallah, n.d.

Iliffe, John. "The Creation of Group Consciousness among the Dockworkers of Dar es Salaam, 1929-1950." In *The Development of an African Working Class: Studies in Class Formation and Action*, edited by Richard Sandbrook and Robin Cohen. London: Longman Group, 1975.

International Center for Peace in the Middle East. *Research on Human Rights in the Occupied Territories, 1979–1983*. Tel Aviv: ICPME, 1985.

International Labour Office. "Report on the Situation of Workers of the Occupied Arab Territories." In *Report of the Director-General*. Geneva: International Labour Organisation, 1985–1990.

"Intifada: Year Three." *Middle East Report*, special double issue, nos. 164–65 (May–August 1990).

Jad, Islah. "From Salons to the Popular Committees: Palestinian Women, 1919–1989." In *Intifada: Palestine at the Crossroads*, edited by Jamal R. Nassar and Roger Heacock, 125–42. New York: Praeger Publishers, 1990.

Johnson, Penny, Lee O'Brien, and Joost Hiltermann. "The West Bank Rises Up." In *Intifada: The Palestinian Uprising against Israeli Occupation*, edited by Zachary Lockman and Joel Beinin, 29–41. Boston: South End Press, 1989.

Joseph, Suad. "Women and Politics in the Middle East." *MERIP Middle East Report*, no. 138 (January–February 1986).

Kazi, Hamida. "Palestinian Women and the National Liberation Movement: A Social Perspective." In *Women in the Middle East*, edited by the Khamsin Collective, 26–39. London: Zed Books, 1987.

Khafagy, Fatma. "Women and Labor Migration: One Village in Egypt." *MERIP Reports*, no. 124 (June 1984).

Khalidi, Rashid. "PNC Strengthens Palestinian Hand." *MERIP Middle East Report*, no. 147 (July–August 1987): 38–39.

Kimmerling, Baruch. *Zionism and Economy*. Cambridge, Mass.: Schenkman Publishing, 1983.

Layne, Linda. "Women in Jordan's Workforce." *MERIP Reports*, no. 95 (March–April 1981).

Lesch, Ann Mosely. *Arab Politics in Palestine, 1917–1939: The Frustration of a National Movement*. Ithaca: Cornell University Press, 1979.

———. "The Frustration of a Nationalist Movement: Palestine Arab Politics, 1917–1939." Ph.D. diss., Columbia University, 1973.

———. *Political Perceptions of the Palestinians on the West Bank and the Gaza Strip*. Washington, D.C.: Middle East Institute, 1980.

Lockman, Zachary. "Original Sin." In *Intifada: The Palestinian Uprising against Israeli Occupation*, edited by Zachary Lockman and Joel Beinin, 185–203. Boston: South End Press, 1989.

Lockman, Zachary, and Joel Beinin. *Intifada: The Palestinian Uprising against Israeli Occupation*. Boston: South End Press, 1989.

McDowall, David. *Palestine and Israel: The Uprising and Beyond*. Berkeley and Los Angeles: University of California Press, 1989.

Mansour, Antoine, *Palestine: Une Economie de Résistance en Cisjordanie et à Gaza*. Paris: Editions L'Harmattan, 1983.

Ma'oz, Moshe. *Palestinian Leadership on the West Bank: The Changing Role of the Arab Mayors under Jordan and Israel*. London: Frank Cass and Co., 1984.

MERIP. "Abd el-Jawad Saleh: 'Abu Ammar's Biggest Mistake Was Gambling on the Americans.'" *MERIP Reports*, no. 119 (November–December 1983).

———. "Abu Leila: Confronting the Dilemmas of the PLO in Lebanon and Jordan." *MERIP Reports*, no. 83 (December 1979).

———. "Hussein Hangover: The West Bank after the PNC." *MERIP Reports*, no. 131 (March–April 1985).

———. "Interview with the Palestine National Front." *MERIP Reports*, no. 32 (November 1974).

———. "Interview with the Palestine National Front." *MERIP Reports*, no. 50 (August 1976).

————. "Israeli Military Authorities Ban 'Illegal' Palestinian Organization." *MERIP Reports*, no. 83 (December 1979).

————. "Khalid al-Hassan: Our Strategy Is to Help Our People Stay on Their Land." *MERIP Reports*, no. 83 (December 1979).

————. "Open Door in the Middle East." *MERIP Reports*, no. 31 (October 1974).

————. "The Palestinian National Front." *MERIP Reports*, no. 25 (February 1974).

Metzger, Jan, Martin Orth, and Christian Sterzing. *This Land Is Our Land: The West Bank under Israeli Occupation*. London: Zed Press, 1983.

Migdal, Joel S. "The Effects of Regime Policies on Social Cohesion and Fragmentation." In *Palestinian Society and Politics*, edited by Joel S. Migdal, 3–96. Princeton: Princeton University Press, 1980.

Ministry of Defense, Coordinator of Government Operations in Judaea and Samaria, Gaza District, Sinai, Golan Heights. *A Thirteen-Year Survey (1967–1980)*. Jerusalem: State of Israel, 1981.

Moffett, Martha Roadstrum. *Perpetual Emergency: A Legal Analysis of Israel's Use of the British Defence (Emergency) Regulations, 1945, in the Occupied Territories*. Ramallah: Al-Haq, 1989.

Mogannam, Matiel E. T. *The Arab Woman and the Palestine Problem*. London: Herbert Joseph, 1937.

Moore, Barrington, Jr. *Injustice: The Social Bases of Obedience and Revolt*. White Plains, N.Y.: M. E. Sharpe, 1978.

Myntti, Cynthia. "Yemeni Workers Abroad: The Impact on Women." *MERIP Reports*, no. 124 (June 1984).

Paige, Jeffery. *Agrarian Revolution: Social Movements and Export Agriculture in the Underdeveloped World*. New York: Free Press, 1975.

————. "Social Theory and Peasant Revolution in Vietnam and Guatemala." *Theory and Society* 12, no. 6 (November 1983): 699–737.

Palestine Focus. "An Interview with Rita Giacaman: Women, Resistance, and the Popular Movement." *Palestine Focus* (San Francisco), no. 24 (July–August 1987).

Peteet, Julie. "Women and the Palestinian Movement: No Going Back?" *MERIP Middle East Report* 16, no. 1 (January–February 1986): 20–44.

Playfair, Emma. *Administrative Detention in the Occupied West Bank*. Ramallah: Al-Haq, 1986.

————. "The Legal Aspects of the Occupation." In *Occupation: Israel over Palestine*, 2d ed., edited by Naseer H. Aruri, 101–76. Belmont, Mass.: Association of Arab-American University Graduates, 1989.

Quandt, William B. "Political and Military Dimensions of Contemporary Palestinian Nationalism." In *The Politics of Palestinian Nationalism*, edited by William B. Quandt, Fuad Jabber, and Ann Mosely Lesch. Berkeley and Los Angeles: University of California Press, 1973.

Quandt, William B., Fuad Jabber, and Ann Mosely Lesch, eds. *The Politics of Palestinian Nationalism*. Berkeley and Los Angeles: University of California Press, 1973.

Rekhess, Elie. "The Employment in Israel of Arab Labourers from the Administered Areas." *Israel Yearbook on Human Rights* 5 (1975).

Rifkin, Lena. "Notes from the Occupation: Peace Treaty Sharpens Struggle on West Bank." *MERIP Reports*, no. 83 (December 1979).

Rishmawi, Mona. "Finding Security in Subterfuge: The Uses of an Argument." Article provided by the author, Ramallah, April 1987.

Rockwell, Susan. "Palestinian Women Workers in the Israeli-Occupied Gaza Strip." *Journal of Palestine Studies* 14, no. 2 (Winter 1985).

Roy, Sara M. *The Gaza Strip: A Demographic, Economic, Social, and Legal Survey.* Jerusalem: West Bank Data Base Project, 1986.

Ryan, Sheila. "Israeli Economic Policy in the Occupied Areas: Foundations of a New Imperialism." *MERIP Reports*, no. 24 (January 1974).

———. "The West Bank and Gaza: Political Consequences of Occupation." *MERIP Reports*, no. 74 (January 1979): 3–8.

Samed, Amal. "The Proletarianization of Palestinian Women in Israel." *MERIP Reports*, no. 50 (August 1976): 10–26.

Sandbrook, Richard, and Robin Cohen, eds. *The Development of an African Working Class: Studies in Class Formation and Action.* London: Longman Group, 1975.

Sayigh, Rosemary. "Encounters with Palestinian Women under Occupation." *Journal of Palestine Studies* 10, no. 4 (Summer 1981): 3–26.

———. "Looking across the Mediterranean." *MERIP Reports*, no. 124 (June 1984).

———. *Palestinians: From Peasants to Revolutionaries.* London: Zed Press, 1979.

Schiff, Ze'ev, and Ehud Ya'ari. *Intifada: The Palestinian Uprising—Israel's Third Front.* New York: Simon and Schuster, 1990.

Semyonov, Moshe, and Noah Lewin-Epstein. *Hewers of Wood and Drawers of Water: Noncitizen Arabs in the Israeli Labor Market.* Ithaca: ILR Press, 1987.

Shehadeh, Raja. *Occupier's Law: Israel and the West Bank.* 2d ed. Washington, D.C.: Institute for Palestine Studies, 1988.

Simon, Roger. *Gramsci's Political Thought: An Introduction.* London: Lawrence and Wishart, 1982.

Siniora, Randa George. "Palestinian Labour in a Dependent Economy: The Case of Women in the Sub-Contracting Clothing Industry in the West Bank." Master's thesis, American University in Cairo, 1987.

Stephens, Marc. *Taxation in the Occupied West Bank, 1967–1989.* Ramallah: Al-Haq, 1990.

Taggert, Simon. *Workers in Struggle: Palestinian Trade Unions in the Occupied West Bank.* London: Editpride, 1985.

Tamari, Salim. "Building Other People's Homes: The Palestinian Peasant's Household and Work in Israel." *Journal of Palestine Studies*, 11, no. 1 (Fall 1981): 31–66.

———. "In League with Zion: Israel's Search for a Native Pillar." *Journal of Palestine Studies* 12, no. 4 (Summer 1983): 41–56.

———. "The Palestinian Demand for Independence Cannot Be Postponed Indefinitely." *MERIP Reports*, nos. 100–101 (October–December 1981): 28–35.

———. "What the Uprising Means." *Middle East Report*, no. 152 (May–June 1988): 24–30.

Taqqu, Rachelle. "Peasants into Workmen: Internal Labor Migration and the Arab

Village Community under the Mandate." In *Palestinian Society and Politics*, edited by Joel S. Migdal, 261–85. Princeton: Princeton University Press, 1980.

Taraki, Lisa. "The Development of Political Consciousness among Palestinians in the Occupied Territories, 1967–1987." In *Intifada: Palestine at the Crossroads*, edited by Jamal R. Nassar and Roger Heacock, 53–71. New York: Praeger Publishers, 1990.

————. "Mass Organizations in the West Bank." In *Occupation: Israel over Palestine*, 2d ed., edited by Naseer H. Aruri, 431–63. Belmont, Mass.: Association of Arab-American University Graduates, 1989.

Taylor, Elizabeth. "Egyptian Migration and Peasant Wives." *MERIP Reports*, no. 124 (June 1984).

Tilly, Charles. *From Mobilization to Revolution*. Reading, Mass.: Addison-Wesley, 1978.

Vitullo, Anita. "Uprising in Gaza." In *Intifada: The Palestinian Uprising against Israeli Occupation*, edited by Zachary Lockman and Joel Beinin, 43–55. Boston: South End Press, 1989.

Wallerstein, Immanuel. *Africa, the Politics of Independence: An Interpretation of Modern African History*. New York: Random House, 1961.

————, ed. *Social Change: The Colonial Situation*. New York: John Wiley and Sons, 1966.

"We Are Political Prisoners with Certain Rights." *Journal of Palestine Studies* 14, no. 2 (Winter 1985).

Documents

Construction and General Institutions Workers' Union (CGIWU). *Bylaws of the Construction and General Institutions Workers' Union in Ramallah/al-Bireh* (in Arabic). 1983.

Federation of Palestinian Women's Action Committees. "All Efforts toward Organizing Housewives and Women in Villages and Camps." In *Women's Struggle* (in Arabic), a one-time publication of the FPWAC. 1985.

————. *Amended Bylaws*. 1985.

————. *Amended Program of the Federation of Palestinian Women's Action Committees in the Occupied Territories* (in Arabic). Jerusalem. N.d.

————. "Basic Committees in the Locations of the Women's Work Committees: How to Organize Them, How to Set Them Up, and How to Arrange Their Work." In *Women's Struggle* (in Arabic), a one-time publication of the FPWAC. 1985.

————. "The Fighting Woman Alongside the Man" (in Arabic). Article in a publication of the FPWAC on the occasion of International Women's Day. N.d.; probably March 1985.

————. "The Fourth General Conference of the Federation of Palestinian Women's Work Committees: The Distinct Deep-Rootedness of the History of the Palestinian Women's Movement in the Occupied Territories." In *Women's March* (in Arabic), a one-time publication of the FPWAC. 1986.

————. *FPWAC Bylaws* (in Arabic). Pamphlet. N.d.

————. "The Palestinian Working Woman and the Problems of Unionist Work." In *Women's Struggle* (in Arabic), a one-time publication of the FPWAC. 1985.

————. "Spotlight on the Fourth General Conference of the Federation of Palestinian Women's Work Committees." In *Women's March* (in Arabic), a one-time publication of the FPWAC. 1986.

————. "The Women's Work Committee in the West Bank and Gaza." Second bulletin. Jerusalem. 1984.

————. "Working Women and the Law." In *Women's Struggle* (in Arabic), a one-time publication of the FPWAC. 1985.

Federation of Women's Committees for Social Work (FWCSW). *Bylaws* (in Arabic). 1985.

Gaza Building Workers' and Carpenters' Union (GBWCU) and Gaza Commercial and Public Services Workers' Union (GCPSWU). "Violations against the Right to Organise by Israeli Authorities in the Occupied Gaza Strip." Complaint submitted to the ILO, 2 June 1987. In the files of Al-Haq.

General Committee of Government School Teachers (GCGST). "Statement by the General Committee of Government School Teachers in the West Bank." Press release. 1 August 1987.

General Federation of Trade Unions (GFTU). *Bylaws of the General Federation of Trade Unions in the West Bank* (in Arabic).

In'ash Al-Usra. *The Society of In'ash Al-Usra.* Brochure. Al-Bireh. 1985.

Israel Defense Forces. "Military Order 825 (Order Concerning the Labor Law, Law No. 21 of 1960, Amended)." (In Hebrew). West Bank. 20 February 1980.

————. "Military Order 101 (Order Regarding Prohibition of Acts of Incitement and Hostile Propaganda)." (In Hebrew). West Bank. 27 August 1967.

————. "Military Order 378 (Order Concerning Security Regulations)." (In Hebrew). West Bank. 20 April 1970.

"Memo from the WUB, the PUAF, and the WVB 'to Secretary-General 'Adel Ghanem' and the PWB" (in Arabic). Handbill. 6 October 1985.

Municipality and General Institutions Workers' Union (MGIWU). "Statement of the Municipality and General Institutions Workers' Union (WYM) in Nablus" (in Arabic). Handbill. 9 July 1985.

Printers' Cooperative Association (PCA) and Printers' Union (PU). "Statement by the Printers' Cooperative Association and the Printers' Union in Jerusalem" (in Arabic). 31 July 1987.

"Provisional Labour Law of the Hashemite Kingdom of Jordan (Law No. 21 of 1960)" (in Arabic). *Official Gazette,* no 1491 (May 21, 1960).

Union of Palestinian Women's Committees. "Maha Nassar on Hunger Strike." Press release. 10 October 1989.

————. "The March of the Federation of Palestinian Women's Committees." In *Women's Sail* (in Arabic), a one-time publication of the UPWC. 1985.

————. *May.* A one-time publication of the UPWC. May 1983.

————. "The Palestinian Woman Breaks Her Fetters and Bursts Forth." In *Our Struggle Continues* (in Arabic). 1989.

————. "A Pioneering Experiment of One of the Committees." In *The UPWC and March 8* (in Arabic), a one-time publication of the UPWC. 1984.

————. "What Is the Federation of Palestinian Women's Committees?" In *The UPWC and March 8* (in Arabic), a one-time publication of the UPWC. 1984.

Union of Palestinian Working Women's Committees. "The Federation and the Unionist Domain." In *Working Women's Struggle* (in Arabic), a one-time publication of the UPWWC. 1986.

————. "Kindergartens." In *Working Women's Struggle* (in Arabic), a one-time publication of the UPWWC. 1986.

————. "The Statement of the Palestinian Women under Israeli Occupation, Presented to the International Conference on Women, Nairobi, July 1985." Paper presented at the conference of the International Decade for Women, Nairobi. In *International Decade of Women, 1975–1985*. West Bank. March 1986.

————. *Union of Palestinian Working Women's Committees, West Bank and Gaza Strip, 1987*. Pamphlet. 1987.

Women's Committees for Social Work. *Association Bulletin No. 2: The Association Achievements, 1983–1984*. Ramallah. 1984.

Women's Work Committee. "First Social Field Study: The Conditions of Palestinian Working Women" (in Arabic). In *On the Condition of Palestinian Women in the Occupied Territories*. Ramallah/al-Bireh. 1980.

————. *On the Condition of Palestinian Women in the Occupied Territories* (in Arabic). Ramallah/al-Bireh. 1980.

————. "Second Social Field Study: The Conditions of Housewives" (in Arabic). In *On the Condition of Palestinian Women in the Occupied Territories*. Ramallah/al-Bireh. 1980.

Workers' Unity Bloc. *Workers' Unity Bloc in the West Bank and Gaza Strip*. Pamphlet. West Bank. 1985.

INDEX

British Mandate, 57–60, 114, 120–21, 128–29
Budeiri, Musa, 59, 222n.72
Budeiri family, 128
Burhan, 241n.119

Camp David Accords, 46, 47, 48, 49, 51, 68
Canada, 140
cardboard unions. *See* trade unions
Caritas Hospital, 189
Carpenters and Building Workers' Union in Gaza, 123–24
Carpentry Workshop Workers' Union in Hebron, 82
Central Bureau of Statistics, 188
charitable societies, 71, 78, 128, 129, 130–31, 132–33, 134, 136, 139, 168
child labor, 189
Cinema Al-Hamra, 108
Civil Administration, 22, 31, 90, 127, 133
civil disobedience, 40, 45, 59, 201, 206, 236n.6
class consciousness, 4
class structure, 7, 37
class struggle, 8, 12, 63, 76, 93, 214, 215
Cobban, Helena, 61
collaboration, 51, 97, 103–4, 112, 122, 127, 140, 166–67, 170
collaborators. *See* collaboration
collective agreements, 88, 89–90, 96, 158, 162, 182–83, 186, 189, 191, 192, 206
colonialism, during Mandate, 58; and Israel's occupation, 30, 174, 208, 209, 212–13; and nationalism, 4, 5, 8, 11, 50, 77, 216
Commercial and Public Services Workers' Union in Gaza, 123–25, 178
Committee on Freedom of Association, 115–16, 124
Communists. *See* Palestine Communist Party
consumer cooperatives, and trade unions, 79, 88, 89; and women's committees, 150, 151
Construction and General Institutions Workers' Union, in Abu Dis, 72–73, 100, 157, 159; in Deir al-Ghussoun, 107, 115; in Hebron, 88; in Ramallah/al-Bireh (PWB), 69, 84, 87, 90, 94, 99, 105, 106–7, 197–8, 155, 181; in Ramallah/al-Bireh

(WUB), 84, 155, 159, 182; in Ya'bad, 115
Construction Workers' Union, in Amman, 60–61; in Jerusalem, 72–73, 86; in Nablus (PWB), 84; in Nablus (WUB), 84

Dagher, 'Adnan, 107, 178, 181
Dajani company, 159
Dakkak, Ibrahim, 18, 38, 40, 49
al-Darabi, Muhammad, 121–22
Al-Darb, 112
Dayan, Moshe, 18–19, 20, 43
Deduction Fund, 22
Defense (Emergency) Regulations, 114, 177
Deheisheh refugee camp, 98, 147, 169, 181
Deheisheh stonecutting company, 189
Democratic Front for the Liberation of Palestine (DFLP), xiii; and factionalism, 79; founding of, 39; and popular mobilization, 65–66; repression against, 111, 115; role in PLO of, 45, 48, 49, 51, 52, 178, 237n.18; and trade unions, 64, 67; and women's committees, 134
Democratic Youth Association, 60
Department of Professional Unions, 23
Department of Social Affairs, in Israel, 133; in Jordan, 90, 91
deportations. *See* Israel's military occupation
devaluation of dinar, 183–84, 188
Diana sweets company, 189
Dib, Karima, 155, 158
Diplomat Hotel, 100–101
Drivers' Union, in Gaza, 125; in Jerusalem, 103
Dweik, Mahmoud, 190

East Jerusalem, 95, 100, 108, 134, 136, 138, 140, 141, 146, 147, 152, 156, 157, 168; annexation of, 23, 44, 62, 103, 184, 188, 220n.29; under Jordan, 6; in the uprising, 175, 181, 184, 200
Egypt, 120, 128, 129, 222n.65
Ehrlich, Avishai, 32
'Ein Beit al-Ma' refugee camp, 169
Electricity Workers' Union in Hebron, of the WUB, 84; of the WYM, 84
Employment Service, 22–23, 24, 101, 179, 184
Employment Service Law, 21, 184
Erez settlement, 121